COMMODITY MODELS
FOR FORECASTING
AND POLICY ANALYSIS

COMMODITY MODELS
FOR FORECASTING
AND POLICY ANALYSIS

WALTER C. LABYS
AND
PETER K. POLLAK

Routledge
Taylor & Francis Group

LONDON AND NEW YORK

First published in 1984 by Croom Helm Ltd.

This edition first published in 2024
by Routledge
4 Park Square, Milton Park, Abingdon, Oxon OX14 4RN

and by Routledge
605 Third Avenue, New York, NY 10158

Routledge is an imprint of the Taylor & Francis Group, an informa business

British Library Cataloguing in Publication Data
A catalogue record for this book is available from the British Library

ISBN: 978-1-032-69509-9 (Set)
ISBN: 978-1-032-69353-8 (Volume 4) (hbk)
ISBN: 978-1-032-69370-5 (Volume 4) (pbk)
ISBN: 978-1-032-69364-4 (Volume 4) (ebk)

DOI: 10.4324/9781032693644

Publisher's Note
The publisher has gone to great lengths to ensure the quality of this reprint but points out that some imperfections in the original copies may be apparent.

Disclaimer
The publisher has made every effort to trace copyright holders and would welcome correspondence from those they have been unable to trace.

Commodity Models for Forecasting and Policy Analysis

Walter C. Labys
& Peter K. Pollak

CROOM HELM
London & Sydney

NICHOLS PUBLISHING COMPANY
New York

© 1984 W.C. Labys and P.K. Pollak
Croom Helm Ltd, Provident House, Burrell Row,
Beckenham, Kent BR3 1AT
Croom Helm Australia Pty Ltd, First Floor,
139 King Street, Sydney, NSW 2001, Australia

British Library Cataloguing in Publication Data

Labys, W.C.
    Commodity models for forecasting and policy
    analysis.
    1. Markcting–Mathematical models
    I. Title   II. Pollak, P.K.
658.8'00724.   HF5415.122

ISBN 0-7099-1616-7

First published in the United States of America 1984
by Nichols Publishing Company, Post Office Box 96,
New York, NY 10024

Library of Congress Cataloging in Publication Data

Labys, Walter C.
    Commodity models for forecasting and policy analysis.

    Includes index.
    1. Commodity exchanges–Mathematical models. I. Pollak,
Peter. II. Title.
HG6046.L23   1984   332.64'4'0724   84-4706
ISBN 0-89397-193-6

Printed and bound in Great Britain

CONTENTS

TABLES

FIGURES

PREFACE

The oil crises of the 1970s and more recently the growing international debt burden have again highlighted the extent to which events in primary commodity markets continue to influence alike the economies of developing and industrialized countries. Policy makers, business leaders, consumers and producers of primary commodities accordingly have intensified their efforts to reduce the fluctuations in these markets or at least to make the markets more predictable. As we are well aware, few of these efforts have thus far proven successful. This, in turn, has led to increasingly greater attempts to understand and to predict the behavior of these markets. One vehicle which has helped in these attempts has been that of commodity modeling. Through advances in the fields of econometric modeling, mathematical programming and computer science, commodity modeling has not only become a useful means for market analysis but has also received extensive application.

The purpose of this book is to provide an overview of the nature of the different types of commodity models as well as their diverse applications. In non-technical language the reader will be introduced to the underlying modeling methodologies, including their advantages, limitations and commodity specific implications. A reader with sufficient background will also be able to use this information to begin actual model construction. The book should thus be of interest to commodity economists, commodity traders and analysts, commodity managers, economic planners and forecasters, financial analysts, and government officials in commodity-related areas. The book can also serve as a supplementary text for a variety of courses such as agricultural, mineral and energy modeling; econometrics, mathematical programming and operations research; and business forecasting and industrial management.

Thanks are due to a number of persons who helped with this effort. Several colleagues as well as graduate students at West Virginia University kindly offered corrections on early drafts of the manuscript. The *Journal of Policy Modeling* and *Energy Economics* gave permission to reprint materials for Chapters 3 and 4. Finally, Nancy Ireland rendered a great service in typing the manuscript through to its completion.

Walter C. Labys
Peter K. Pollak

1 COMMODITY MARKETS AND MODELS

Increases in the price of oil and other major primary commodities during the mid 1970s has sparked a renewed interest in the behavior of international commodity markets. It has also led to a growing awareness that a large number of our current economic problems, such as inflation, sluggish economic growth in developing as well as industrial countries, instability in international trade and international financial markets as well as the specter of food and raw materials scarcities, have been seriously affected by the changing conditions in international commodity markets. Commodity model construction and application have thus emerged as a distinct area of economic analysis to provide a basis for the analysis of these markets. The fact that Chapter 7 lists more than four-hundred commodity models illustrates the growth of economic research in this area.

Commodity models provide a systematic and comprehensive approach for analyzing and forecasting the behavior of commodity markets. They also permit the analysis of a wide range of policy decisions. Over the years, commodity models have thus become indispensable tools for forecasters and policy analysts. Since models represent a simplified abstraction of a rather complex real world, they do have obvious limitations. For one, even the most complex models cannot capture all the intricate relationships that shape the behavior of a commodity market; then, in order to generate forecasts with the help of a model, the forecaster has to make assumptions about all of those variables for which the model does not provide answers. Usually, these are variables, such as economic growth, population, crop yields or the weather. Any 'errors' in the assumptions about these variables result in a corresponding error in the forecasts. Although commodity models have become increasingly sophisticated in recent decades, few, if any, provide consistently correct forecasts. This has led many forecasters to discard this approach all together and rely instead on 'judgmental analysis'. If used properly, commodity models can greatly enhance the quality of market forecasts, and provide valuable insights into the behavior of commodity markets as well as the effectiveness of various economic policy measures. As with any other tool, it is important to be aware of its capabilities and limitations. It is our hope that this study will illustrate the usefulness of commodity models.

This first chapter serves as an introduction to the need for commodity models by focussing on the nature of commodity markets and the kinds of commodity analysis that can be performed with a modeling approach. The definition, distribution and structure of these markets are considered first. Price movements are also considered, including their role in international trade and economic development. Traditional approaches to analyzing these markets are then reviewed. The chapter closes with a discussion of the needs for commodity modeling.

Commodity Market Characteristics

Primary Commodities Defined

Traded goods are frequently categorized — depending on the degree of processing embodied in them — as primary commodities or manufactures. The boundaries between these two groups of commodities are obviously vague. Few primary commodities enter the markets without some form of processing. Just to trade, store and transport commodities, requires a certain degree of processing, and it is sometimes unclear as to where processing ends and manufacturing begins. For example, grain crops have to be threshed, cotton crops have to be ginned to separate the seed from the lint, sugar cane and beets have to be converted to sugar, natural rubber has to be smoked and separated into sheets, and metallic minerals have to be separated or beneficiated, melted and refined. Obviously, traded goods represent a continuum that extends from completely unprocessed commodities on the one end (e.g., iron ore, raw diamonds, coal) to highly processed products in which the raw material content is minimal (e.g., electronics).

Why is it so important to differentiate between primary commodities and manufactures? The answer lies in the fact that raw materials, that is unprocessed primary commodities, are more homogeneous than manufactures, that is primary commodities that have undergone extensive processing. The markets for (nearly) homogeneous raw materials are usually easily identifiable and, unlike those for manufactures, can be analyzed quite readily. With the exception of a few raw materials[1] (e.g., diamonds, oil and gas, some metals), many of these markets are characterized by a highly competitive structure, the direct result of the large number of buyers and sellers trading in a particular market. Information about prices and quantities traded are for most raw materials readily available, which is another factor that eases the analysis of these markets. By comparison, the markets for most manufactures (e.g., cars, aircraft, chemicals, electronics) are dominated by a small number of producers, which trade often with a small number of highly specialized buyers (aircraft, chemicals) or sell their products through specialized dealers to a mass market (cars, electronics). Many of these markets are characterized by special trading arrangements, and much of the information on prices and trade volumes remains with the trading companies. This makes these markets less transparent and thus more difficult to analyze. Hence, much of the analysis of the behavior of markets has been focused on the markets of largely unprocessed primary commodities.

Sources of Primary Commodities

Primary commodities are usually grouped into four broad categories: agricultural food products (e.g., grains, coffee, cocoa, tea, fruits and vegetables, fats and oils), agricultural raw materials (e.g., cotton, jute, rubber, tobacco, tropical hardwood), metals and minerals (e.g., copper, tin, aluminum, bauxite), and fuels (e.g., petroleum as well as petroleum products, coal, natural gas). Table 1.1 provides a list of primary commodities that are traded internationally.

With the exception of some agricultural products that require specific climatic conditions (e.g., coffee, cocoa, coconuts, oil palm products), primary products are produced and consumed in almost every country. However, the industrial countries remain the major market for primary commodities, although in recent years the developing countries have emerged as an increasingly important market for these commodities. The traditional concept of the 'North' as the buyer of primary commodities and the 'South' as their producer is gradually corrected by the rapidly growing 'South-South' trade in primary commodities. Rising *per capita* incomes and a comparatively rapid industrialization in a growing number of developing countries are the main forces behind this shift in the traditional trading pattern.

Although industrial countries dominate the production of some primary commodities (e.g., grains), they depend heavily on the deposits of minerals, metals and hydrocarbons (oil and natural gas) in developing countries. Because some of these commodities are of vital importance in the manufacture of key industrial products, several industrial countries maintain 'strategic stockpiles' to reduce the risk of supply interruptions. The oil crisis of the 1970s has heightened the awareness of a 'global interdependence' that rests, to a large extent, on the international trade of primary commodities. The struggle for the ownership of the primary commodity resource base or, more precisely, the battle for their economic rents spilled over into the political arena. Political objectives

Table 1.1: Primary Commodities Traded Internationally[a]

Agricultural Food Products	Agricultural Raw Materials	Metals and Minerals
Beverages	Abaca	Aluminum
Cocoa	Burlap	Asbestos
Coffee	Cotton	Bauxite
Tea	Hides and Skins	Beryllium
	Jute	Bismuth
Cereals	Linseed	Cadmium
Maize	Sisal	Cement
Rye	Timber	Chromite
Sorghum	Rubber	Clays
Wheat	Wool	Cobalt
		Columbium
Fruit		Copper
Apples	Fuels	Diamonds
Bananas		Fertilizers
Dates	Coal	Gallium
Grapes	Gas	Gem Stones
Olives	Peat	Gold
Oranges	Petroleum	Graphite
	Propane	Gypsum
Meat	Uranium	Iron
Beef		Lead
Lamb		Magnesium
Pork		Manganese
Poultry		Mercury
		Mica
Oilseeds, Oils, Meals		Molybdenum
Copra		Nickel
Coconut Oil/Meal		Phosphate
Cottonseed Oil/Meal		Platinum
Fish Oil/Meal		Potash
Groundnut Oil/Meal		Salt
Palm Kernel Oil/Meal		Sand
Palm Oil/Meal		Silicon
Soybean Oil/Meal		Silver
Tung Oil		Stone
		Sulfur
Rice		Thorium
Spices		Tin
Sugar		Titanium
Tobacco		Tungsten
Vegetables		Vanadium
Wine		Zinc

Note: [a]This is intended to be representative rather than exhaustive.

overshadowed in some instances the economic interests of primary commodity producers. Oil producers applied their 'oil weapon' against selected oil importing countries and grain producers imposed grain embargoes at various times for political motives. Hence, political factors could no longer be safely ignored in analyzing commodity markets. The steep rise in oil prices resulted in yet another link, namely to financial markets. Production decisions in oil exporting countries that were unable to absorb all of their oil revenues domestically became increasingly dependent on the returns they received from their investments abroad. Hence, interest and exchange rates and inflation joined the more traditional variables, such as *per capita* incomes and economic growth rates.

A thorough knowledge of the geographical distribution of the main producers and consumers of a commodity is prerequisite for any formal or informal modeling of its markets. It provides clues to the market structure and the likely behavior of buyers and sellers. Table 1.2 shows the geographic distribution of major exporters and importers of selected primary commodities.

Major Markets

The terms markets and industries have thus far been used interchangeably. The differences between them derive from microeconomics. That is, industries refer to the firms involved in producing and transforming commodities. Markets refer to institutions that surround commodity exchange and trade. Commodity markets tend to be located near the major geographical nodes of production and consumption. Deviations from this pattern normally result from historical circumstances, such as that of previously important trading routes or communication centers. An attempt to specify the major commodity markets has been made in Table 1.3, which specifies centers of major price making activity. For the industrial countries, Chicago, London, New York, and Hamburg are the most important. For the developing countries, Calcutta, Manila, and Buenos Aires are significant.

Markets can also be characterized according to the nature of the underlying contractual arrangements. Markets can be identified as spot markets when they feature physical exchange of the commodity and contracts specifying delivery on the spot. They are termed futures markets when they involve the exchange of paper contracts that specify forward delivery accompanied by terms permitting easy transfer of liability. These markets are popularly known for the hedging and speculative needs they accommodate. Forward markets are more difficult to

Table 1.2: Geographic Distribution of Major Commodity Exporters and Importers

Commodity	Major Exporters	Major Importers
Wheat	United States Canada France Australia Argentina	Japan United Kingdom Italy Egypt Brazil
Maize	United States Argentina Netherlands France S. Africa	Japan Netherlands Spain United Kingdom Italy
Rice	United States Thailand Pakistan Italy Burma	Indonesia Iran Hong Kong Sri Lanka Nigeria
Soybeans	United States Brazil Argentina Paraguay Netherlands	Japan FR Germany Netherlands Spain Italy
Coffee	Brazil Colombia Ivory Coast El Salvador Mexico	United States FR Germany France Italy Netherlands
Cocoa	Ghana Nigeria Brazil Ivory Coast Netherlands	United States FR Germany Netherlands United Kingdom France
Tea	India Sri Lanka Kenya United Kingdom Indonesia	United Kingdom United States Pakistan Egypt Canada
Sugar	Cuba Australia Brazil Philippines	United States United Kingdom Japan FR Germany France
Bananas	Costa Rica Ecuador Honduras Philippines Martinique	United States France FR Germany Japan United Kingdom

Commodity	Major Exporters	Major Importers
Palm Oil	Malaysia	India
	Indonesia	United Kingdom
	Singapore	United States
	Netherlands	FR Germany
	Ivory Coast	Netherlands
Coconut Oil	Philippines	United States
	FR Germany	FR Germany
	Netherlands	Netherlands
	Singapore	United Kingdom
	Sri Lanka	Italy
Beef	Australia	United States
	Ireland	Italy
	FR Germany	France
	France	FR Germany
	Netherlands	United Kingdom
Cotton	United States	Japan
	Egypt	FR Germany
	Sudan	Korea
	Turkey	Italy
	Syria	France
Wool	Australia	Japan
	New Zealand	Italy
	France	United Kingdom
	S. Africa	FR Germany
	United Kingdom	France
Jute	Bangladesh	United Kingdom
	Thailand	France
	Nepal	Pakistan
	India	Belgium-Lux.
	Belgium-Lux.	Egypt
Bauxite	Australia	United States
	Jamaica	USSR
	Surinam	Japan
	Guinea	Canada
	Guyana	FR Germany
Copper	Chile	FR Germany
	Zambia	United States
	Belgium	Belgium
	FR Germany	France
	Zaire	United Kingdom
Iron Ore	Australia	Japan
	Canada	FR Germany
	Brazil	United States
	Sweden	United Kingdom
	India	Belgium-Lux.

Table 1.2 (*cont.*):

Commodity	Major Exporters	Major Importers
Tin	Malaysia	United States
	Bolivia	Japan
	Thailand	FR Germany
	Indonesia	France
	United Kingdom	United Kingdom
Zinc	Canada	United States
	Belgium-Lux.	United Kingdom
	Australia	FR Germany
	FR Germany	France
	Netherlands	Italy
Lead	Australia	United Kingdom
	United Kingdom	United States
	FR Germany	FR Germany
	Canada	Italy
	Belgium-Lux.	Netherlands
Petroleum	Saudi Arabia	United States
	Iran	Japan
	Nigeria	France
	Libya	FR Germany
	Iraq	Italy
Coal	United States	Japan
	Australia	France
	FR Germany	Italy
	Canada	Canada
	S. Africa	Netherlands

Source: United Nations, *Yearbook of International Trade Statistics*, 1978, United Nations, New York, 1979.

identify, since forward contracts that specify delivery at some time forward are most often negotiated privately. Spot markets tend to be located at points of production, such as in the developing countries. Futures markets are located in major financial centers, such as Chicago, London, and New York.

Market Structure

Commodity markets vary widely in the degree to which they reflect the basic concept of a competitive market in which prices are determined by the free interaction of supply and demand forces. These markets can be highly competitive, involving a number of producers and consumers, such as for soybeans. Markets can also feature administered and quasi-administered pricing, such as that of the OPEC cartel, or they can contain a single monopoly or dominant producing firm that influences

Table 1.3: Locations of Major Commodity Markets

Markets[a]	Bananas	Barley	Beef	Boneless Beef	Broilers	Cattle	Cocoa	Coconut Oil	Coffee	Copper	Copra	Cottonseed	Citrus	Corn	Cotton	Eggs[b]	Feeder Cattle	Fishmeal	Flaxseed	Grain Sorghums	Gold	Hogs	Iron Ore	Jute	Lead	Lumber	Lumber (Stud)	Linseed	Groundnuts	Mercury	Oats	Palladium[c]	Palm Oil	Pepper	Plywood	Pork Bellies	Potatoes	Propane	Rapeseed	Rice	Rubber	Rye	Sheep/Lambs	Silver	Soybeans	Soybean Meal	Soybean Oil	Sugar	Tea	Tin	Wheat	Wool	Zinc
London	S	SF	S				SF	S	SF	F	S				SF						F			S	S				S	F		S		S			F	F		S	S	F		F		F	F	SF	S	S	SF	SF	F
New York			S	F			SF	S	SF	SF	S				S	S					F			S	S					F		S					F	F			S			F		F	F	SF	S	S	S	SF	F
Hamburg										S																																							S		S		
Calcutta																								S										S						S	S								S		S		
Chicago														SF		S	F			F	F	F				F	F				S				F	F	F					S			SF	F	F				S		
Rotterdam										F																							S						SF							F	F				S		
Manila								S			S																													S												
Marseilles				F																																																	
Winnipeg		SF																	F																				S			F									SF		
Buenos Aires				F		F											F																									F									S		
Colombo																																		S							S								S				
Singapore											S																						S								S							S		S			
Minneapolis																																										S									SF		
Bangkok																																								S											S		
Chittagong																								S																													
Djakarta											S																																										
Istanbul																																		S																			
Montevideo				S																																																S	
Sao Paulo																																																						
Amsterdam														S																																							
Kansas City														SF																																					S		
Le Havre										S				S																																		S					
Liverpool															S																																						
Melbourne																																																				S	
Sydney																																											S										
Paris										F																			F												F							F			SF	SF	
West Coast				F						F						F					F																											F					

Note: [a] S = Spot market, F = Futures market
[b] Frozen and Fresh
[c] And platinum

Source: W. C. Labys, 'Commodity Markets and Models: the Range of Experience' in F. G. Adams and S. Klein (eds.), *Stabilizing World Commodity Markets*, Lexington, MA: Heath Lexington Books, 1978, pp. 6–7.

prices and quantities to ensure profit maximization, such as for cobalt. Cognizance of these factors has led to the identification of market structure as an important characteristic of commodity markets whether they be agricultural (McCalla, 1981), mineral (Labys, 1980) or energy (Aperjis, 1982). Market structure refers to factors ranging from the number of firms on the supply and demand side of a market and the degree of cooperation among them to the limits of a market determined by the degree of substitutability among commodities.

Concerning the first of these, one can examine the conditions associated with a commodity marketing system. The latter consists of firms engaged in the production, marketing, shipping, processing and distribution activities through which commodities pass from producers to ultimate consumers. Each of these activities or stages generally coincides with recognized industry units or other intermediaries. Between the firms or economic intermediaries operating at each stage, there is normally sufficient trading so that different vertically related markets are established. The determinants underlying commodity supply and demand flows within this system such as prices, industrial activity, etc. constitute the market conditions.

Market structure in international commodity markets is often described according to the number of actors or major exporters and importers in a market. This sometimes takes the form of origin-destination matrices that identify not only the major participants but also the relative importance of flows between them, e.g., (Demler and Tilton, 1980). Related to market structure is market power which refers to the ability of an actor or set of actors to influence market outcomes with their actions. While the size of a mineral exporter or importer relative to the total market provides some indication of potential power, the actual exercise of that power need not take place. In some cases a government can influence a market through supply restriction or perhaps the operation of export quotas. A principle advantage of focussing on market conditions, market structure and bargaining power is that it helps us to assess the nature of price behavior in a particular commodity market. Market structure is thus an important element in examining agricultural markets such as for wheat and coarse grains as well as for minerals such as bauxite, cobalt and tungsten, and for fuels such as petroleum.

Concerning the market limits determined by commodity substitution, one normally determines the technical characteristics of a commodity which determine the degree of interchangeability it possesses with other commodities or with synthetic substitutes. These characteristics, in fact, determine the boundary of commodities when they are defined in terms of properties such as conductivity, energy, or protein content.

Technical characteristics, together with economic and quality or taste considerations, determine the relative substitutability of commodities on the demand side. Where synthetic substitutes exist, there is the danger that a commodity's market share will be eroded by a synthetic with lower and more stable prices. Where a number of substitutes with similar characteristics exist, changes in market share occur with only small changes in relative prices. This is particularly true for mineral commodities that compete closely in product composition at the intermediate demand level.

On the supply side, substitution relates more to the return obtained from investing productive capital in one commodity as compared to another. When the price of soybeans increases, for example, land planted in cotton will be taken over for soybeans. One can also think of investments shifting from mining operations in one mineral to another.

Price Movements

Price movements have often been considered as one of if not the major factor which separates primary commodity markets from those for manufactured goods. Commodity prices have tended to grow more slowly than the latter over time. They also have been known to fluctuate more violently. The relative growth in commodity prices can be assessed from Table 1.4 which presents the evolution of commodity prices based on weighted price indexes (constant dollars, 1977-9 = 100) for several commodity groupings and in aggregate. The aggregate commodity price index shows declining prices since 1950 with the exception of the Korean price boom in the early 1950s and the recent inflationary boom as petroleum prices rose rapidly in the 1970s. The same pattern is reflected in the agricultural food index and to a lesser extent in the agricultural raw materials index. Metals and minerals prices to the contrary have not declined as sharply and short term upward fluctuations have occurred around the trend. Of course, petroleum prices have continued upwards.

The relative instability of commodity prices can be assessed from Table 1.5 which reflects the short term variations of actual market prices around the longer term price trends. The degree of variation found among the commodities is substantial. Among those with more substantial price fluctuations are coffee, cocoa, sugar, oranges, rice, copra and coconut oil, jute, rubber, copper, lead, zinc and phosphate rock. Among the lowest are bananas, nickel, bauxite and aluminum, and iron ore.

Table 1.4: Indices of Commodity Price Movements[a] (Constant Dollars, 1977-1979 = 100)

	Aggregate of 33 Commodities (Excluding Energy) (100.0)	Agriculture							Petroleum	Metals & Minerals (24.3)
		Total (70.6)	Food					Materials (14.1)		
			Total (56.5)	Beverages (28.1)	Cereals (8.0)	Fats & Oils (9.2)	Other (11.2)			
1950	144	154	137	102	192	159	167	222	43	131
1951	146	152	130	95	175	159	159	243	36	138
1952	132	128	113	88	170	129	123	188	35	156
1953	127	125	118	95	179	137	116	152	39	148
1954	138	139	136	136	168	129	118	153	42	144
1955	135	129	115	106	146	117	114	184	41	165
1956	135	128	120	109	145	118	129	164	40	170
1957	126	123	116	98	132	114	154	152	39	146
1958	108	105	98	82	127	101	114	133	35	128
1959	113	109	97	77	127	115	113	158	32	131
1960	111	106	92	72	118	107	114	162	30	130
1961	105	99	89	65	127	112	105	138	30	128
1962	105	99	89	64	141	104	103	138	28	126
1963	113	111	107	63	140	109	193	128	28	122
1964	117	109	105	74	137	111	152	128	25	148
1965	113	97	91	69	131	121	93	123	25	166
1966	114	95	89	65	144	115	88	121	24	174
1967	106	95	90	63	151	107	101	114	24	144

Year										
1968	114	101	95	66	157	110	110	126	26	158
1969	122	107	100	69	154	109	134	134	25	171
1970	115	102	98	72	127	116	130	115	23	162
1971	100	91	88	58	113	109	127	107	28	128
1972	97	92	90	58	109	95	153	99	31	116
1973	123	118	115	61	188	161	160	133	36	141
1974	141	138	143	57	220	157	291	119	112	155
1975	100	96	98	47	150	90	193	90	95	117
1976	105	104	103	89	120	93	131	112	101	112
1977	114	119	122	141	101	107	102	105	101	105
1978	92	93	92	88	103	96	93	95	86	91
1979	97	92	90	80	96	98	105	101	111	104
1980	102	98	96	65	105	81	180	105	166	106
1981	90	85	84	56	116	82	133	92	193	99
1982	80	74	72	56	88	70	103	83	180	93

Note: [a]Index of purchasing power of exports of developing countries. Computed from unrounded data. Weighted by 1977–1979 developing countries' export values. Percent of aggregate index consumption is in parenthesis.

Note: The commodities included in each group are beverages — coffee, cocoa, tea; cereals — maize, rice, wheat, grain sorghum; fats and oils — palm oil, coconut oil, groundnut oil, soybeans, copra, groundnuts, soybean meal; other foods — sugar, beef, bananas, oranges; non-foods — cotton, jute, rubber, tobacco; timber — logs; metals and minerals — copper, tin, nickel, bauxite, aluminum, iron ore, manganese ore, lead, zinc, phosphate rock.

Source: World Bank, *Commodity Trade and Price Trends*, Economic Analysis and Projections Department, Commodities and Export Projections Division, Washington, D.C., 1982.

Table 1.5: Indices of Fluctuations in Commodity Prices (Percentages in 1981 Constant $)

	Deviations from Moving Averages[a]		Annual Average Change[b]
	3-Year	5-Year	
Petroleum	6.3	9.4	17.7
Coffee	7.1	12.1	17.8
Cocoa	10.2	16.8	25.3
Tea	4.8	6.2	9.7
Sugar	18.8	30.3	41.6
Beef	5.9	7.2	11.8
Bananas	3.4	5.9	7.0
Oranges	6.6	8.5	15.4
Rice	7.0	14.1	16.6
Wheat	4.5	7.9	10.2
Maize	4.6	6.9	9.5
Grain Sorghum	4.2	5.9	8.7
Palm Oil	7.7	10.7	13.9
Coconut Oil	11.5	16.4	20.3
Groundnut Oil	7.3	10.8	14.2
Soybeans	6.0	8.3	10.8
Copra	11.8	18.4	22.8
Groundnuts	6.0	9.6	12.6
Soybean Meal	7.5	10.8	13.2
Cotton	4.7	6.8	10.1
Jute	6.9	9.2	15.6
Rubber	7.9	12.1	16.3
Tobacco	6.1	5.8	10.8
Logs (Lauan)	6.6	8.9	14.0
Copper	9.1	15.3	18.5
Tin	5.3	8.1	10.4
Nickel	2.6	4.6	7.1
Aluminum	2.4	4.6	6.2
Lead	9.2	14.7	18.8
Zinc	8.4	14.4	17.8
Iron Ore	4.1	5.7	8.4
Bauxite	3.7	5.6	8.0
Manganese Ore	4.0	7.2	10.3
Phosphate Rock	6.7	13.8	17.4

Notes: For the calculation of the indices of fluctuation in commodity prices, annual price data in 1981 constant dollars for 1955–81 were used. Formulas used are as follows:

[a]The average percentage deviation from the moving average.

Sum $[(|Pt - P't|)/P't]/n = 100$

Where Pt = the price in year t

$P't$ = the moving average centered on the year t

n = the number of observations of the relevant moving average

[b]Average of annual percentage changes, devoid of sign.

Source: World Bank, *Price Prospects for Major Primary Commodities*, Economic Analysis and Projections Department, Commodities and Export Projections Division, Washington DC, 1982.

Identifying the factors responsible for fluctuations in these and other commodity markets requires an analysis of the particular characteristics of individual markets; e.g., see Labys (1973) and Labys and Granger (1970). In brief, commodity markets can be distinguished from other markets such as those for manufactured goods in that they display low price elasticities of supply and demand. That is, amounts supplied and demanded are relatively unresponsive to changes in prices, at least in the short run. Consequently, even slight disturbances in supply or demand conditions may require substantial price changes to move the market towards equilibrium.

Where agricultural commodities are concerned, for example, fluctuations in prices tend to occur because of disturbances in supply conditions. In the long run, the supply from tree crops cannot be easily adjusted since current output is heavily dependent upon the stock of trees. Thus wide and lengthy price swings result from attempts to optimally adjust this stock. In the medium run, supply from annual crops will vary depending on the situation between the period of planting and of harvest. If farmers' expectations of next year's demand are in error, price fluctuations result from over- or under-supply. In the short run, factors such as weather during the growing or harvest season often cause price fluctuations.

For the case of mineral commodities, supply can also be seen as price inelastic, since production capacity cannot be easily increased. Because of the long lead time required between exploration, mine development and mineral production, the perceived profitability of a price increase cannot readily increase production. Fluctuations in mineral demand, usually the result of short or long run fluctuations of the business cycle in industrialized countries, thus lead to mineral price fluctuations.

The volatility of these price fluctuations has had severe effects on the economies of developing as well as industrialized countries. It is for this reason that commodity price stabilization schemes such as buffer stocks have been an important subject of policy analysis in recent years. The use of models to analyze this particular problem thus receives attention in Chapter 5.

World Trade

Primary commodities play a major role in world trade. In value terms, agricultural commodities constitute about 17 percent, ores and minerals including fuels about 25 percent, and manufactures about 58 percent. The aspect of primary commodity trade that has received most interest recently has been that of the direction and magnitude of that trade. Some idea of the direction of commodity trade flows has been obtained from Table 1.2. A broader perspective can be obtained from Table 1.6 which shows the percentage composition of both the direction and magnitude of that trade. Foodstuffs and manufactured products have also been included to emphasize certain aspects of trade. Regarding sectors of destination, primary commodities constitute about 48 percent of the import values of industrialized countries and about 42 percent of the import value of developing countries. Concerning sectors of origin, industrialized countries export about 67 percent of manufactured products and only 33 percent of primary commodities. Developing countries, in turn, export about 80 per cent of primary commodities and only 19 percent of manufactured products. It is the tendency of developing countries to export mostly primary commodities and to import mostly manufactured ones that has led to the recent 'North-South' debate, the call for a 'new international economic order', and the 'UNCTAD Integrated Program for Commodities', e.g., see Nappi (1979), Brown (1981) and Brandt (1980).

Economic Development

A final aspect of recent attention on primary commodity markets related to trade patterns is the impact that these commodities have on the export earnings and economic growth of developing countries. Among reasons offered to substantiate the role played by exports are the following: (1) an increasing level of exports provides a country with the means to step-up its imports; (2) export-led development tends to concentrate investment in the most efficient sectors of the economy, those in which the country enjoys a comparative advantage; (3) the country also gains from economies of scale because the international market added to the domestic market increases the scale of operation possible; (4) the necessity of remaining competitive in international markets tends to maintain pressure on the export industries to improve efficiency; (5) for primary commodities, the country exports those goods most suitable to its natural resource, agricultural, and cultural base; and (6) secondary benefits are generated that result in increased investment, consumption, and flow of technology.

For this theory of export linkage to influence economic growth positively, the prices of these exports (taken relative to imports) must grow over time and be relatively stable. The latter implies that governments will not experience substantial fluctuations in exchange earnings and revenues necessary to finance imports, improve the level and

Table 1.6: Structure of World Exports by Products and by Sectors of Origin and Destination (Percentages in 1973 and 1979)

Export	Year	World	To Developed Countries	To Developing Countries	To Countries with a Planned Economy	
					Europe	Asia
Food	1973	14.9	15.0	14.7	13.7	20.2
	1979	11.8	11.5	11.7	14.9	15.8
Agricultural Materials	1973	6.0	6.3	4.6	6.0	12.6
	1979	4.2	9.4	3.1	4.2	9.7
Ores and Metals	1973	10.5	10.7	8.2	12.8	22.9
	1979	8.6	8.4	7.3	12.3	22.5
Fuels	1973	11.0	12.3	8.4	5.9	2.0
	1979	20.3	22.6	15.4	12.6	2.6
Manufactured Goods	1973	55.5	54.6	59.7	58.4	39.5
	1979	53.2	51.6	58.4	53.8	47.1
All Products	1973	100.0	100.0	100.0	100.0	100.0
	1979	100.0	100.0	100.0	100.0	100.0

Export	Year	World	From Developed Countries	From Developing Countries	From Countries with a Planned Economy	
					Europe	Asia
Food	1973	14.9	13.7	21.3	10.2	30.4
	1979	11.8	11.4	13.9	6.8	27.1
Agricultural Materials	1973	6.0	5.1	9.3	5.8	13.7
	1979	4.2	3.8	4.7	4.5	9.6
Ores and Metals	1973	10.5	10.8	8.8	11.8	9.2
	1979	8.6	9.8	5.3	9.2	6.8
Fuels	1973	11.0	3.5	39.6	10.7	1.3
	1979	20.3	5.9	56.6	24.2	10.7
Manufactured Goods	1973	55.5	65.6	20.0	52.4	44.1
	1979	53.2	67.2	19.0	48.3	45.3
All Products	1973	100.0	100.0	100.0	100.0	100.0
	1979	100.0	100.0	100.0	100.0	100.0

Source: United Nations Conference on Trade and Development (UNCTAD), *Handbook of International Trade and Development Statistics*, Geneva, 1976 and 1981.

structure of employment, establish the economic infrastructure and elaborate upon planning programs. In the section on prices we have seen that the behavior of commodity prices has worked adversely for these countries. Prices in constant terms were shown in Table 1.4 to have grown only slightly if at all for primary commodities. And price instability was shown in Table 1.5 to be quite severe for a large group of primary commodities.

Now the effect of this price behavior might not be too drastic if the developing countries also exported a host of other products whose prices were stable and growing. However, the tendency is for developing countries to have their total export earnings highly concentrated in primary commodities. Table 1.7 shows the relative share of the principal primary commodity exports in the total export earnings of a representative group of developing countries. The percentages provided indicate that for many countries more than 50 to 90 percent of earnings are vested in a single export. For example, coffee accounts for 85 percent of the earnings in Burundi; cocoa 76 percent for Ghana; sugar 68 percent for Mauritius; and petroleum 90 percent or more for a number of countries.

This export structure has given rise to the need for a number of commodity model developments and applications as described in Adams and Behrman (1982) and Labys, Nadiri and del Arco (1980). A description of the nature of these modeling requirements is provided in Chapter 2.

Traditional Approaches to Market Analysis

The economic analysis of primary commodity markets has been traditionally based on the microeconomic concept of market equilibrium between demand and supply. When a commodity is exchanged in a market, the determinant of both the quantity demanded and the quantity supplied is price. For a given commodity, within a given market and specific time frame, the relationship between quantity demanded and price is expressed as a demand schedule. Under normal conditions, demand is inversely related to price. Consumers will desire more of a commodity if its price is low than they will if its price is high. In Figure 1.1 the linear curve D is a demand schedule, the negative slope of which reflects the decrease in quantity demanded with an increase of price. A supply schedule similarly embodies the relationship between quantity supplied and price, given the same restrictions. It is given by curve S, positively sloped to reflect the increased quantity producers

Table 1.7: Primary Commodity Exports as a Percent of Export Earnings

Country	Export	Percent of Total Export Earnings, 1978
Algeria	Petroleum	89.0
Barbados	Sugar	28.7
Bolivia	Tin	27.8
Burma	Rice	31.2
Burundi	Coffee	85.3
Chad	Cotton	43.3
Chile	Copper	48.1
Colombia	Coffee	65.5
Congo (Brazzaville)	Petroleum	62.8
Dominican Republic	Sugar	30.0
Equador	Petroleum	40.0
Egypt	Cotton	20.4
El Salvador	Coffee	35.4
Gabon	Petroleum	72.5
Gambia	Groundnuts	31.9
Ghana	Cocoa	75.6
Guatemala	Coffee	43.0
Guyana	Bauxite & Alumina	33.7
Haiti	Coffee	39.2
Honduras	Bananas	25.8
Indonesia	Petroleum	60.3
Iran	Petroleum	93.7
Iraq	Petroleum	98.1
Jamaica	Bauxite & Alumina	52.9
Jordan	Phosphates	30.3
Kuwait	Petroleum	75.2
Libya	Petroleum	92.8
Malagasy Rep.	Coffee	40.6
Malawi	Tobacco	57.9
Mali Rep.	Cotton	36.7
Mauritania	Iron Ore	69.9
Mauritius	Sugar	67.6
Morocco	Phosphates	32.5
Nicaragua	Cotton	22.6
Philippines	Sugar	6.4
Rwanda	Coffee	60.7
Saudi Arabia	Petroleum	94.2
Sierra Leone	Diamonds	62.5
Sri Lanka	Tea	48.6
Sudan	Cotton	51.9
Syria	Cotton	20.2
Togo	Phosphates	39.2
Tunisia	Petroleum	36.7

Source: UNCTAD, *Trade and Development Handbook*, Supplement, 1981, United Nations, New York, 1982.

are willing to supply at higher prices, exactly the opposite of the situation with demand.

Figure 1.1: Commodity Market Equilibrium Process

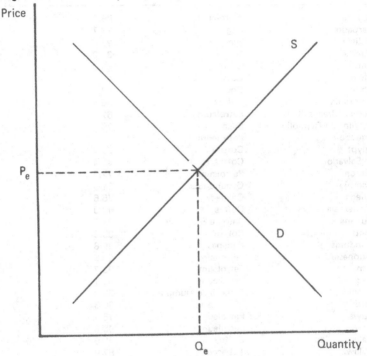

When demand and supply schedules intersect (demand equals supply) as shown in Figure 1.1, the market is said to be in equilibrium. Both producers and consumers are satisfied with the price (Pe) and exchange the agreed upon quantity (Qe). (Pe) is usually referred to as the equilibrium price at which the 'market is cleared'. This term can be traced back to the markets for agricultural products in earlier times when agreement on a certain price — usually for the whole lot — meant that the seller could leave or 'clear the market'. As long as demand and supply, represented by D and S, maintain their relative position, equilibrium price (Pe) and quantity (Qe) will not change. Over time, both the supply and demand schedules will change their position, slope or shape. Many factors contribute to these changes. Increasing *per capita* incomes will tend to shift the demand schedule to the right; a recession which reduces *per capita* incomes will have the opposite effect; techno-logical advances, for example, that increase the availability of substitute products tend to flatten the slope of the schedule. Hence, as synthetic liquid fuels come on the market in growing quantities, oil exporting countries are likely to face an increasingly flatter or more elastic demand for their oil. This clearly has consequences for their market power. Whenever producers face a steep (or inelastic) demand, they can raise their joint revenue (and in all likelihood) their profit by producing less and raising their prices. This is the main reason behind OPEC's decision *not* to lower its prices in times of a weakening demand. Jointly, OPEC faces an inelastic demand for its oil, and would thus stand to lose rev-enues from any price reduction. Changes in the market conditions, in particular government policies, can also alter the shape of the demand schedule. Consider, for example, a situation in which the government imposes a price ceiling. The portion of the demand schedule above this price would be irrelevant, and producers would face a 'kinked' demand schedule.

Similar changes also occur in supply schedules. Changes in the pos-ition, slope and shape of these schedules are usually a reflection of underlying changes in the cost of production, technological advances, the discovery of new resources, etc.

Hence, the 'price pattern' or 'price path' of a commodity is a reflec-tion of the simultaneous changes in the demand and supply schedules that occur over time. While it is always true that a decline in prices in-dicates that supplies exceed demand (and *vice versa*), this change in prices may have been caused by a (downward) shift of the demand schedule, a downward shift of the supply schedule or a combination of these two shifts.

In analyzing a commodity market, and as will be shown later, in modeling such a market, many analysts will prepare a flow chart, similar to the one presented in Figure 1.2 for the US soybean market, that captures the physical movement of a commodity from its production through the various marketing and processing stages to its final con-sumption. In preparing this chart, the analyst determines the prices of the commodity in question at the various intermediate transfer points (e.g., producer prices, import prices, wholesale prices) and identifies, to the extent possible, the key economic variables that will affect prices at the various marketing levels. If the analysis covers several regional mar-kets, he will also establish the relationship of prices in each of these markets and decide on a world market price quotation. He will also explore the extent to which speculation as well as the transactions in forward and futures markets influence the formation of commodity prices.

There are many approaches to analyzing a commodity market. By far the most widely used approach rests on the judgmental evaluation of a market situation or a change in the market by the commodity analyst. The judgmental approach is inexpensive and does not require any quantitative expertise. Its quality tends to reflect the caliber and experience of the analyst. Experience and familiarity with a particular commodity market hone and sharpen the instincts of analysts. The judgmental approach is frequently criticized, because it appears to lack the precision of approaches that use quantitative techniques. This criticism may not be entirely justified. It is true, that judgment replaces the formal model in this approach. However, most analysts who use this approach base their judgment or forecasts on some simplified abstraction of the market. In contrast to the formal modeling approach that clearly spells out the various behavioral and technical relationships the analyst has used to describe the market, an analyst using a judgmental approach employs what could be called an informal model of the market. Unlike the formal econometric models which contain precise estimates or assumptions about the relative strength of the various market forces, the informal models provide the judgmental analyst with 'intuition' and 'gut feeling'. Informal models are updated automatically every time the analyst observes the market or compares his forecasts with actual market developments. Econometric models are generally more difficult to update and to maintain. However, while econometric models can be used by many analysts, informal models remain the personal property of the analyst.

Another approach to forecasting is the so-called balance sheet analysis. Unlike the use of formal or informal forecasting models which focus only on the major elements of the market (the key producers or key consumers), balance sheet analysis attempts to compile relevant market information on a country-by-country basis. Hence, this forecasting approach is frequently refered to as the 'bottom-up approach', while the use of models is called the 'top-down approach'. The first step in the balance sheet approach consists in drawing up commodity balances — that is, a picture of the supply, domestic demand in its various processed forms, the exports, imports and if available changes in inventories — for all (or at least the most important) countries for the forecast period.

These commodity balances are constructed in such a way that supply (composed of production and imports) equals demand (composed of

Figure 1.2: Demand and Price Structure of the Market for US Soybeans. The arrows indicate major directions of influence.

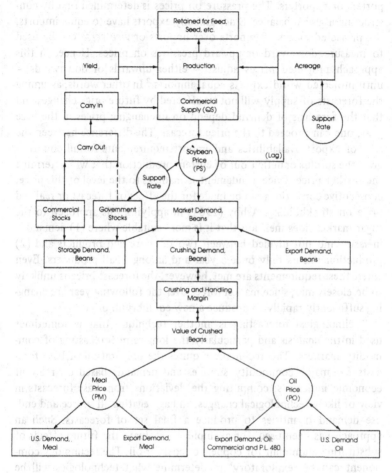

consumption, exports and inventory changes). The country balances are usually further divided according to whether countries are net importers or exporters. The pressure on prices is determined first by constructing a global balance. Since globally exports have to equal imports, the projected excess of exports over imports or *vice versa* can be used to measure downward or upward pressures on prices. Hence, in this approach projected prices adjust – either upwards or downwards – until projected world exports equal imports.[2] In other words, assuming the forecasts of supply will not be affected by future price changes and that the forecasts of demand depend on unchanging prices in the base year, one can proceed to the price forecast. The difference between the sum of export availabilities and import requirements for all countries gives the surplus or deficit out of current production that will determine the market price. Once a judgment is made as to the level of this price, consecutive corrections can be made for the effect of forecast or realized price on stockholding. Ashby (1964) in applying this approach to the sugar market does mention that it is more suitable where (1) demand is inelastic and not divided between two or more end products and (2) production occurs only once a year and among small producers. Even where these requirements are met, however, the forecast price is unlikely to be closely met, since market forces over the following year are changing sufficiently rapidly to produce a new equilibrium price.

Technological forecasting is another technique that is sometimes used in the analysis and particularly the long-term forecasting of commodity markets. This technique requires the preparation of base forecasts for major commodity supplies and demands based on relevant economic indicators, computing the deviations from base forecasts in view of likely technological changes, and aggregating all source and end-use demand quantities to produce a final set of forecasts. Such an approach has been used, for example, to evaluate the future effects of substituting aluminum for copper, or coal for oil. The technology component can be 'exploratory' to determine what technologies will be forthcoming or 'normative' to determine which technologies will be needed. This is achieved through methods such as consensus, Delphi, monitoring or trend and logistic extrapolation. More recently the concept of technology has been expanded to take account of the exploration for and discovery of unknown resources, i.e., mineral endowment evaluation.

Charting is another form of market analysis. It is the preferred tool of traders and analysts of commodity futures markets. It is also used by stock market analysts who refer to it as 'technical analysis'. The analyst who decides to use charting as his primary forecasting tool assumes that any attempt to follow supply, demand, or new information leads to substantial forecast error. Market action is the best guide to forecasting prices; accordingly, the patterns which develop in price formation provide the best indication of whether prices are going to rise or fall. Furthermore, it is only these patterns which furnish a reasonable estimate of the relative strength of demand and supply. While such an approach may be irrelevant for quarterly or annual price movements, some speculators believe that it is useful for predicting shorter-run price movements.

Forecasting price changes by the charting method depends in essence on the successful identification of the regular geometric patterns which prices form. These may take the form of triangles, head and shoulders, or tops and bottoms. The basic assumption that lies behind charting is that patterns will repeat themselves. By identifying a particular pattern or trend development, one can subsequently predict the extent of price movement as well as the timing of turning points. Two basic types of charts are generally used. On the first type of chart the analyst plots the high, low, and closing price against time; on the second one the analyst disregards time, and records price changes on swing, point or figure charts to identify the amplitude and frequency of price changes. The analysis of these charts consists either in a subjective interpretation of recurring patterns or in an objective computation of trends. These trends are normally estimated in terms of simple moving averages.[3]

Conceptually closely related to the charting technique is another approach to commodity market analysis and forecasting, namely time series analysis. Like charting, the objective of this technique consists in identifying regularities in the fluctuations of market variables. In its basic form time series analysis is largely mechanical. The analyst examines a series of observations for an underlying trend and for regular (cyclical) fluctuations, with the help of moving averages, exponential smoothing, adaptive filtering or Box-Jenkins (Autoregressive Integrated Moving Averages).[4] The trend as well as all the cyclical fluctuations that could be identified are then captured in a mathematical model which can be used for forecasting. This forecasting procedure has been enhanced by relating the fluctuation of some economic variable, such as the price, demand or supply of a commodity not only to time, but to economic factors.[5] Regression techniques are often used in conjunction with the techniques of time series analysis to quantify the influence of the various economic factors. The use of these more sophisticated time series techniques and regression methods leads to the kind of mathematical structures that make up the essence of commodity modeling.

The Need for Commodity Models

The increasingly widespread use of commodity models reflects not only our deeper understanding of the complexities of commodity markets but also our ability to measure the various influences which economic and non-economic factors exert in these markets and to capture their behavior in mathematical relationships.[6] During the 1950s and 1960s model builders turned their attention increasingly to the markets for primary commodities. Several factors accounted for this. First, the post World War II economic boom in industrial countries generated a steep increase in the demand for primary commodities and hence a greater need to predict these markets more accurately. In short, commodity models provided the appropriate framework for the investment, production and selling decisions of producers as well as the purchasing decisions of buyers. Although models by themselves are not able to predict market developments consistently, they tend to narrow the range of likely outcomes and thus reduce the risks and uncertainties of investing, trading and speculating in commodities.

Second, the need for more accurate market forecasts led to the in-depth analysis of commodity markets. Commodity models provided a powerful analytical tool to explore the complexities of these markets. Through commodity models analysts were able to build increasingly complex replicas of commodity markets. For the analyst the model represents a hypothesis about the way he assumes the market operates. He could test his model or hypothesis by checking how accurately it simulated market developments in the past or, at times, by the most frequent market behavior during the most recent period.[7] By changing the structure of the model, by choosing different mathematical or statistical models for the various behavioral relationships in the model, or by adding (or deleting) variables in these relationships, the analyst can examine alternative specifications of his model and his perceptions about the way the market functions. Commodity modeling uses a wide variety of analytical techniques including most of those discussed above. What differentiates modeling from the other techniques is its objective, namely to arrive at single quantitative representation of a market or industry.

Third, commodity models made it possible to evaluate the costs and benefits of alternative market policies. Models provided not only answers to 'what-if' questions, they also told the analyst the economic costs and benefits associated with the question. Models increasingly became instrumental during recent decades in shaping domestic market policies particularly in the agricultural sector. They also played an important role in UNCTAD's decision to establish an international buffer stock program.

The remainder of this study examines the various methods of commodity modeling, the applications of such models, as well as their advantages and limitations.

Notes

1. For example, 'fish' as well as 'hides and skins' represent a heterogeneous group of commodities of very different sizes and varieties. 'Wines' can be fine wines of great value or simple table wines.

2. The relative strengths of supply and demand are defined in this approach in terms of exports and imports: (1) 'export availability' implies an excess of production over demand and (2) 'import requirements' implies an excess of demand over production.

3. Most of this analysis – charts as well as the estimation of trends – is now provided, largely mechanically, by computers.

4. Many of the techniques used in time series analysis were taken from the analysis of electronic signals in physics. Many terms, such as 'filtering' or 'white noise' (the unexplained residual movement of a signal or a variable that can no longer be decomposed in any regular cyclical components) illustrate this close link.

5. Regressions or equations for important market variables, such as demand, for example, relate that variable to its underlying determinants such as prices, industrial activity, technologies, substitutes, etc.

6. An equally important factor in the emergence of econometric models was the availability of inexpensive electronic computers which made it not only possible to estimate a large number of economic relationships using increasingly sophisticated statistical methods, but also to simulate the behavior of complex markets under varying assumptions.

7. Of course, the most recent period was not used in the estimation of model parameters.

References

Adams, F. G. and Behrman, J. R. (1982) *Commodity Exports and Economic Development*, Lexington, MA: Heath Lexington Books

Aperjis, D. G. (1981) *Oil Market in the 1980s, OPEC Oil Policy and Economic Development*, Cambridge, Ballinger

Ashby, A. (1964) 'On Forecasting Commodity Prices With the Balance Sheet Approach', *Journal of Farm Economics*, 46:633–43

Brandt, W. (1980) *North-South*, Cambridge: The MIT Press

Brown, C. P. (1980) *The Political and Social Economy of Commodity Control*, London: The Macmillan Press

Labys, W. C. (1973) *Dynamic Commodity Models: Specification, Estimation and Simulation*, Lexington: Heath Lexington Books

—— Nadiri, I, and del Arco, J. Nunez (1980) *Commodity Markets and Latin American Development*, New York: National Bureau of Economic Research

— (1980) *Market Structure, Bargaining Power and Resource Price Formation*, Lexington: Heath Lexington Books

McCalla, A. F. (1981) 'Structural and Market Power Considerations in International Agricultural Markets' in A. F. McCalla and T. Josling (eds.), *Imperfect Markets in Agricultural Trade*, Montclair, NJ: Allanheld, Oswan, & Company

Nappi, C. (1979) *Commodity Market Controls*, Lexington: Health Lexington Books

2 COMMODITY MODELING METHODOLOGIES

This chapter presents the basic theory and methods of constructing commodity models. The approach which is essentially a modeling review involves two levels. At the first level, the chapter provides an introduction to the major forms of commodity models. At the second level, the chapter involves sufficient theoretical and mathematical depth that it might serve as a spring-board to model formulation itself. The starting point is a brief history of the evolution of commodity modeling. Because of the diverse nature of commodity models, their underlying methodologies are then compared in purpose and function using a taxonomical approach. The basic structure of commodity models is then explained by focussing first on individual model components and secondly on their integration into unified model structures. Finally, each of the major methodologies or techniques is described in detail: econometric market models, econometric process models, system dynamic models, spatial equilibrium and programming models, optimization models, input-output and other related models.

History of Model Evolution

Temporal Market and Industry Models

A commodity model is a quantitative representation of a commodity market or industry; the behavioral relationships included reflect demand and supply aspects of price determination as well as other related economic, political, and social phenomena. Models of this type stem from the basic microeconomic framework considered over some period of time $(t=1,\ldots,n)$.

$$D_t = d(P_t, A_t)$$
$$Q_t = q(P_t, N_t)$$
$$D_t = Q_t$$

Demand D is a function of prices P and industrial activity A; supply Q depends also on prices P and a resource shift variable N; and the identity calls for market clearing quantities and prices.

The history of these models can be first traced to early studies regarding the demand for agricultural commodities. Often mentioned in this regard are the empirical works of Moore (1919), Working (1927), and Schultz (1938). The first recognition of a commodity market as a dynamic system appears in the work of Ezekiel (1938) who summarized and advanced the theory of the cobweb. The possibility of obtaining an equilibrium solution from solving sets of demand and supply equations was suggested by Tinbergen (1939). This led to work on problems of identifying and estimating these equations as studied by Haavelmo (1943) and Koopmans (1953).

Most of the progress in the 1950s involved applying statistical inference to microeconomic market theory. Wold and Jureen (1943) critically examined problems associated with demand analysis, and Nerlove (1956) introduced dynamics into supply analysis. Suits (1955) extended this dynamic approach to include stability analysis, producing one of the first estimated commodity models. As in earlier years, considerable research in commodity modeling was fostered by the US Department of Agriculture. Publications by Meinken (1953), Fox (1953a), and Foote (1958) are often cited in this regard. Among other notable works, Hildreth and Jarrett (1955) and Judge and Wallace (1959) are recognized for their models of livestock markets, and Cohen (1960) produced an evolutionary simulation model related to the leather and hide industry.

Developments followed along similar lines during the 1960s although several new approaches emerged. Brandow (1961) investigated methods of demand analysis by constructing a linear demand system whereby the demands for all commodities are interrelated. Zusman (1962) expanded dynamic analysis to also include disequilibrium in the form of dynamic discrepancy, while Witherell (1967) was one of the first to apply dynamic delay and cumulative multipliers. The role played by expectations and futures markets was explored by Weymar (1968) in his refinement of the supply of storage theory.

Among other developments in market models which occurred during that period and later, a very large number could be cited. This results from the fact that this methodology has provided the basis for developing most other commodity modeling methodologies that are time dependent in some form. Thus, we must limit our comments to only the more important modeling extensions. One of these is concerned with the way in which market clearing prices are reached. The models mentioned above are basically price equilibrium models in which a single world commodity market price is determined through global market equilibration of supply and demand. Among other examples of such a model is the world fats and oils model constructed by Adams (1975) where a single global oils price to which each individual oil price is related reflects the equilibration of global supply and demand. Reutlinger's (1976) stochastic simulation for global grain reserve stocks also obtains one world wheat price from the intersection of world supply and demand schedules.

Thompson (1981) shows that two other subclasses of models stem from the basic price equilibrium model, depending on the inclusion of regional markets and prices. The first of these would link the prices in all regions but one through transport costs in that one region. For example, Williams' (1977) world soybean, oil and meal market model aggregates all importers into one region and links the price of soybeans, soy meal and soy oil back through transport costs and policy decisions to internal market prices in Brazil and in the United States. The second subclass of models includes pairwise price linkages among countries along the principal historical trade flows. Such an approach has been followed by Rojko and Schwartz (1976) in building the USDA's Grains-Oils-Livestock (GOL) model of world agriculture and in the Quance and Mesarovic (1980) version of the Agricultural and World Integrated Model (AGWIM).

The remaining methodological developments of interest go beyond price equilibrium and price linkages to focus on the market as functioning in a particular way. The consideration of commodity supply and demand instead as inputs and outputs of an industry can be found in the process models of Adams and Griffin (1969) and of Higgins (1969). The work on industrial dynamics by Forrester (1965) was adapted to commodity modeling by Meadows (1970) with his generalized dynamic commodity cycle model. Finally, the extensive application of computer techniques led to the construction of commodity models which blended econometric methods and/or optimization algorithms with decision rules. Of interest are system simulation models of the type constructed by the US Department of Agriculture (1970) and the computer simulation models of Naylor and his colleagues (1971). These methodologies actually comprise a broad group of commodity model applications. Most of these have been thoroughly evaluated in a survey by Johnson and Rausser (1977).

Spatial Equilibrium and Optimization Models

An alternative approach to commodity modeling features spatial or interregional efficiency in commodity production, distribution and utilization. The recognition of the transportation of commodities between regions extends the commodity modeling approach to spatial analysis. Among early developments, Enke (1951) built an electric analog in which prices were represented by voltages and physical commodity flows by amperages, and then solved the interspatial trade problem with a set of linear trading functions. He began with a model of n commodities (i=1,2,. . .,n) such that

$$E_i = b_i(P_i - R_i)$$

where E_i equals local production minus local consumption for the ith region (negative quantities indicate imports), P_i is the local price level, and R_i is the price in region i before trade. The coefficients b_i along with prices R_i and the transportation costs between regions i and j are given. Equilibrium conditions require that total net exports be equal to zero and that import prices be the sum of unit transportation costs and export prices. Given this information, the equilibrium price P_i and shipments E_i were solved by an iterative method with the aid of electric circuits.

Samuelson (1952) reformulated Enke's problem in which the sum of producers' and consumers' surplus, termed the 'net social payoff' or NSP, is maximized. Among other advantages, this formulation aids the convergence of the system through its numerical iterations. He established the equivalence between the Cournot-Enke and the Koopmans formulations of the transportation problem which led to the possibility of driving a programming solution to the point of competitive equilibrium with respect to quantities marketed at each location. In dealing with the livestock feed market, Fox (1953b) and Fox and Tauber (1955) solved the equilibrium problem by using an iterative computational procedure to arrive at market-clearing prices and shipments. The model contained regional demand and supply functions, with quantities and prices treated endogenously. Several years later both Judge and Wallace (1959) and Tramel and Seale (1959) proposed iterative, non-optimizing tatonnement procedures to find equilibrium solutions for the interregional shipment problem.

With the introduction of price-elastic demand functions into the spatial model, researchers such as Schrader and King (1962) found that iterative procedures were excessively time consuming for larger models. Iterations, of course, are necessary because the objective function is basically nonlinear in models such as this, being dependent on price times quantity which are both endogenous. Takayama and Judge (1964) were the first to solve the spatial equilibrium problem with quadratic programming, subject to linear interdependent demand functions. The modified simplex algorithm was applied through reformulation of the problem as a combined primal-dual linear program. Now incorporating price sensitive regional demand and supply equations, the model yielded a set of solutions consistent with competitive equilibrium and zero profit conditions. They also showed how monopolistic equilibrium could be replicated in this context.

Developments of this approach have been numerous. Takayama and Judge (1964) showed how it could be applied to multicommodity models and Bawden (1966) extended the multicommodity approach to embody international trade problems. A special iterative market simulating procedure applicable to spatial equilibrium which allowed price adjustment was applied by Dean and Collins (1967) as well as by Zusman, Melamed and Katzir (1973). And Bjarnason, McGarry and Schmitz (1969) showed how the study of tariffs and quotas could be extended to include impact analysis of changes in exchange rates.

A change of focus to disequilibrium and comparative dynamics can be seen in Bawden's (1966) study which featured a recursive programming solution to the interregional equilibrium problem. Here regional production is represented by econometric equations that depend on price, the latter being determined by a transportation model that optimizes the short run trade problem. Schmitz and Bawden (1973) later applied this approach to their model of the world wheat market. Temporal as well as spatial optimization was achieved by Takayama and Liu (1975) who built a wheat trade model to analyze alternative reserve stock proposals. Stock adjustment was also solved by Martin and Zwart (1975) who extended spatial equilibrium dynamically by including inventory relationships linked over time.

However, it was the attention to the production response problem where aggregation over individual producers was preferred to regional totals that led to formal work on recursive programming. Based on Henderson's (1959) use of programming to solve this problem, Day (1963) developed his recursive programming algorithm which represents a sequence of optimization problems in which the parameters of a linear model depend on optimal solutions of the model obtained earlier in the sequence. While a full description of the methodology can be found in Day and Nelson (1973), its particular extensions to agricultural process appear in Singh and Ahn (1972) and to mineral engineering process in Nelson (1971).

Not all spatial price equilibrium models have been cast in a quadratic programming framework. Moore, Elassar, and Lessley (1972) cast the grain and beef trade problem as a classical transportation problem of merely minimizing transport cost, with fixed export and import quantities. Blakeslee, Heady and Framingham (1973) built a linear programming model of world trade in grains, fertilizer, and phosphate rock. Further work on the linear programming model itself continued with Yaron (1967) including income in addition to price as a variable in the demand function. While this still required dependence on an iterative solution, Martin (1972) showed how step-wise demand and supply functions could be used to obtain linear programming solutions with iteration. This approach saw further improvement in the work of Duloy and Norton (1974) who solved the QP problem which normally includes endogenous supply and demand relations as an LP problem) now including commodity interdependence in demand, demand dependence also on income and population, and approximations of nonlinear demand functions. This approach was developed in the context of large-scale agricultural planning programs. One application which it received was in Radhi's (1979) world nitrogen fertilizer model which solved the underlying LP model as a separable programming problem with grid linearization of the demand schedules.

More Recent Developments

During the 1970s, the development of commodity modeling methodologies has grown slowly relative to the extensive modeling applications that took place. Two studies can be seen as consolidating the methodologies to establish commodity markets as a formal modeling area. Labys (1973) in his *Dynamic Commodity Models* traced the structure from model specification and estimation to model simulation and forecasting. While that work concentrated on econometric approaches, his follow-up study (1975), *Quantitative Models of Commodity Markets*, expanded the methodological framework to include engineering or programming and other forms of models.

Several other works also influenced model development. Adams and Behrman (1976) presented a study describing the use of small or 'mini' commodity models that could be integrated with larger model systems and applied this structure to several international agricultural commodity markets. Adams and Klein (1978) then edited the results of a Ford Foundation Conference designed to analyze how commodity models could be used to analyze international commodity stabilization policies. This was also followed by a related study of Adams and Behrman (1978) that presented more recent developments in commodity modeling methodologies. Finally, attention has recently been drawn specifically to forecasting with commodity models in a study edited by Rausser (1980) and another oriented towards price forecasting by Driehuis (1976).

Regarding developments in spatial equilibrium models, the time dimension has been explored more deeply in the form of intertemporal price equilibrium models as well as of intertemporal spatial price equilibrium models. Takayama and Onishi (1976) have provided a suitable algorithm which has been applied by Pant and Takayama (1973) to analyze commodity price stabilization problems. Since an optimal decision at any point in time inevitably requires revision as time evolves, Takayama, Judge and Guise (1971) combine the spatial and the adaptive revisions problem, exploring spatial equilibrium within the context of optimal control. In addition, Quirk and Smith (1969) dealt with optimal control approaches to fisheries, and Burt (1969) utilized Bellman's dynamic programming framework to produce a more general theory of production and investment for natural resources. Another dimension of solving the temporal problem has been to interrelate the behavior of several commodities at once. Thus, Takayama and Hashimoto (1976) have extended the QP approach to the multicommodity problem. Later applications also to agricultural trade were that of Nguyen (1977) and Whitacre and Schmidt (1980).

One area of recent interest has been that of solving nonlinear spatial equilibrium models. Warner (1979) has used the fixed-point nonlinear multi-regional model. An alternative solution to a similar problem also has been posed by Holland and Pratt (1980). The ability of these solution methods to utilize a separable programming approach has permitted larger models to be built than with conventional QP. For example, Polito, McCarl and Morin (1980) have shown that Benders' decomposition can be applied to break large nonlinear models down into a small nonlinear and a large linear programming model. The two can be solved iteratively at a much lower cost than by solving the large model by nonlinear programming. Problems of building large-scale energy models have also led to the development of more efficient computer solution methods. In particular Hogan and Weyant (1980) show how optimization can take place in a network of combined (linear and nonlinear) energy models.

Finally, attention should be drawn to the increased use of the multiperiod linear mixed integer programming model, first by Kendrick and Stoutjesdik (1978) for evaluating investments in the fertilizer industry and second by Dammert (1980) in the world copper market.

One major event of the 1970s which spawned a major model development was the price hike of crude oil instigated by OPEC at the end of 1973. This led economists in general and modelers in particular to consider the importance of noncompetitive market structures and institutions in modeling commodity resource markets. Thus, resource optimization models were developed as a class separate from spatial equilibrium and programming optimization models. The roots of this development can be seen in the early work of Hotelling (1931) on exhaustible resources and the work of Cournot (1838), von Stackelberg (1952), and Nash (1953) on oligopolistic market behavior and bargaining processes. It was Salant (1976) who showed how the range of market structures between price competition and monopoly could be structured within a common framework using a Nash-Cournot approach. Pindyck (1978) was one of the first to build a simple control-optimization model of cartel behavior in the aluminum and copper as well as the crude oil markets. His use of the Nash-Cournot approach can be further seen in the OPEC model of Hnyilicza and Pindyck (1976). Finally, the Stackelberg approach has also been employed, principally in the work of Cremer and Weitzman (1976), Gilbert (1978), and Salant (1979). A good review of this modeling approach can be found in Salant (1980) and Aperjis (1981).

As we move into the 1980s the model developments of most interest other than programming center upon model dynamics and control. An important study in this respect is that by Rausser and Hochman (1979) that deals with deterministic, stochastic and adaptive control formulations of models in the agricultural area. And Labys (1980a) has questioned the basic specification of dynamic commodity models. The applications of disequilibrium methods hold promise for better dynamic modeling of the kinds of fluctuations characterizing commodity markets. Further discussion of these developments appears in Chapter 6.

Range of Commodity Applications

The proliferation of model application to a variety of commodities can be viewed in the bibliography provided in Chapter 7. Some examples of more formal studies published during that period are best presented by commodity type or area. The area which probably saw the greatest expansion in models is that of energy. Some collections of energy models were provided by Searl (1973), *Energy Policy* (1973), and Charpentier (1974). Among methodologies emphasized were large-scale energy system models, electricity supply network models, and spatial equilibrium models. These various developments as well as other advances were then compared in a model survey by Limaye (1974). The particular modeling problem of relating an energy inter-industry model to a macroeconomic model of the US economy was presented by Jorgenson (1976). Macavoy and Pindyck (1975) dealt with particular modeling aspects of the natural gas shortage. One of the most large scale modeling efforts was that of the US Energy Information Agency (1979) in its construction of the PIES model. The latter based on Hogan and Weyant (1980), featured interregional equilibrium through iterations between a linear programming model of energy supply and an energy demand econometric model. Other accounts of modeling efforts can be found in Mackrakis (1974), Roberts (1976), and Hitch (1977). The most recent review dealing specifically with international energy models is that of Labys (1982).

The modeling of mineral markets also became a growing area of application. Vogely (1975) acting on behalf of Resources for the Future reviewed the different types of mineral models, including an introduction to geostatistics and resource base modeling. This overview was broadened into a state of the art survey by Labys (1977). Two books dealing with models of individual markets, tungsten and cobalt, were published by Burrows (1971a and 1971b). A later study also conducted by Charles River Associates (1978) was the first to be truly long term, integrating a reserve and mine development model based on geostatistical theory with the supply side of a copper model. Mikesell (1979) also provided a study dealing with the modeling of the copper market. And Smithson (1979) has described world mineral models of importance to the Canadian economy.

One mineral application which also led to the further development of techniques is the engineering process model. Both material process optimization models and material direct demand models received application in copper, stainless steel and other industries. A thorough description of them can be found in the recent review of *Mineral Demand Modeling* published by the National Academy of Sciences (1982).

As mentioned above, agricultural commodity modeling provided the major stimulus to general model development and this impetus still continues. Houck, Ryan and Subotnik (1972) provided a market structure approach to building international commodity models, with applications in the fats and oils area. Canadian developments were also consolidated in a CAES (1974) symposium volume, and international models were prepared within the World Bank (1981). Programming models also proliferated during this era. Following the survey in this area by Judge and Takayama (1973), individual studies appeared on spatial agricultural sector models first by Bishay (1974) and by Heady and Srivastava (1975). A work on spatial models of the grain trade followed by Grennes, Johnson and Thursby (1978). Kendrick and Stoutjesdijk (1978) also presented the integer programming approach to development planning for particular commodities. Finally, Johnson and Rausser (1977) surveyed these and more general systems models as part of the American Agricultural Economics Association general literature review. The most recent review which describes international agricultural modeling developments and applications is that of Thompson (1981).

A Taxonomy of Methodologies

Why speak of a 'taxonomy' of commodity models? This is necessary because the models can take a number of different analytical forms and their applications to commodity analysis differ considerably. Here the basic purposes and methodologies of commodity modeling are introduced so that the different modeling methodologies presented might be better evaluated. We start with a general definition of commodity modeling. It is then expanded by contrasting the different aspects of commodity behavior to be analyzed against the methodologies or modeling processes which can be employed.

As defined above, a commodity model is a formal representation of a commodity market, industry or firm, where the behavioral relationships included reflect the underlying economic, political, and social institutions. To make this definition more meaningful, let us consider it from three points of view: Why build a commodity model? What information is needed? And what procedure do we follow?

Why build a commodity model? We do this to explain market behavior or market history, to analyze commodity policies, to make commodity decisions, or to forecast and predict important commodity variables.

What information is needed? Although this depends on the inherent structure of a model, knowledge of the following is usually required:

1. The actors involved in the market and their decision-making framework, e.g., the competitive versus noncompetitive structure of a market.
2. The surrounding economic political, social, and legal institutions.
3. Technical, social, and other forms of constraints which influence production processes, consumption patterns, etc.

4. Relevant principles of economic theory which can be applied to explain production, consumption, inventory holding, etc.
5. Methodologies which can be appropriately employed, including their relative advantages and disadvantages.
6. The availability and accuracy of market data.

What procedure do we follow? The above information is normally applied according to the following procedure:

1. Identification of the policy problems to be solved.
2. Adoption of a modeling approach to their solution based upon available methodologies or the design of new ones.
3. Specification of the model incorporating the above institutions and constraints; selection of the most appropriate model based on statistical and judgmental observations.
4. Validation and refinement of the model so that it best reflects reality and best meets the requirements of the user.
5. Application of the model to the policy problems selected.

These steps are further described in Figure 2.1, using the example of a market equilibrium form of model. That the commodity models of interest can be validated is a most important part of the procedure. As compared to general systems or programming models for which validation is sometimes difficult, most of the models considered here are of a type whose effectiveness in explaining market behavior or forecasting can be determined. Otherwise, no way exists of distinguishing the quality of one model from another. An equally important feature of the procedure is that its steps are related in an iterative manner. That is, if the model does not explain well the behavior of a particular variable, or if the model does not provide the type of answers needed given the policy problems posed, then the model designer returns to an earlier stage either to improve the model specification or to suggest that other types of policy problems be examined.

Table 2.1 shows how commodity models can be applied to a variety of problems or situations in its depicting of the interplay between behavioral analysis and modeling process. The former refers to that particular aspect of commodity behavior which we want to analyze. The latter has been shown as answering a number of questions: What do the modeling techniques or methodoligies describe? What is modeled? What aspects of commodity behavior are emphasized? And what forms of policy analysis are possible?

Table 2.1: Commodity Behavioral Analysis and the Modeling Process

Behavioral Analysis / Modeling Process	What Do the Modeling Techniques Describe?	What is Modeled?	What Aspects of Commodity Behavior Are Emphasized?	What Forms of Policy Analysis are Possible?
Market environment at decision level	Economic decision making	Actual decision making process	Consumption, production, stock holding, investment	Impact of individual decisions on consumption or production
Market environment at interaction level	Simultaneous economic decision making	Interaction between decision makers within markets	Market equilibrium and disequilibrium	Impact of decisions on market adjustments
National and International Levels				
1. Market stabilization	Short run economic and institutional behavior	Interaction between market behavior and stabilization goals	Market stabilization and control, speculation and hedging	Impact of buffer stocks, production schemes, cartels on price behavior
2. Market planning	Long run economic and institutional behavior	Interaction between market behavior and private and national goals	Future consumption, production, prices	Impact of investment, technology, incomes on markets
3. Supply restriction	Long run strategic and economic behavior	Interaction between market behavior and national military and strategic goals	Future supply availability subject to geopolitics	Impact of international conflict and strategies on commodity supply

Market Environment at				
4. Agricultural process	Economic and agricultural behavior	Interaction between market behavior and agricultural activities	Transformation between resource inputs and commodity outputs	Impact of technology, profits, weather, area, plantings on output
5. Industrial process	Economic and industrial behavior	Interaction between market behavior and manufacturing/ processing activities	Sales, input requirements, transformation between outputs and inputs	Impact of national economic activities on industries and commodities
6. Spatial Flows	Economic behavior over space	Interaction between regional or national markets	Imports, exports, prices, tariffs, quotas, transportation costs	Impact of tariffs, transportation technology, exchange rates on commodity transfers
7. Economic growth	Economic development and growth processes	Interaction between commodity production/ processing/diversification and national growth	Investment, resource allocation, changes in income and employment	Impact of commodity investment on national economic growth
8. Interdependent systems	Economic, biological, social, and ecological behavior	Interaction between market behavior and supporting or constraining systems	Biological life cycles, pollution, energy demands, resource exhaustion	Interdependency of commodity and other systems, world interdependency
Nonmarket environment	Social, political, and cultural processes	Processes such as those found in sociology, anthropology, international relations	Cultural, social, geo-political, environmental	Impact of national trade, environmental policies

Figure 2.1: Procedure for Developing and Applying Commodity Models

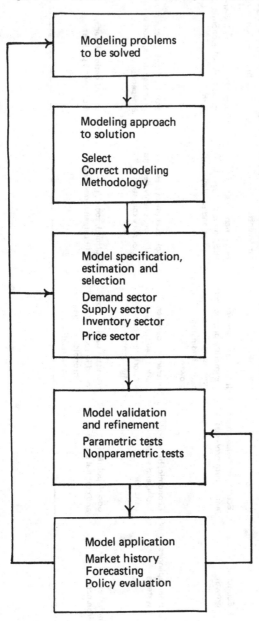

The different forms of commodity analysis possible have been ordered such that Table 2.1 delineates a number of steps in which a commodity decision maker or planner becomes progressively involved in a market environment of increased complexity. The behavioral analysis performed at the first or decision level would require explaining or predicting the activities of a single group of decision makers such as producers, consumers, or investors. This environment becomes only slightly more complex at the second or interaction level where the simultaneous interaction of a number of decision makers is analyzed.

Up to this point, we have considered the behavior of market participants whose activities are relatively independent of a broader set of economic influences at the national or international level. But what if we want to analyze this behavior as it related to national and international economic activities? Here we arrive at forms of commodity analysis which have been of most interest in studies recently carried out or planned for the near future. Let us examine each of these more thoroughly.

1. Market stabilization analysis involves finding those control mechanisms or forms of market organization which lead to more stable price or equilibrium positions.
2. Market planning analysis related to the forecasting of long run outcomes, depending on the policy problems or market strategies of interest.
3. Supply restriction analysis requires that a probabilistic theory describing the possibilities of sudden supply or import disruptions can be integrated with domestic market analysis.
4. Agricultural process analysis explains the influence that farm level decisions, technology, aggregate demand and prices have on agricultural output.
5. Industrial process analysis describes the relationship that exists between national activities, technical transformation processes within industries, and commodity input demands.
6. Analysis of spatial flows requires the application of spatial economic theory at the commodity level so that the relations of demand, supply and transportation costs to commodity flows can be determined.
7. Economic growth analysis can solve problems of planning for growth where commodities represent the 'engine' or primary sector of country growth. Analyses such as the impact of investment

or exchange rate changes on commodity development also fall into this category.

8. Analysis of interdependent systems implies consideration of commodity markets in relation to other important related spheres of activity such as biological, geological, environmental or social systems, or considerations of the future international distribution of commodity resources.

Other forms of commodity analysis could be added to this list, but the present selection covers the major work done thus far. The nonmarket environmental situation which is more complex has not yet been the subject of modeling analysis, except for some research on endogenizing political forces.

Let us now consider how one applies the modeling process to problems involving the market environment at national and international levels. Take, for example, the problem of analysing commodity stabilization. Table 2.1 indicates that this problem requires use of modeling techniques that are capable of describing short run market and institutional behavior. One would thus make use of a market equilibrium model now containing an inventory variable to permit incorporation of an inventory control mechanism. To stabilize the market of interest, one might begin by examining the impact of instigating futures market activity or speculation and hedging operations, but if the welfare goals of interest call for a much lower price variance, this approach would have to be abandoned. Policy analysis might then be directed to learning how a buffer stock scheme could lower price variance to the desired level.

The above attempt to interrelate commodity analysis and the modeling process can be extended to provide yet another perspective. In Table 2.2 the basic methodologies or model types employed in commodity model building are contrasted against the modeling process. Note that there are similarities between the forms of analysis previously selected and the methodologies to be employed. For example, econometric process models have been developed to analyze the industry process, and spatial equilibrium models are intended to analyze commodity trade flows. Table 2.2 also represents a pivotal point in providing an explanation of the modeling process as related to each of the methodologies of interest. It should be referred to as we answer questions about that process: What economic behavior is specified? What quantitative method is used? And what is the purpose of the methodology?

Table 2.2: Commodity Modeling Methodologies and the Modeling Process

Methodologies	Modeling Process: What is the purpose of the methodology?	What quantitative method is used?	What economic behavior is specified?	Examples of Commodity Applications
Market Model	Demand, supply, inventories interact to produce an equilibrium price in competitive or noncompetitive markets	Dynamic micro econometric system composed of difference or differential equations	Interaction between decision makers in reaching market equilibrium based on demand, supply inventories, prices trade, etc.	Cobalt, Energy, Lauric Oils, Rubber, Soybeans, Sugar, Tungsten
Process Model	Demand and production determined within an industry, focussing on transformation from product demand to input requirements	Dynamic micro economic difference equation system suitable for integrating linear programming on production side	Interaction between decision makers in industries, markets, national economies based on demand, inventories, production, investment, capacity utilization, commodity inputs, prices, etc.	Petroleum Steel
Systems Dynamics Model	Demand, supply, inventories interact to produce an equilibrium price emphasizing role of amplifications and feedback delays	Dynamic micro econometric differential equation system which features lagged feedback relations and variables in rates of change	Interaction between decision makers in adjusting rate of production to maintain a desired level of inventory in relationship to rate of consumption	Aluminum Broilers Cattle Copper Hogs Orange Juice

Table 2.2 (*cont.*):

Modeling Process / Methodologies	What is the purpose of the methodology?	What quantitative method is used?	What economic behavior is specified?	Examples of Commodity Applications
Spatial Equilibrium and Programming Models 1. Linear and Quadratic Programming	Spatial flows of demand and supply and equilibrium conditions assigned optimally in equilibrium depending on configuration of transportation network	Activity analysis of a spatial and/or temporal form. Degree of complexity depends on endogeneity and method of incorporation of demand and supply functions	Interation between decision makers in allocating shipments (exports) and consumption (imports) optimized through maximizing sectoral revenues or minimizing sectoral costs	Bananas Broilers Livestock Oranges Palm Oil Wheat
2. Recursive Programming	Production conditions and input revenue determined through primal/dual of linear program. Recursivity introduced through feedback component which includes profit, capital and demand	Activity analysis involving a sequence of constrained maximization problems in which objective function, limitation coefficients depend on optimal primal/dual solutions attained earlier in the sequence	Interaction between decision makers in reaching market equilibrium involves adaptive intertemporal processes related to production, investment and technological change	Coal Iron, steel Wheat, corn Soybeans
3. Mixed Integer Programming	Spatial and temporal equilibrium embodying production-process, transportation, and project investment components	Activity analysis involving spatial and temporal optimization but also including integer (0.1) variables to represent capacity additions	Interaction between decision makers in finding minimum discounted costs of meeting specific market requirements, i.e., project selection	Aluminum Copper Fertilizers

Optimization Model	Supply and demand analyzed in relation to optimal resource exhaustion over time and cartel behavior	Dynamic micro econometric system featuring formal cartel-fringe models such as that of monopoly, Stackelberg and Nash-Cournot	Interaction between decision makers in optimizing resource allocation and prices over time in non-competitive markets involving bargaining activity	Aluminum Copper Crude Oil
Input-Output Model	System regarded as process that converts raw materials into intermediate and final products via intermediate processes. Investment strategies evaluated in terms of raw materials supply and demand	Input-Output model combined with macro economic framework or disaggregated raw materials balance framework	Interaction between non-fuel and fuel commodities and macro markets in reaching materials and energy balance including supply-demand determination	Minerals Energy Agriculture
System Simulation Model	Demand, supply and other major variables and objectives considered as a complete system rather than a single market	Dynamic micro econometric equation system which when formed into a simulation framework is coupled with activity analysis and/or decision rules	Interaction between decision makers belonging to the system environment based on performance variables such as revenues, costs as well as market variables such as demand, supply, prices, etc.	Beef Energy Fish Livestock Multi-commodity Rice

Structure of Commodity Models

Most commodity models are composed of a number of components which reflect various aspects of demand, supply and price determination. Figure 2.2 presents an example of these components and their typical interrelation in the case of a simple commodity market model.

Figure 2.2: Model Representation of a Commodity Market

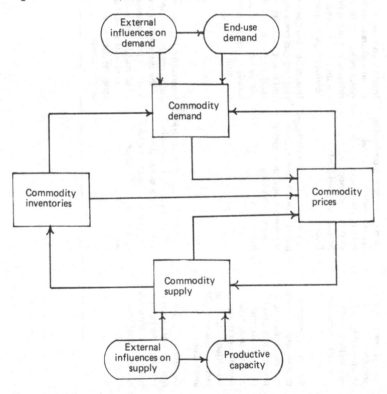

Commodity demand depends on commodity prices as well as external influences such as economic activity. Commodity supply depends on prices as well as external influences such as agricultural yields, geological rank, or climate. Changes in capital stock also affect commodity production. Inventories normally exist on the demand and supply sides of the market and these are held for precautionary, transactions' or speculative motives. Depending on the relative elasticity of demand and supply, inventories play a smaller or greater role in price adjustments.

Of course, these relationships also involve feedback effects. As shown in Figure 2.2, demand and supply are determined by prices, but the effects of demand and supply on prices must also be included.

Before describing each of these components and their integration, it should be noted that some theoretical background is helpful for understanding this process. Although such a presentation is beyond the scope of this work, interested readers should consult Labys (1978), Adams (1978b) or Behrman (1978).

Demand

Modeling of international demand behavior begins with an interpretation of basic demand responses to prices and income, i.e. the associated price and income elasticities. Direct price elasticities vary between commodities and markets. They tend to be lower for commodities without close substitutes (coffee or cocoa) than for those with such substitutes (natural rubber and synthetic rubber, copper and aluminum). More critically, these elasticities vary with time as well as with the actual excess demand or excess supply state of the market. This, coupled with the relative instability of commodity prices, makes measurements of demand behavior difficult. This measurement is further complicated by income fluctuations. The degree to which demand responds to changes in income or industrial activity depends on the income elasticity of the end products to which the primary commodities serve as inputs. Those products with a relatively low income elasticity tend to experience less demand fluctuations than those with higher elasticities. Thus the transmission of international demand cycles to commodity producing countries comes through these stage-of-process effects as well as through exchange rates and trade arrangements.

Demand measurement is also influenced considerably by commodity substitution patterns. The price elasticity of a competitive or complementary commodity, termed the cross-elasticity, also varies with commodities, markets, and time. Where commodities easily substitute for one another, as in the case of soybean oil and cottonseed oil, cross-price elasticities are relatively high. Substitution tends to be of an economic as well as a technical and quality or taste nature. Economic substitution normally results where material costs can be reduced by varying the proportions of a material used in the products. It can also take place between a natural commodity and its synthetic equivalent because the price of the former tends to be relatively higher and more unstable. Technical substitution, being of a more long run nature, occurs because of a change in the production process which permits the utilization of a less costly commodity. Quality substitution arises because of consumer influence on the end-product composition, such as the recent interest in biodegradable soaps or polyunsaturated margarines. Other factors influencing substitution may be the vertical integration of fabricating enterprises in consumer countries or changes in strategic policies.

Supply

Approaches utilized in modeling supply vary with the agronomic, biological, geological or technological nature of the production process. They also depend on the time span between investment and production, distinctions between short and long run price response being difficult to capture. Approaches also vary because commodities with similar technical characteristics such as fats and oils originate in different geographic areas under different climatic conditions and with varying harvest dates. For example, soybean oil is derived from a temperate annual crop, palm oil from a tropical tree crop, animal fats from livestock production, and marine oils from fishing.

Agricultural commodities of an annual nature comprise most of the world's agricultural production. Output from crops such as wheat, corn or rice depends on influences arising since the previous harvest. This is considered a form of short run response in which producers regulate their planting according to their perception of present prices and their expectation of future ones. But in a number of cases, especially for crops originating in developing countries, it is difficult to detect this lagged price response. Such is the case where farmers are near subsistence levels of income and the commodity is a staple food, or where farmers do not have access to credit for investment in improved variable inputs such as fertilizers. Another form of short run response occurs in relation to perennial tree crops. As the harvest cycle nears, prices can affect the intensity of the harvest or the quality of the crop, i.e., through over or under picking. Where production is relatively more capital intensive, short run production response becomes more rigid. Although the impact of some short run influences such as fertilization, irrigation or labor intensification can be measured, the impact of more irregular influences such as climatic conditions or strikes cannot. But recently, increased use has been made of forecasts from international satellite weather reporting systems.

Problems of measuring long run price response are related more to the production of perennial crops and of fuel and nonfuel minerals. The planting of perennial crops requires a fixed investment for a long period of time and careful consideration must be given to alternative uses of the land and capital in planting. Commodity output is influenced by both the stock of plants or trees and the yields. The stock depends on producer's expectations of future prices, a higher expected price leading to more planting with higher output anticipated at the end of the gestation period. Once again, the availability of credit as well as the perception of risk are significant. Yields from new plantings vary with the amount of interplanting, method of planting, variety of plant, and the quality of the land. Any final modeling of output also requires an understanding of the effect of diseases and tree removals on the stock of trees existing at any point in time.

While combined short and long run responses can be analyzed in agricultural production, they are more difficult to perceive in the mining of fuel and nonfuel minerals. Supply analysis is more cost-oriented; it is difficult to provide a linkage between long run costs of exploration and environmental disruption with short run costs of production. Conventional theory suggests that some finite stock of exhaustible resources is allocated over individual production periods, such that the present value of price minus marginal cost be equal in all production periods. Alternatively, a necessary condition for allocation is that the resource price net of extraction costs should rise at a rate equal to the rate of return on other assets.

Normally, it is possible to recognize the long run response of the intention to invest in a mining operation. Changes in current output reflect a response to invest because of higher prices in some past period. However, short run price response may not reflect the optimal rate of depletion. Mines of high capital intensity encountering low prices will continue to function, just as long as operating costs are being covered. Similarly, other mines encountering these price conditions may not close simply because of the relatively high costs of reopening. Nor may such prices elicit a response because of geological factors such as switching from a richer to a poorer vein of ore. Where short run price increases stimulate output, the degree of the response depends on the intensity of capacity utilization possible.

Inventories and Prices

A most crucial aspect of price determination in commodity models is the interrelationship between inventory and price adjustments. The modeling of inventory behavior particularly in international markets is made difficult by lack of both available data and of data classified into appropriate categories. Agricultural inventories, for example, can exist in the form of national and international food reserves and buffer stocks as well as in private stockholdings. Some confusion also exists because producers, consumers and traders each may hold commodity inventories for transactions, precautionary or speculative purposes.

Where suitable inventory data exist for model building, it is sometimes difficult to discover the particular price most crucial for market clearing and adjustment. Although the spot price on the market featuring the largest volume of trading often serves this function, other prices need to be taken into account: forward prices, futures' prices, auction prices, local supply prices, local demand prices, and occasionally support prices. Prices also are indicators of complex adjustments taking place in the international system such as inflation, exchange rate alignments, speculation, and military, natural or political crises.

Integrating the Components

Modeling of commodity markets entails integrating all of the above components into the overall market or industry structure. But before reaching the complete market or model structure, one must first deal with a number of conceptual problems.

To begin with, the time span of the model of interest must be decided. Is the market behavior to be analyzed or forecast of a short, medium or long run nature? If it is short run, then the relevant market structure includes spot trading as well as futures trading. This becomes critical for a number of commodities where the annual volume of futures trading can be ten to twenty times the volume of annual production. Most econometric market models of a supply-demand nature with a temporal or spatial configuration work best in the medium run. But this approach becomes less effective for the long run. Here, goal seeking, feedback relationships and technological forecasting are helpful in predicting long run market behavior.

There is also the need to re-examine conventional notions about adjustment mechanisms which move the market towards equilibrium. Price may not be the result of competitive adjustments; consequently, market structures reflective of monopolistic competition must be investigated. This appears to be more frequent in mineral markets where production is not competitively determined and supply behavior must be based on cost relationships. Some markets may also never attain equilibrium in the sense that supply always equals demand at different points in time; thus the disequilibrium characteristics of the market must be modeled. Part of the problem may be in defining the market framework. Perhaps modeling the properties of such commodities like conductivity or protein content may lead to more realistic models.

Finally, the market represents more than an economic mechanism. Other information needs to be introduced, which relates to the institutions and organization of the market, the behavioral patterns of industries and firms, and the government policies affecting the industry. These institutions and policies differ widely from country to country and they must be included in international modeling. It would even be reasonable to introduce behavioral relationships reflecting political and government activities in a market — the fuels market being a case in point.

Econometric Market Models

The most basic type of microeconomic model from which other commodity methodologies have developed is the market model. Focussing on the price mechanism which serves to clear the market, the rudiments of a market model can be summarized in four equations, although much more complex structures are used in practice.

$$
\begin{aligned}
D_t &= d(D_{t-1}, P_t, P_t^c, A_t, T_t) \\
Q_t &= q(Q_{t-1}, P_{t-\theta}, N_t, Z_t) \\
P_t &= p(P_{t-1}, \Delta I_t) \\
I_t &= I_{t-1} + Q_t - D_t
\end{aligned}
\tag{1}
$$

Definition of variables:

D = Commodity demand
Q = Commodity supply
P = Commodity prices
P^c = Prices of substitute commodities
$P_{-\theta}$ = Prices with lag distribution
I = Commodity inventories
A = Income or activity level
T = Technical factors
N = Agronomic or geological factors
Z = Policy variable influencing supply

Demand is explained as being dependent on prices, economic activity, prices of one or more substitute commodities, and possible technical influences such as the growth of synthetic substitutes. Other possible influencing factors and the customary stochastic disturbance term are omitted here and elsewhere to simplify presentation. Accordingly supply would depend on prices as well as underlying productivity factors such as agronomic or geological influences, and a possible policy variable. A lagged price variable is included since the supply process is normally described using some form of the general class of distributed lag functions.

Prices are explained by changes in inventories, although this equation is sometimes inverted to explain inventory demand. The model is closed using an identity which equates inventories with lagged inventories plus supply minus demand. Where the price equation is inverted to represent inventory demand, the identity can be recognized as the equivalent supply of inventories equation.

The econometric description of the model can be found in Labys (1973, 1975 and 1978) who presents it as a general system of first or higher order difference equations, solvable within a simulation framework. This requires that its variables be classified as endogenous variables or targets: D, S, I and P; lagged endogenous variables: D_{-1}, S_{-1}, I_{-1} and P_{-1}; and exogenous variables: P^c, A, N, T and Z. Of the latter group, Z is also known as an instrument or policy controllable variable. We normally refer to the above equation system in its matrix form

$$\Gamma Y + B_1 Y_{-1} + B_2 X = U \tag{2}$$

where Y = a $G \times n$ matrix of current endogenous variables; Y_{-1} = a $G \times n$ matrix of lagged endogenous variables; X = a $M \times n$ matrix of exogenous and policy controllable variables; U = a $G \times n$ matrix of current disturbance terms; Γ and B_1 = $G \times G$ matrices of coefficients on the current and lagged endogenous variables respectively; and B_2 = a $G \times M$ matrix of coefficients on the exogenous and policy variables. The equivalent reduced form is given by

$$Y_t = \Pi_1 Y_{t-1} + \Pi_2 X_t + V_t \tag{3}$$

where

$$\pi_1 = -\Gamma^{-1}\beta_1, \ \pi_2 = -\Gamma^{-1}\beta_2, \ V_t = \Gamma^{-1}U_t$$

Π_1 = a $G \times G$ matrix of reduced form coefficients on the lagged endogenous variables, Π_2 = a $G \times M$ matrix of reduced form coefficients on the exogenous and policy variables X, and V = a G X n matrix of stochastic disturbance terms.

The reduced form provides a basis for analyzing model stability where in the limit all endogenous variables approach their equilibrium levels. This is normally determined by:

$$|\pi_1 - \lambda I| = 0 \tag{4}$$

The λ's will be the characteristic or latent roots of the matrix. The condition for stability requires the real roots to lie within the unit circle. If the roots are imaginary or $\lambda = a + bi$, stability requires that the modulus $|z| = \sqrt{a^2 + b^2} < 1$. If the λ's are stable, then the general solution will converge to the equilibrium values of Y as $t \to \infty$.

Another useful derivative of the reduced form (3) is the final form defined to be:

$$Y_t = \sum_{\tau=0}^{\infty} \pi_1^{\tau} \pi_2 X_{t-\tau} + \sum_{\tau=0}^{\infty} \pi_1^{\tau} V_{t-\tau} \tag{5}$$

The principal use of the final form in commodity modeling is that it permits us to compute several types of multipliers that can be employed in policy analysis. Definitions of these multipliers can be obtained from successive components of the exact part of the final form: π_2, $\pi_1\pi_2$, $\pi_1^2\pi_2$ . . $\pi_1^{\tau}\pi_2$. As described in Labys (1973), the definitions include: static short and long run multipliers, and dynamic delay and cumulative multipliers.

The use of these multipliers has lessened as simulation methods have developed as a superior tool for policy analysis. Model simulation can take place (in the case of a temporal model) over the historical period or over some future period. One normally bases simulation on the model structural form given by (2), where the stochastic disturbance terms can be suppressed or generated. For models which are dynamic, nonlinear and simultaneous, a numerical solution is typically imposed. Interpreting the model as a set of n equations (j = 1, 2, . . . , n) any one can be written as:

$$Y_{jt} = f(Y_{1t}, Y_{2t}, \ldots, Y_{gt}; Y_{1,t-1}, Y_{2,t-1}, \ldots, Y_{g,t-1}; \\ X_{1t}, X_{2t}, \ldots, X_{mt}) \tag{6}$$

Guess a set of starting estimates (0) to be used for the dependent variables on the right side of the equation; values of the exogenous variables are given. Solve each equation to obtain a new set of estimates (1) for the dependent variables.

$$Y_{jt}^{(1)} = f(Y_{1t}^{(0)}, Y_{2t}^{(0)}, \ldots, Y_{gt}^{(0)}; Y_{1,t-1}, Y_{2,t-1}, \ldots, Y_{g,t-1};$$
$$X_{1t}, X_{2t}, \ldots, X_{mt}) \tag{7}$$

One then uses the estimates (1) on the right side of each equation to obtain estimates (2).

$$Y_{jt}^{(2)} = f(Y_{1t}^{(1)}, Y_{2t}^{(1)}, \ldots, Y_{gt}^{(1)}; Y_{1,t-1}, Y_{2,t-1}, \ldots, Y_{g,t-1};$$
$$X_{1t}, X_{2t}, \ldots, X_{mt}) \tag{8}$$

This procedure can be continued for up to r iterations such that:

$$Y_{jt}^{(r)} = f(Y_{1t}^{(r-1)}, Y_{2t}^{(r-1)}, \ldots, Y_{gt}^{(r-1)}; Y_{1,t-1}, Y_{2,t-1}, \ldots,$$
$$Y_{g,t-1}; X_{1t}, X_{2t}, \ldots, X_{mt}) \tag{9}$$

where

$$\left| \frac{Y_{jt}^{(r)} - Y_{jt}^{(r-1)}}{Y_{jt}^{(r-1)}} \right| \leq C \tag{10}$$

The value of r is selected as a critical percentage so that at convergence the finally estimated value does not differ from the previously estimated value by more than, for example, $C = 0.1$ or 0.001. When the critical value is not met, the r estimates are placed on the right hand side of each equation and the procedure is continued. Note that the critical value applies to each variable and to each equation until the full set of equations is solved for a particular period. A complete set of values for all endogenous variables can be obtained by forming successive solutions through time. Note that since the model is dynamic, the solution is evolutionary and generates its own values for the endogenous variables with only the exogenous variables given. Naylor (1971) and Epps (1975) have shown how to extend commodity simulation analysis by conducting stochastic simulation which involves a series of replications, each spanning multiple observation intervals.

While policy decision making can be simulated by changing values of the exogenous policy variables contained in X and observing their impact on variables in Y, the *ex ante* prediction problem is normally one of obtaining Y_{+k} from

$$Y_{t+k} = \Pi_1 Y_{t+k-i} + \Pi_2 X_{t+k} \tag{11}$$

where values of X_{t+k} are assumed. The values of Y_{t+k-i} can be given or generated in previous periods. The latter is preferable for dynamic prediction. *Ex post* forecasts known as 'backcasts' also can be made based on actual values of the lagged variables and the exogenous variables; this permits disaggregation of *ex ante* forecast error into information and model error.

Simulation can also facilitate the investigation of the stability and cyclical properties or commodity models. Typically investigation of these properties has been based on the linear nonstochastic representation of the model (2) given above. But these properties can also be investigated based on stochastic simulation. Stochastic behavior normally arises from random variation in the equation disturbances and/or the exogenous variables. Evaluating the performance of a model subject to stochastic shocks stems from the work of Adelman and Adelman (1959), as witnessed in commodity studies, for example, of Zusman (1962) and Desai (1966). Howrey and Witherell (1968) also have shown that a more complete description of the cyclical properties of a model can be obtained using 'analytical simulation', which features spectral representation of the stochastic component of the final form. More recently, Arzac (1976) has applied the spectral approach to interpret the stochastic dynamics of the US grain market.

Finally, simulation can be extended to include optimization by using optimal control theory to steer the endogenous or state variables Y close to some target A, through the appropriate choice of some policy or control variables Z. The market model now referred to as the system or motion or transformation equations is rewritten to distinguish the exogenous variables X not subject to control from the variables Z subject to control.

$$Y_t = B_1 Y_{t-1} + B_2 Z_t + B_3 X_t + U_t \tag{12}$$

Performance of the system will be measured by deviations of Y from the target vector A, as embodied in some objective or welfare function W. For the simplest case of a finite horizon, discrete interval, deterministic control problem, one searches for the optimal sequence of controls Z^* from the set of admissible sequences C which will transform the commodity system Y from its initial conditions Y(0) through the control region R, in such a way that the welfare function W is optimized. In this case, minimize

$$W = w(Y_1 - A_1, Z_1; \ldots; Y_T - A_T, Z_T) \tag{13}$$

subject to

$$Y_t = f(Y_{t-i}, Z_t, X_t)$$
$$Y(0) = Y_0$$
$$Y \epsilon R; Z \epsilon C$$

where T is the length of the horizon. Developments in the application of control theory to commodity models can be found in works by Kim, Goreux and Kendrick (1975), Sequra (1973), Rausser and Freebairn (1974), Klein (1978), Mariano (1978), and Rausser and Hochman (1979).

As stated in the section on market model history, the application of the econometric market model has been the most extensive of all the methodologies employed in commodity modeling. Applications to agriculture, minerals and energy have been cited as well. Interested readers can refer to the many works suggested as well as more theoretical model studies such as that of Labys (1973 and 1975) and Adams and Behrman (1976 and 1978). Further model examples can also be found in the bibliography of Chapter 7.

Econometric Process Models

Commodity models of the process type, although econometric models, have been designed to supplant market models in several respects. Process models deal with supply and demand within an industry rather than across a market; they thus focus on the transformation of commodity inputs into finished products. Whereas market models balance supply and demand to produce an equilibrium price, prices in a process model are normally a function of production and material costs. The emphasis is also different: process models concentrate on the industrial production process, requirements for raw materials, and labor and plant capacity.

To construct the simplest form of process model, one begins with four equations.

$$DO_t = d(PP_t, A_t) \text{ or } \overline{DO}_t \tag{14}$$
$$QO_t = q(K_t, L_t, E_t, M_t) \tag{15}$$
$$QO_t = DO_t \text{ or } \overline{DO}_t \tag{16}$$
$$PP_t = p\left(\frac{K_t}{QO_t} PK_t + \frac{L_t}{QO_t} PL_t + \frac{E_t}{QO_t} PE_t + \frac{M_t}{QO_t} P_t\right) \tag{17}$$

Definition of variables:

QO = Product output
DO = Demand for output
PP = Product price
A = Activity or GNP
L = Labor inputs
K = Capital inputs
E = Energy inputs
M = Commodity inputs
P = Commodity price
PL = Wage rate
PK = Price of capital
PE = Energy price

Demand for the product output can be assumed to be exogenous $\overline{DO}_t$. Alternatively as in the case of Adams and Griffin (1972), it can be endogenously determined by the demand relation (14) where the income variable is obtained from a macroeconometric model. The supply equation becomes an equation linking the output of a product to capital stock, inputs or labor, inputs of energy, and raw materials or commodities. The identity (16) shows that production is scheduled to equal demand requirements. The final equation explains product prices as a mark-up on the costs of inputs. An advantage of introducing price determination in this manner is that it enables the modeling approach to be applicable to industries with an oligopolistic structure.

More recent experiments have involved improving the structural representation of these models. On the supply side, Adams and Griffin (1972) have shown how engineering data can be introduced by utilizing a linear programming model to explain transformation from refined petroleum product outputs to the demand for inputs in the petroleum industry. Such an attempt has also been made more recently by Eckbo, Jacoby and Smith (1978). On the demand side, Tsurumi (1976) criticizes the use of industrial activity variables to explain demand in modeling the Japanese steel industry. Instead, he hypothesizes that activity variables follow some form of distributed lag pattern and that the related lag structure can be determined from the future production planning of steel consumers.

Both the petroleum refining and the steel industries have proven highly suitable for process modeling. However, it is the modeling of the steel and related metal industries which has stimulated further methodological developments in this area. For example, Kopp and Smith (1980) have used the steel industry process model of Russel and Vaughan (1976) to evaluate factor substitution capabilities of neoclassical cost functions. Moreover, a recent report by the National Academy of Sciences (1982) describes engineering process models as a major area of mineral demand modeling. Since these models use econometric process methods as a minor component of overall model formulation, we delay discussion of process models until their methodology is more fully discussed in the sections on linear programming and system simulation models.

System Dynamics Models

The dynamic aspects of econometric market models constitute the basis for the industrial dynamics methodology. As associated with the work of Forrester (1965), this methodology focuses on attributes of commodity systems which lend themselves to engineering or systems analysis: amplification and time delays, feedback and control, and stability and damping. Meadows (1970) further developed this approach with his 'Dynamic Commodity Cycle Model' which emphasizes the inventory formation aspect of market models. Two coupled negative feedback loops — consumption and production — each act to adjust inventory coverage to desired levels. When exogenous factors cause inventories to deviate from desired levels, there are changes propagated in the production and/or consumption sectors which influence prices, thus causing inventories to return to their normal position. Further features of the model include extending the lagged response of production to consumption, at least implicitly in the form of partial expectations. In addition, functional relationships are expressed in continuous time with 'period' analysis being replaced by 'rate of change' analysis, implying that all relationships are cast into the form of differential equations.

The structuring of a Dynamic Commodity Cycle Model normally, but not always, requires the 'Dynamo' simulation format. Thus, the programming statements featured in the original formulation have been adapted to provide difference equation examples comparable to the above econometric models. Model formulation begins with the inventory component; stocks are assumed to adjust to differences between rates of production and consumption

$$I_k = I_j + T(Q_{jk} - D_{jk}) \tag{18}$$

where j refers to a point in time previous to k and production and consumption rates are taken over the intervening period. The parameter T is a time adjustment constant. The stocks variable is also considered in terms of actual as well as relative (length of) time coverage of consumption.

$$IC_k = I_k/D_k^* \text{ and } RIC_k = IC_k/IC_k^d \tag{19}$$

Here D_k^* is the expected consumption rate and IC_k^d is a desired stock coverage. Relative stock coverage then provides the mechanism for price determination.

$$P_k = p(RIC_k) \tag{20}$$

The production component is organized around the ability of capacity to adjust to meet production needs. For commodities, capacity is reflected in variables such as breeding stock, acres, trees, mines, or refining and processing facilities. Desired production capacity which is the rate to be maintained in the long run is a function of prices P_k^* expected by producers.

$$QC_k^d = q(P_k^*) \tag{21}$$

These prices are normally assumed to follow adaptive expectations. Between a change in desired production capacity and a corresponding change in actual production capacity, two processes intervene: capacity ordering and capacity arrival. The former or capacity-transfer-initiation rate is the difference between desired capacity and that which is available or being transferred.

$$QCT_{kl} = (OC_k^d - QC_k - QCB_k)/CD \tag{22}$$

Important here is the delay factor CD which is the time period required for producers to initiate transfer of capacity to eliminate the above difference as well as the transference variable QCB defined as:

$$QCB_k = QCB_j + T(QCT_{jk} - QCC_{jk}) \tag{23}$$

The second or capacity-transfer-completion rate (capacity arrival) also includes a delay factor CTD, which implies that capacity to be used will not immediately affect commodity initiation.

$$QCC_{kl} = L(QCT_{jk}, CTD) \tag{24}$$

Production capacity itself is defined as being equal to the above arrival rate less the rate of capacity depreciation, where the latter reflects depletion, biological aging, or physical deterioration

$$QC_k = QC_j + T(QCC_{jk} - CDR_{jk})$$

where $CDR_{kl} = QC_k/AQC$. Finally, using the commodity-initiation rate $QI_{kl} = QC_k \cdot CU_k$, an expression can be reached for commodity output expressed as the production rate

$$Q_{kl} = L(QI_{jk}, \theta) \cdot QU_k \tag{25}$$

The production response lag featured in the cobweb is introduced here using θ. Equations explaining the utilization factor CU have been omitted for simplicity.

Less detail is contained in the consumption sector where the consumption rate is the product of *per capita* consumption requirements and population

$$D_{kl} = (D/N)_k \cdot N_k \tag{26}$$

the former assumed to follow a partial adjustment process

$$(D/N)_k = (D/N)_j + B_1 T [(D^*/N)_j - (D/N)_j] \tag{27}$$

where $(D^*/N)_k = d(P_k)$ and B_1 is equivalent to the partial adjustment coefficient. The endogenous variables in the model can then be simulated for historical explanation or predictive purposes.

Definition of variables

I   = Commodity stocks (units)
Q   = Commodity production rate (units/time)
D   = Consumption rate (units/time)
IC = Stock coverage (time)
RIC = Relative stock coverage
P   = Commodity price (dollars/unit)
QC = Production capacity (units/time)
QCT = Capacity-transfer-initiation rate (units/time/time)
QCB = Capacity-being-transferred (units/time)
CD = Capacity-transfer-initiation delay (time)
QCC = Capacity-transfer-completion rate (units/time/time)
CTD = Capacity-transfer-delay (time)
CDR = Capacity-depreciation rate (units/time/time)
AQC = Average life of production capacity (time)
QI = Commodity initiation rate (units/time)
CU = Capacity utilization factor
QU = Production utilization factor
D/N = *Per capita* consumption requirements (units/time/person)
DD = Consumption-requirements-adjustment delay (time)

To apply the industrial dynamics framework, the conventional wisdom has been to select only those commodities which display some form of cyclical behavior in production and prices. These cycles, furthermore, should result from certain amplifications and delays within the system. In the original Meadows (1970) study, models were constructed for the hog, cattle and broiler markets. Since then, Naill, Mass, Randers and Simpson (1973) have revamped the hog model and Raulerson and Langham (1970) have applied industrial dynamics to the frozen concentrated orange industry. More recent applications, however, have tended to diverge from the originally specified model structure, requiring neither differential equation formulation nor pronounced cyclicality. Ferrari (1978) has also published a system dynamics modeling guide which facilitates model construction.

Current applications are largely in the mineral and energy areas. For example, Strongman, Killingsworth and Cummings (1976) and Wolstenholme (1979) have built models of the copper industry, and Krallmann (1979) a combined systems dynamics/input-output model of the chemicals industry. Applications in the energy area include the Dartmouth (1977) model of the US energy market, and the Choucri

(1980) model of the world oil market. A large-scale model featuring systems dynamics is the Hughes and Mesarovic (1978) energy component of the 'World Integrated Model'.

Spatial Equilibrium and Programming Models

An important aspect of dealing with commodity markets is examining spatial or interregional efficiency in production, distribution and utilization. As shown by Day and Sparling (1977), optimization and programming techniques have proven particularly effective in modeling such phenomena. The logical process for describing this class of models would be to begin with problem formulation and then to apply some form of convex programming to its solution. However, several distinct programming approaches have emerged that modelers tend to apply to commodity problem solutions. The most popular of these are linear and quadratic programming models which have the specific advantage of recognizing transport costs and market constraints in the formulation of an equilibrium system. Since it it often necessary to concentrate on processes involving optimization over time, recursive progamming and mixed integer programming models also are important. One other recent approach of interest is that of combined or hybrid models.

Linear Programming Models

This class of spatial (transportation) models normally involves the following components: (1) a set of demand points or observations and a set of supply points, (2) the distribution activities over space, and (3) the equilibrium conditions. These components are represented in the following mathematical definition.

$$\text{Minimize } L = \sum_{i=1}^{n} \sum_{j=1}^{n} T_{ij} Q_{ij} \tag{28}$$

Subject to

$$D_i \leq \sum_{j}^{n} Q_{ij} \qquad i = 1, \ldots, n \tag{29}$$

$$S_j \geq \sum_{i}^{n} Q_{ij} \qquad j = 1, \ldots, n \tag{30}$$

$$T_{ij}, Q_{ij} \geq 0 \qquad \text{all } i, j \tag{31}$$

Definition of variables:

D_i = Commodity demand in region i
S_j = Commodity supply in region j
T_{ij} = Transportation cost of shipping a commodity between region i and region j
Q_{ij} = Quantity shipped between region i and region j

The model operates such that transportation costs are minimized by allowing commodities to transfer until demand equals supply in every spatially separate market. The cost minimization process is established by the objective function (28). The constraint relations (29 and 30) reflect the conditions that regional consumption cannot exceed the total shipment to the region and that the total shipments from a region cannot exceed the total quantity available for shipment. Relation (31) assures the lack of negative shipments.

Applications of LP models to agricultural commodity analysis have been very extensive. In fact many of the developments of commodity models in this area stem from the early work on agricultural production analysis previously cited in this chapter. Surveys of modeling in this area can be found in Day and Sparling (1977) and in Takayama and Judge (1971), while reviews of applications in agricultural planning can be found in Bishay (1974) and in Heady and Srivasta (1975).

A more recent area of application is that of mineral commodity analysis. Some of these LP applications can be termed conventional ones. They include domestic models such as that of Libbin and Boehlji (1977) for coal, and international ones such as that of Copithorne (1973) for nickel and Kovisars for copper (1975) and zinc (1976). However, a much wider area appears to be that of engineering process optimization models described by the National Academy of Sciences (1982). These models normally are based on LP models of a production process which account for the physical quantities of processed and furnished materials derived from mineral inputs. Some model components of special interest include production technology and non-mineral inputs such as labor and energy.

Where the activity component is distinguished as an intermediate conversion process, these models are considered specialized process models rather than just LP models. An explanation of this specialized formulation can be found in Sparrow and Soyster (1980), while related model examples of the steel industry include Nelson (1971), Tsao and Day (1971), and Clark and Church (1981).

Quadratic Programming Models

This class of spatial model replaces the exogenously given demand and supply observations with observations that are endogenously determined. While other nonlinear formulations of an LP are possible, the quadratic programming (QP) model represents a specific formulation that features spatial equilibrium characteristics. The QP model normally is specified to include the following components: (1) a system of equations describing the aggregate demand for one or more commodities or interest in each of the included markets as well as the aggregate supply of the commodities in each of the markets, (2) the distribution activities over space, and (3) the equilibrium conditions. While the demand and supply equations imply a structure similar to that of an econometric market model, the equilibrium process is more adequately represented through the identification of the profits to be realized from the flow of commodities, i.e., the excess of a price differential between two points minus transportation costs. Profit maximization is assured through the use of a computational algorithm which allows commodities to transfer until demand equals supply in every spatially separated market. So that policy decisions can be evaluated more realistically, the equilibrium conditions and other definitional equations can be used to impose constraints on the model parameters.

The system of demand and supply equations necessary for transforming the linear to a quadratic programming model is given below. The equations are written in linear form to help specify the quadratic objective function necessary for solution. Identifying variables are assumed to be computationally embodied in the constant terms.

$$D_i = b_{0i} - b_{1i}P_i \qquad (32)$$
$$S_j = b_{0j} - b_{1j}P_j \qquad (33)$$

where P_i = commodity demand price in region i and P_j = commodity supply price in region j. Because the formulation of this model by Takayama and Judge (1971) expresses these equations in their inverse form, the above equations can be alternatively written as

$$P_i = a_{1i} + a_{2i}D_i \qquad \text{for all i} \qquad (34)$$
$$P_j = a_{3j} - a_{4j}S_j \qquad \text{for all j} \qquad (35)$$

where $a_1, a_2, a_3, a_4 > 0$ over all observations.

The constraints imposed on the supply and demand relations are the same as in the linear programming model.

$$D_i \leqq \sum_j^n Q_{ij} \qquad \text{for all i} \tag{36}$$

$$S_j \geqq \sum_i^n Q_{ij} \qquad \text{for all j} \tag{37}$$

Transport costs and shipments are assumed to be non-negative.

$$T_{ij}, Q_{ij} \geqq 0 \tag{38}$$

The objective function necessary to complete the model goes beyond the cost minimization goal of linear programming. That is, the function maximizes the global sum of producers' and consumers' surplus after the deduction of transportation costs. This form of market-oriented quasi-welfare function has been termed net social payoff (NSP) by Samuelson (1952) and is defined as follows.

$$NSP = \sum_i^n \int_0^D P_i(D_i)dD_i - \sum_j^n \int_0^S P_j(S_j)dS_j - \sum_i^n \sum_j^n Q_{ij}T_{ij} \tag{39}$$

The objective function for the present model is a restatement of the above after substitution of the linear demand and supply relations.

$$\text{Max (NSP)} = \sum_i^n a_{1i}D_i - \sum_j^n a_{3j}S_j$$
$$- \tfrac{1}{2} \sum_i^n a_{2i}D_i^2 - \tfrac{1}{2} \sum_j^n a_{4j}S_j^2$$
$$- \sum_i^n \sum_j^n T_{ij}Q_{ij} \tag{40}$$

where D_i and $S_j \geqq 0$.

Applications of quadratic programming possess the advantage of simultaneous interaction between prices and quantities, an adjustment not normally possible in linear programming. The use of a nonlinear objective function also prevents the erratic changes in spatial flows that sometimes occur in LP model adjustments. As indicated in the discussion of model history, applications of QP models have been extensive. These range from temporal model extensions of wheat trade by Takayama and Liu (1975) to multicommodity agricultural models by Takayama and Hashimoto (1976). More recent applications have been in energy with the Kennedy (1974) world oil refining model and the Labys and Yang (1980) coal model. Most recently, a model applications package has been made available by Apland, McCarl, Thomspon and Santini (1982) at Purdue University.

Recursive Programming Models

These can be considered a special case of adaptive intertemporal spatial equilibrium models. Applications to commodity markets thus far have not been extensive, mainly because emphasis on processes of production, investment and technological change is nor normally a feature of commodity studies. Data used also are normally disaggregated below the market level. A recursive program can be described as a sequence of constrained optimization problems in which one or more objective functions, constraint or limitation coefficients of a given problem depend functionally on the optimal primal and/or dual solution vectors of one or more problems earlier in the sequence. To obtain this recursive dependence of the coefficients on preceding solutions, a set of feedback functions are used. The rationale behind this approach is that it emulates a decision maker who proceeds according to a succession of behaviorially conditioned, suboptimizing decisions. The decision marker in protecting himself from errors of estimation and forecasting reviews his maximization plans each period based on current information. The sequence of decisions as a whole must then converge to some desired optimum.

The formulation of an elementary recursive programming model can be explained using Day's (1973) generalized cobweb example. (For a survey of more complex models and some of the results obtained, refer to Day and Nelson, 1973.) Two homogenous agricultural commodities are produced by two farms or decision units, each requiring land and working capital. Their production levels as well as resource allocation are decided by maximizing gross short run profits. Thus the decision problem for each unit at the beginning of a period t can be described by the linear programming problem

$$\text{MAX}_{Q_1,Q_2} \quad [V_1^*(t)Q_1 + V_2^*(t)Q_2] \tag{41}$$

subject to

$$Q_1 + Q_2 \leq L$$
$$C_1Q_1 + C_2Q_2 \leq K(t)$$
$$Q_1, Q_2 \geq 0$$

With L and K(t) representing aggregate amounts of resources available, decision makers are considered identical in their behavior and the linear program represents the sum of the decisions of all units.

The marginal net revenue values associated with L and K(t) are given by the solution values R_1 and R_2 of the dual (to the above) which is

$$\text{MIN}_{R_1,R_2} \quad [R_1L + R_2K(t)] \tag{42}$$

subject to

$$R_1 + C_1R_2 \geq V_1^*(t)$$
$$R_1 + C_2R_2 \geq V_2^*(t)$$
$$R_1, R_2 \geq 0$$

And recursivity is introduced through a feedback component consisting of three equations which describe anticipated unit profits per area, working capital, and prices

$$V_i^*(t) = P_i(t-1) - C_i \qquad i = 1, 2 \tag{43a}$$
$$K(t) = \Sigma_i P_i(t-1)Q_i(t-1) - H \qquad i = 1, 2 \tag{43b}$$
$$P_i(t) = \text{MAX}(0, a_i + b_iQ_i(t)) \qquad i = 1, 2 \tag{43c}$$

The feedback component can be said to follow the principle of the cobweb. That is, current price is expressed as a function of past prices, reflecting naive expectations; it can also be determined concurrently with demand, when the market is in equilibrium. Thus, anticipated profits $V_i^*(t)$ are computed from current expected prices expressed in terms of past values $P_i(t-1)$. Total capital available for production at the beginning of a year K(t) also depends on last year's activities. The value of sales $P_i(t-1)Q_i(t-1)$ minus payments for overhead H is derived from the linear programming definition of supply. Finally prices $P_i(t)$ are determined, assuming a temporary equilibrium in markets where those commodities produced are also sold. Linear demand functions are used with $P_i(t)$ expressed as a function of current demand $Q_i(t)$, no price substitution effects being included. Policy analysis performed with this type of model can answer questions regarding stability of behavior, cyclical patterns, growth and equilibrium.

So far, the commodity related studies based on recursive programming have concentrated on applying the basic method to explain substitution patterns during agricultural transition as well as to describe the role of technological change in commodity extractive industries. See studies by Day and Tab (1972), Nelson (1971), Singh and Ahn (1972), and Abe (1973) related to commodities such as iron, steel, coal, wheat, corn and soybeans. Latest developments as reported by Day and Sparling (1977) relate to constructing multi-sector models as well as extending the approach to embody general equilibrium.

Mixed Integer Programming Models

The multiperiod linear mixed integer (MIP) programming model of the type described by Kendrick (1967) and Kendrick and Stoutjesdijk (1978) represents an alternative methodology for describing optimization over time. Like recursive programming, it represents an application of linear programming; only the integer characteristic is introduced to accommodate combinations of 0–1 variables which can refer to the non-existence or existence of a production facility. The background to MIP stems from attempts to cope with a number of commodity-oriented analyses including shipping and transportation, industrial process, and project selection. Several of these functions are typically combined to study market adjustments, as exemplified in Dammert's (1980) study of copper investment in Latin America.

Formulating such a model begins with the transport component which resembles the spatial equilibrium transportation model studied earlier. A process component is necessary when modeling commodity industries such as minerals or energy where one can produce one or more products from a primary commodity or where one can produce a single product by more than one process. In the first case, copper can be semimanufactured in the form of wire, tubes and rods, or sheet strip and plate. In the second case, coal, natural gas, or petroleum can be used to generate electric power. Finally, the project selection component can be introduced by incorporating investment to augment capacity as well as economies of scale and exports.

A model that embodies these components and is operated intertemporally attempts to find the minimum discounted cost of meeting specified market requirements over the period covered by the model. This search involves the selection of activity levels for the following variables: (1) increments to capacity, (2) shipments from plants to markets and among plants, (3) imports and exports, and (4) domestic purchases of raw materials, miscellaneous material inputs, and labor. A simplified structure of such a model is presented below, following the formulation of Kendrick and Stoutjesdijk (1980, pp. 50-5). Because of its relative complexity, the specification is divided according to (1) the objective function (2) the cost components, and (3) the model

Table 2.3: Definition of Variables — Mixed Integer/Programming Model

Symbol	Definition
INDEXES	
i	Plant sites (I)[a]
j	Domestic market areas (J)
l	Export market areas (L)
m	Productive units (M)
q	Productive processes (Q)
λ,t	Time intervals and time periods (T)
c	Commodities used or produced in the industry, (final products of the industry (CF), intermediate products (CI), and raw materials, miscellaneous inputs, and labor (CR))
VARIABLES	
Q	Process levels (production levels)
X	Domestic shipments
R	Domestic purchases materials and labor
Y	0-1 investment decisions
H	Continuous investment decisions
$\overline{H}$	Maximum capacity expansion per time period
CK	Capital costs
CR	Recurrent costs
CT	Transportation costs
TC	Total costs
D	Domestic sales
K	Initial capacity
S	Retirements of capacity
W	Market requirements
PARAMETERS	
a	Process inputs (—) or outputs (+)
b	Capacity utilization rate
ρ	Discount rate per time interval
δ	Discount factor
σm	Capital recovery factor for productive unit m
ω	Fixed-charge portion of investment costs
υ	Linear portion of investment costs
β	Recurrent costs related to capacity
π	Prices
μ	Unit transportation costs

Note: [a]Total or limit indicated within parenthesis.

constraints. Definitions of the symbols and variables are provided in Table 2.3.

Objective Function. This function minimizes the total discounted costs of production where these costs consist of three cost components: capital costs, recurrent costs, and transport costs.

$$\text{Minimize } TC_t = \sum_t^T \delta_t (CK_t + CR_t + CT_t) \tag{44}$$

Cost Components. 2a. The capital cost component equals fixed charges plus the linear portion of capital costs.

$$CK_t = \sum_{\lambda=1}^t \sum_i^I \sum_m^M \sigma_m (\omega_{mi\lambda} Y_{mi\lambda} + \nu_{mi\lambda} H_{mi\lambda}) \tag{45}$$

2b. The recurrent costs equal recurrent costs related to capacity plus local raw materials and labor costs.

$$CR_t = \sum_{\lambda=1}^t \sum_i^I \sum_m^M \beta_{mi\lambda} H_{mi\lambda} + \sum_c^{CR} \sum_i^I \pi_{cit} R_{cit} \tag{46}$$

Here β represents the portion of recurrent costs that is not proportional to actual production levels but rather is proportional to the capacity installed. Examples are the maintenance costs and insurance payments on any piece of capital equipment.

2c. The transport cost component equals final product shipment costs, plus intermediate shipment costs. Raw materials are assumed to be prices inclusive of domestic transport cost.

$$TC_t = \sum_c^{CF} \sum_i^I \sum_j^J \mu_{cijt} X_{cijt} + \sum_c^{CI} \sum_i^I \mu_{cii't} X_{cii't} \tag{47}$$

Material Balance Constraints. 3a. Final Commodity Constraint: The production Q of commodity c by all processes p at plant i must at least equal the shipments of commodity c from plant i to all markets j. The typical process that provides final commodities can be assigned a coefficient $a_{cpi} = 1.0$ in the final commodities' constraint (48), because the unit of capacity can be arbitrarily defined in terms of one of the inputs or outputs.

$$\sum_q^Q a_{cpi} Q_{pit} \geq \sum_j^J X_{cijt} \tag{48}$$

3b. Intermediate Commodity Constraint: The output of intermediate commodities at plant i must be greater than or equal to shipments of intermediate commodities from plant i to plant i'.

$$\sum_q^Q a_{cpi} Q_{pit} \geq \sum_i^I X_{cii't} \tag{49}$$
$$i' \neq i$$

3c. Raw Materials and Labor Constraint: The production of intermediate and final products requires raw materials and labor. The coefficient a_{cpi} in constraint (50) thus will normally be negative. Purchases of raw material and labor R_{ci}, in turn, will have to be positive for the constraint to hold.

$$\sum_q^Q a_{cpi} Q_{pi} + R_{ci} \geq 0 \tag{50}$$

Capacity Constraints. Capacity required is less than or equal to expansion less capacity retirements

$$\sum_q^Q b_{mpi} Q_{pit} \leq K_{mi} + \sum_\lambda^T (H_{mi\lambda} - S_{mi\lambda}) \tag{51}$$
$$\lambda \leq t$$

Here K_{mi} = initial capacity for productive unit m at plant i, parameter b_{mpi} = units of capacity used on productive unit m per unit of output of process p, and $S_{mi\lambda}$ = expected retirement of capacity in productive unit m at plant i in time period λ. The S variables are chosen exogenously to the model. For example, if a productive unit manufactures steel, the initial capacity might include a number of open hearth furnaces that were slated for retirement during the period covered by the model. Then $S_{mi\lambda}$ would represent the capacity to be retired in each time period λ. The effect of the summation over λ for λ less than or equal to t in (50) is to permit all capacity installed in previous periods to be available for use in period t.

Investment Constraints. Two additional constraints are needed to complete the specification of investment in the model. These two constraints introduce the integer side conditions directly into the model

$$Y = 0 \text{ when } H = 0,$$
$$Y = 1 \text{ when } H > 0,$$

which are used in specifying the investment cost function. These constraints are:

$$H_{mit} \leq \bar{H}_{mit} Y_{mit} \tag{52}$$
$$Y_{mit} = 0 \text{ or } 1 \tag{53}$$

where H_{mit} = an upper bound on the size of capacity unit that can be added to productive unit m at plant i in period t.

The effect of (52) and (53) is to prohibit any addition to capacity unless the fixed charge is incurred, and the fixed charge is only incurred if Y_{mit} is equal to 1. From (52) it follows the Y_{mit} must be placed at 1 if H_{mit} is positive for the constraint to hold. If H_{mit} is 0, Y_{mit} will be forced to 0 by the model as the cost minimization objective of the model leads to a preference not to incur the fixed charge.

Market Requirements. The summation of shipments from all plants i to each market j must be equal to or greater than the product requirement of market j

$$\sum_{i}^{T} X_{cij} \geq W_{cj} \tag{54}$$

Nonnegativity Constraints. $X_{cij}, Q_{pi}, W_{ci}, H_{mi}, R_{ci}, S_{mi} \geq 0$ (55)

Applications of this model have involved mostly the planning of commodity investment programs in developing countries. Important factors involved in this process that can be dealt with in the model are the determination of efficient investment patterns, project and program evaluation, economic integration plans, and industry regulations. A comprehensive explanation of the application of this approach can be found in Kendrick and Stoutjesdijk (1979). The mentioned study of Dammert (1980) deals specifically with the world copper market and copper investment planning in Latin America. One can also see the potential usefulness of the model for energy planning purposes, such as in the application of Schinzinger (1974).

One interesting aspect of Dammert's approach is that of dealing with reserve levels and reserve limits within the context of mineral exhaustion. This is accomplished by including the following constraints on processing different ore grades.

$$Z_{pit} \leq Q_{cpit} \tag{56}$$

This constraint places an upper limit on the annual exploitation of high-grade ores and of second-grade ores where Q_{cpit} = annual availability of ore grade c. This constraint can also be extended to include the total reserve limit.

$$\sum_{t}^{T} Z_{pit} \leq V_{pi} \tag{57}$$

where V_{pi} = total reserves of ore grade in processing area i.

Finally, there are several extensions of the model, which when developed, will add considerably to its application. While the model has so far dealt only with fixed demands, the possibility exists of endogenizing demands, for example, in the context of the quadratic programming model where an objective function involving social surplus is now maximized. Since the fixed-demand specification also implies no substitution between final products, the inclusion of appropriately specified demand functions may permit this possibility. Related also to demand, the prices of some inputs and outputs are fixed. One could thus combine an algorithm with the model that would associate a different price with different commodity specifications. Kendrick and Stoutjesdijk (1978) also report on other alternatives such as collapsing the model to represent other forms of programming problems and the reader may want to refer to their text.

Hybrid Programming Models

This special class of commodity model does not refer to a specific model type but rather to various approaches combining various models in a single framework or of constructing large-scale multi-commodity models. The models to be combined have tended to be of a programming nature, often also linked to some form of econometric model. The most comprehensive effort to develop a methodology for hybrid commodity models in the 'combined' energy model approach of Hogan and

Weyant (1980). A theoretical as well as a computational approach is presented for reaching equilibrium solutions with a combined set of models. The most well known application of this approach is the Project Independence Energy Evaluation System (PIES) constructed for EIA (1979). It contains energy supply engineering models, an energy demand econometric model, and a linear programming model that integrates over supply and demand to generate a set of equilibrium energy prices. Other energy models which represent hybrid forms of models, although not of the above type, are the Hughes and Mesarovic (1978) world integrated model (WIM), the Herrera and Scolnik (1976) version of the Bariloche model, the Linneman (1976) MOIRA system, and the IIASA set of models described by Basile (1979).

Optimization Models

As a modeling methodology, optimization models are normally studied in the same class of models as programming models. The survey of Day and Sparling (1977) mentioned above takes this general combined approach into regard. However, optimization models have also been developed as a special group of international commodity models designed to explain and predict cartel behavior in the case of mineral markets as well as the crude oil markets. According to Salant (1980), the theoretical background to this group of models stems from the economic literature on exhaustible resources, which dates back to Hotelling (1931). Prior to 1975, contributions to that literature assumed either perfect competition or a single monopoly, despite historical examples of market structures intermediate between the two.

By 1975 several attempts to integrate the theory of imperfect competition and exhaustible resources were made. Pindyck (1978) presented a model of resource market behavior capable of analyzing the impacts of the cartelization of exhaustible resources. Salant (1976) showed how the polar cases of perfect competition and pure monopoly, as well as the continuum of intermediate market structures, could be structured within a common framework by using a dynamic analogue of the Cournot (1838) equilibrium concept (formally an open-loop, Nash non-cooperative, non-zero-sum differential game). In essence, the Nash-Cournot approach assumes duopoly market behavior in the form of a non-uniform cartel, but changes the behavioral pattern of the fringe from that of followers to that of bargainers. Applications of this approach to resource commodities can be found in the work of Ulph

(1980), Hnyilicza and Pindyck (1976), Lewis and Schmalensee (1979), and Loury (1981).

At the same time, a conceptually distinct approach utilizing a dynamic (open-loop) analogue of the von Stackelberg (1952) solution concept was initiated by Cremer and Weitzman (1976), with subsequent contributions by Gilbert (1978), Gilbert and Goldman (1978), and Salant (1976). The Stackelberg duopoly theory reflects a cartel and fringe interaction less than bargaining. The cartel or dominant firm takes the reactions of other firms into account in its pricing policy, while the other firms or fringe take prices as given. Some applications of this approach can be found in Gilbert (1978) and in Ulph and Folie (1978).

Because of the relative complexity of the above models other than that of a simple cartel, we restrict ourselves to the latter formulation to explain this methodology. In particular, the cartel model of Pindyck (1978, pp. 238-90) is presented which consists of a multiplant monopolist or cartel and a competitive fringe. Net demand facing the cartel is

$$X_t = D_t - S_t \tag{58}$$

where D is total market demand

$$D_t = d(D_{t-1}, P_t, A_t) \tag{59}$$

and S is the supply of the competitive fringe

$$S_t = s(S_{t-1}, P_t, N_t) \tag{60}$$

Resource depletion is possible for the competitive fringe and this is modeled by incorporating cumulative production CS into the above equation such that

$$S_t = s(S_{t-1}, P_t, CS_t) \tag{61}$$

where increases in CS defined below move the supply function to the left

$$CS_t = CS_{t-1} + S_t \tag{62}$$

A similar accounting identity is needed to keep track of cartel reserves R.

$$R_t = R_{t-1} - D_t \tag{63}$$

The objective of the cartel is to pick a price trajectory P_t that will maximize the sum of discounted profits

$$\text{Max } W = \sum_{t=1}^{N} (1/(1 + \delta)^t)[P_t - m/R_t]D_t \tag{64}$$

where m/R is average (and marginal) production costs (so that the parameter m determines initial average costs), δ is the discount rate, and N is chosen to be large enough to approximate the infinite-horizon problem. Note that average costs become infinite as the reserve base R approaches zero, so that the resource exhaustion constraint need not be introduced explicitly. The resulting model framework is that of a classical unconstrained discrete-time optimal control problem, where numerical solutions can be easily obtained.

The control solution to this model yields an optimal price trajectory P_t^* as well as the optimal sum of discounted profits W^* for the monopolist. One might like to compare these variables with the optimal price trajectory and sum of discounted profits that would result if the cartel dissolved (or never formed), and its member producers behaved competitively. Optimal here implies that competitive producers must still manage an exhaustible resource, balancing profits this year against profits in future years.

Although competitive producers cannot collectively set price, they each determine output given a price. Pindyck shows that the rate of output should be such that the competitive price satisfies the equation

$$P_t = (1 + \delta)P_{t-1} - \delta m/R_{t-1} \tag{65}$$

If this were not the case, larger profits could be obtained by shifting output from one period to another. In addition, the initial price must be such that two constraints hold. First, the resulting price P and output D trajectories must both satisfy net demand at every point in time as given by equations (58), (59), and (60), i.e., supply and demand must be in market equilibrium. Second, as the price rises monotonically over time, resource exhaustion must occur at the same time that net demand goes to zero. If demand becomes zero before exhaustion occurs some of the resource is wasted and yields no profits; profits would be greater if the resource were depleted more rapidly (at a lower price). If exhaustion occurs before demand becomes zero, depletion is occurring too rapidly and should proceed more slowly.

The computation of the optimal price trajectory for the competitive case is thus straightforward. Pick an initial P_0 and solve over time equation (64) together with equations (58), (59), (60), and (63). Repeat this for different values of P_0 until D_t and R_t becomes zero simultaneously. Results of application of such optimizing models to mineral cartels including OPEC can be found in Pindyck (1978) as well as in Cremer and Weitzman (1976).

Readers interested in some of the more complex optimization approaches can consult a number of studies reviewed by Labys (1982). Among more practical empirical models attempting to explain OPEC behavior, a Stackelberg formulation can be found in Aperjis (1981) and a Nash-Cournot version in Hnyilicza and Pindyck (1976). A modified or 'crippled' optimization model in which a less restrictive formulation of competing and cooperative rules appears is in Kuenne (1980).

Input-Output Models

Input-output, or 'interindustry economics', as it was once formally known, is a conceptualization of economic production systems that has come to be used over the years both as a modeling device and as an element in national economic accounting systems. The input-output model as such cannot be employed directly to explain primary commodity markets. Rather it provides a disaggregated view as to how the demand and supply patterns for different commodities relate to the interindustry structure and aggregate or macroeconomic variables of a national economy.

The basis for input-output modeling is an accounting framework which contains a complete set of relationships between any industry and all of the markets for its product (the provision of a service is also called a 'product'.) The portion of output sold to other industries for further processing is called intermediate demand, because it is used by the purchaser as an input into his production process. The remainder of output is, by definition, sold to final demand. These final demand customers fall into the familiar gross national product (GNP) accounts categories, that is, personnel consumption, investment (in plant, equipment and inventory), government, exports and imports.

This can be expressed symbolically as:

$$Y_i = PC_i + IN_i + G_i + X_i - M_i + IS_i \qquad (66)$$

where Y is output, PC is personal consumption, G is government purchases, X is exports and M is imports. Investment IN has the further interpretation of being the total dollar amount of product i sold to construction activities, to buyers of equipment or to inventory accumulation. Intermediate Sales IS is the only category normally omitted from GNP, since it would double-count many items. For example, consumer purchases of flour and bakery goods enter GNP directly; but the wheat that goes into the flour and the flour that goes into the bakery goods does not. GNP components alone, however, are too broad a measure to be used meaningfully in most commodity analyses. What is needed is information on a myriad of markets, and the more intermediate the nature of the commodity transactions, the more useful input-output becomes.

The most important contribution of input-output analysis is the basic method for computing these intermediate commodity transactions. If we have 200 industries in the input-output system, there is an enormous number (200^2) of possible intermediate sales to other industries, including sales made completely within one industry. To ease the computational burden (because data on these transactions are usually impossible to find), one assumes that the demand for inputs (materials, energy, services) by an industry rises and falls with the output level of that industry. This is a very general law of costs. Then we make use of a large matrix or table, that for a given year shows the distribution of each industry's output, or alternatively the purchases of inputs by each industry. The individual cells of such a matrix, for example, have been estimated for the United States economy by the US Department of Commerce for the years 1958, 1963, 1967, and 1972, e.g. see US DOC (1979).

An example of a simplified input-output transaction matrix has been provided in Table 2.4. The matrix is hypothetical and represents dollar transactions between sectors in the economy. These sectors normally refer to a particular industry such as copper mining, but in this case are highly aggregated: MN (minerals), MFG I and MFG II (two arbitrary manufacturing industries); and services (utilities, transportation, etc.). The entries in this matrix indicate how much one industry sector such as minerals sells to all other sectors, as well as final demand and total domestic output. The output of this industry can be seen as dependent upon both the final demand for that industry's products and the intermediate product demand required to produce all other products (and itself).

This matrix of transactions is normally used to derive a set of coefficients giving us the value of the ith product used as input in the

Table 2.4: Hypothetical Input-Output Transactions Matrix[a]

Buyers / Sellers	MN	MFG I	MFG II	Serv	Total Intermediate Purchases	Gross Final Demand	Imports	Total Domestic Output
Minerals	$ 15	$230	$175	$ 10	$ 430	$ 20	− $ 10	$ 440
Manufacturing I	—	50	200	100	350	500	70	780
Manufacturing II	5	170	35	140	350	350	50	650
Services	20	30	40	20	110	390	50	450
Totals	40	480	450	270	1,240	1,260	180	2,320
Value Added[b]	400	300	200	180	1,080[c]			
Total Output	440	780	650	450	2,320			

1,260 − 180 = 1,080[c]

Notes: a. Dollar figures shown are fictitious and are used only for illustrative purposes.
b. Primary employee compensation, taxes, and profits.
c. GNP.

Source: National Academy of Science, *Mineral Demand Modeling*, Washington, DC: National Academy Press, 1982, p. 95.

production of one dollar's worth of product j. If this transaction between industry i and j is defined as Y_{ij} and the total output of industry
j as Y_j, then the coefficient of interest can be defined as $a_{ij} = Y_{ij}/Y_j$.
For example, Table 2.4 shows that Manufacturing Industry I purchased
$130 of the output of the minerals sector which is a direct input of
$130/650 = 0.20$ to each dollar of the Manufacturing Industry I output.
If we assume that the jth industry's demand for each item on the input
list is proportional to that industry's output, then we can solve equation
(66) simultaneously with similar equations for every other industry, in
this way obtaining outputs that are in balance with all current input
requirements and with final demands.

What makes input-output useful for commodity modeling is its
simple theoretical structure which can interrelate industry inputs and
outputs with the intermediate and final demands for primary commodities. The starting point is the set of input-output coefficients a_{ij} mentioned above. A full tabulation and organization of these coefficients
for all relevant industry transactions leads to a corresponding A matrix,
also known as the technical matrix or set of direct coefficients.

This matrix enters the overall model as follows:

$$Y + AY + D \tag{67}$$

where Y is the gross output of all industries, A is the input-output
matrix translating some of that output into intermediate demand, and
D is final demand. The model as described is basically production
oriented. Technology which is embodied in the fixed input-output coefficients determines what can be produced and what can be used in further production. If one then assumes an identity matrix, I, which is to
say one which consists entirely of zeros except for 1s along the diagonal,
it is possible to substitute IY for Y and rewrite equation (67) as:

$$IY - AY + D, \text{ or } (I - A)Y = D \tag{68}$$

Solved for Y, this becomes

$$Y + (I-A)^{-1} D \tag{69}$$

where $(I-A)^1$ is the inverse, or total requirements matrix. It is often
referred to as the 'Leontief Inverse' or the matrix of 'direct and indirect
requirements per dollar of delivery to final demand'. Its exact calculation depends on computer manipulation employing matrix algebra. It

should also be noted that for these relationships to be applied, the variables need to be expressed in terms of money, and the coefficients therefore represent value relationships. However, they may sometimes be treated as if also representing physical quantities and subsidiary physical relationships may readily be added.

Applications of input-output modeling to primary commodity market analysis have not been extensive. A full-economy input-output model has rarely been used and thus modified or disaggregated models have been employed. These are often referred to as 'electic' input-output models. To illustrate the potential of such modeling, we select examples from major commodity applications in minerals, energy, and agriculture.

Mineral Commodity Analysis

One of the first attempts to apply input-output to primary commodity analysis was in the mineral industry study of Wang and Kokat (1967). This and later studies concentrated mostly on tracing mineral demand. For example, one could use such a model to determine the current period impact upon all or particular mineral industries of a change in automobile sales. We can easily trace the resulting changes in the demand for steel, aluminum, copper, and glass to changes in the demand for automobiles. However, such an application is only a static forecasting application of the model. It does not, for example, evaluate the income effects of this change in auto demand, nor does it tell us anything about resulting changes in investment plans by the auto and steel industries (which would each have further effects on the steel industry in the future), nor does it address the critical issue of possible changes in the coefficients.

Such limited demand analyses have been carried out on several occasions within US governments. Kruegar (1976) has described a model developed by the Federal Preparedness Agency of the GSA to explain how the future consumption of ferrous and nonferrous metals can be forecast by combining projections of material consumption ratios which relate materials' consumption for individual industries to the demand for output of that industry. Components of the modeling structure thus include an estimate of GNP derived from a macro-forecasting model, estimated ratios reflecting materials' consumption per unit of industrial output for individual industries, and an input-output table which converts the economic estimates to production estimates and subsequently to minerals' consumption. Industry outputs derived from the solution of a relation similar to (69) are converted to mineral consumption by employing the mentioned minerals' consumption ratios. Alternatively one can employ the method of Bingham and Lee (1976) which uses output tables to derive the interrelationships between final consumer expenditures and natural resource consumption. The minerals' consumption ratios are estimated based on past levels of mineral consumption and industry output for individual industries. Summing over each industry yields total consumption for each mineral. Thus far the methodology has been applied to the planning of national stockpiles for a number of commodities, e.g. aluminum, chromite, lead, manganese, palladium, silver, tin, tungsten, vanadium and zinc.

A more general or economy-wide application of input-output to mineral demand analysis can be seen in two works in particular. The first of these, the Leontief world model (Leontief, Carter and Petri 1977), was an elaborate exercise designed to determine account of pollution, mineral resource sufficiency, and other factors associated with a variety of hypotheses as to long-range world growth patterns. This model, however, could not be considered a minerals' model specifically, since it also included agricultural, energy and a number of regional components. The second work referred to is more mineral specific. Directed by Ridker and Watson (1980), the SEAS model was designed to provide economic, mineral consumption, and pollution forecasts for the United States through the year 2025. As in the Leontief model, economy-wide interaction also is important, particularly with respect to the minerals actively envisioned in that growth.

Energy Product Analysis

Input-output models have not been applied as extensively to energy analysis, although the methodology required resembles mineral analysis. Input-output has the particular advantage in this case of being able to deal with a larger number of primary and secondary fuels and their various demands all at once. Where it is possible to estimate shifts in the technical coefficient, imports of new technology in energy production and conversion can be determined, including macroeconomic effects. Griffin (1976), in his thorough review of input-output energy applications has indicated the kinds of problems that confront modelers: energy prices tend to vary between sectors, data problems exist in relation to imported goods and in defining investment, and rapid structural changes make the coefficients unstable.

Nonetheless, several modeling experiments have taken place which are worthy of noting. Beneson (1974) reports on attempts at the Lawrence Berkeley Laboratory to analyze the impact on the US economy of a severe energy embargo. Bullard (1975) shows how inter-fuel substitution effects can be analyzed by integrating input-output with the Brookhaven model. Common and McPherson (1982) have computed energy requirements in UK commodity production. And the Hudson and Jorgenson (1974) model to be discussed in the next section interrelates energy demand and supply with growth of the US economy.

Agricultural Commodity Analysis

Among attempts to apply input-output to agricultural commodity analysis, Simpson (1980) has determined how to analyze the impact of individual agricultural commodities on a developing economy. This re-quires disaggregating or opening up the transactions or technical coef-ficients matrix to compute appropriate output and income multipliers. The industry disaggregation took place by obtaining budgets for indus-tries which refer to processed primary commodities and inserting them in the transactions matrix. In this case, the products are beef deriva-tives which were analyzed in input-output tables for four countries: Argentina, Brazil, Paraguay and Uruguay. The importance of these products is their export earnings. Thus, multipliers were calculated showing the backward linkages of these products on the individual economies through the input-supplying industries.

The advantage of this input-output application is that it can provide commodity model builders a short-cut technique for projecting the im-pact of a new commodity industry on an economy (assuming similar behavior to that of existing industries). The multiplier analysis can also be extended as in Labys (1980b) to show forward as well as backward linkages. Finally, the impact of the new industry can be compared to an existing industry or several new alternative industries.

Other Modeling Methodologies

The wide-ranging nature of primary commodity activities requires that we have to address a large number of issues regarding industry analysis, market forecasting, and policy problems. Because of the diversity of these issues, it is obvious that the quantitative or modeling techniques applied would also be diverse. The next stage beyond modeling with the above basic methodologies is to realize that there is considerable overlap among them. In particular, as the modeling profession becomes more sophisticated, there is a tendency for analysts to borrow skills from one another so that modeling techniques begin to merge and become more difficult to classify exactly. The principal ways in which mergers occur are through hybridization and linkage. In this final section we review a long existing form of hybridization known as systems simulation models and then describe several more recent endeavors in this area.

Systems Simulation Models

Systems simulation models can embody any of the methodologies discussed so far. Their advantages rest in being able to study a commodity system when data are inadequate, when an objective function is difficult to specify, or when the system is too complex to be optimized with conventional methods. Formulating commodity models with a system approach usually entails structuring the major objectives and variables to be considered as a complete system rather than constituting a single market or industry; it then incorporates one or more analytical or quantitative methods to produce a model emulating that system. In the system model survey conducted by Johnson and Rausser (1977), the methodologies employed are classified as stochastic/nonstochastic, static/dynamic, open/closed, historical/nonhistorical, decomposable and interaction. Regarding commodity models in particular, the methodologies seem to center around two types which can be distinguished by the way in which the parameters are estimated. They can be of an econometric type which begins with an econometric model and then includes whatever decision rules or quantitative structure are necessary to simulate the market or industry of interest. Or they can be of an engineering programming or optimization type which combines an economic model with an engineering, biological or agricultural model, depending on the range of total system characteristics to be taken into account.

The econometric type of models can be further classified according to whether they describe industrial or agricultural systems. Examples of industry models would be those often referred to as computer simulation models: (1) Cohen's (1960) model of the shoe, leather, and hide sequence; (2) the Naylor, Wallace and Sasser (1967) model of the textile industry; and (3) the Baughman (1974) model of the US energy system. The common properties of these models include the selection of variables that describe the basic flow characteristics of the industry rather than conventional market behavior as well as the adoption of a dynamic structure that permits an evolutionary description of the industry variables extending over a large number of future periods.

Agricultural models embody basic econometric market models which tend to be simultaneous rather than recursive. Where these models have been formulated dynamically, the resulting simulation is still evolution-ary; only decision rules have been added to reflect the general objectives and principles of the system under consideration. Some work on agricultural models within the USDA is reported in its 'Systems Workshop Proceedings' document (1970) and in the beef and pork systems model constructed by Crom (1970). More recently, Haidacher, Kite and Matthews (1975) have constructed a multicommodity systems model which emulates the decision making process involved in the administration of the US surplus commodity removal program.

The optimization type of system model will typically integrate an optimization methodology with a number of decision rules to provide an overall decision-working framework. One such example is the system model of the US rice industry designed by Holder, Shaw and Snyder (1971) which employs linear and nonlinear programming methods to determine optimal locations and quantity flows.

Models which go beyond an econometric structure but still do not include definite least-cost or optimization techniques lie between the mentioned categories. Katarack, King and Clark (1980), for example, have constructed a system simulation model that determines the consumption of stainless steel in the United States based on domestic industrial activity, stainless product and material input prices and a set of engineering relationships that calculate the costs of production for each product shape and grade of stainless steel. There also is a 'direct demand' form of system model which couples econometric equations with engineering analysis. As can be seen in the Charles River Associates' (1980) cobalt model, this is typically done by employing an engineering description of the production process and subsequently by determining how commodity price increases together with process technology changes will affect the demand for that commodity.

Some examples of nonoptimizing agricultural systems models have been based on the methodology proposed by Halter, Hayenga and Manetsch (1971) in simulating developing economies with reference to particular commodity sectors. Their approach which generally avoids using a definite econometric structure relies instead on a mathematical structure which embodies exponential lags, branches, multiplicative variables, etc. Many of the parameters in these models are based simply on technical information. While such models obviously lie on the fringe of methodologies being considered here, they may prove useful as our ability to model the overall social and economic environment improves. Commodity-oriented models based on this approach constructed so far relate to work on the Nigerian economy: the Manetsch, Hayenga and

Halter (1968) model of the beef industry and the Lapido (1973) model of the fisheries industry. Other systems models which employ a similar philosophy relate to research being carried out regarding energy, e.g. see models built by Hughes, Mesarovic and Pestel (1974) as well as several studies in Limaye (1974).

Other Combined Models

While system simulation models provide a good illustration of model hybridization, model linkage involves hooking together two or more distinct models in a systematic fashion. The individual models that are linked can be constructed using the same or different methodologies. There appear to be three main directions in these linkage efforts.

The first direction begins with the realization that common technical properties make certain groups of commodities highly competitive in substitution as product inputs. Rather than consider each commodity in a partial equilibrium context, groups of commodity markets are combined in a general equilibrium framework. For example, in the Model of International Relations in Agriculture (MOIRA) described by Linneman (1979), all agricultural commodities were aggregated into protein equivalent units and general market equilibrium was determined by a single world market 'food price'. On the whole, most attempts to interrelate commodity behavior have involved multicommodity spatial models. Considerable work has taken place to interrelate feed grain markets as viewed in the Guedry (1973) model of the US feed-grain economy and the Kost (1975) model of the EEC grain-livestock economy. Spatial models of international trade in food commodities have also been constructed, such as that by Blakeslee, Heady and Framingham (1973), the USDA (1974) world food model, and the Japanese (1974) agricultural model. More recently, Takayama (1975) has integrated both food and energy commodity behavior within a single spatial model.

Regarding multicommodity nonspatial models of an econometric type, Adams (1975) has constructed a tightly integrated model of the world oils and fats market. Methods for linking minerals models by iterating over price and product input variables have been described by Perlman and Allingham (1975). Actual solutions of such systems have been obtained by Adams (1975) in his ocean floor nodule study involving aluminum, copper, nickel, cobalt and manganese models.

The second major linkage approach would involve eclectic input-output models as previously described, where commodity demand and supply behavior is interrelated with an input-output framework describing the national economy. In this case, the principal economic relationships would be estimated by statistical inference and the input-output tables would be appropriately modified to provide the necessary economic interface. An example of this form of linkage can be seen in the Hudson and Jorgenson (1976) model which relates US economic growth to the demand and supply of energy and other commodities reflected in an interindustry structure. Energy demand and supply not only depend on economic growth but the latter, in turn, is determined by the former. Energy is thus viewed as one of the many interacting parts of the economy, linking energy developments to variables such as employment, income and consumption.

The third major direction of linkage relates to the integration of commodity market models with macro models of the national economy. Once again, some differentiation exists. One approach which is associated with the work of agricultural economics is to combine a number of agricultural commodity models into a single model which describes the agriculture sector of an economy-wide macro model. King (1974) has presented an overview of this approach, and recent advances can be seen in the work of Byerlee and Halter (1974), Roop and Zeitner (1976), and Heien (1976). Both Wharton EFA and Data Resources, Inc. offer computer linked modeling systems for these areas. Mineral commodity models can also be integrated with macro models in this manner, as described by Tinsley (1976).

A second approach which has been advanced in the context of trade and development theory would interrelate a macro-econometric planning model for a developing country with one or more world commodity models. As described by Labys, Nadiri and del Arco (1980), this would provide certain advantages for planning in countries which are typically small but highly specialized in the export of a small number of primary commodities. Such export specialization is revealed not only in the very high proportions of the country's major exports in the total export bill but also in their large contribution to foreign exchange and domestic product. Since foreign exchange earnings as well as tax revenues greatly influence a country's capability for self financed development, it would be valuable to determine to what degree any changed allocation of resources among commodities would influence these and other performance outputs.

The methodological incentive for this combined model structure arises from the premise that the magnitude of exports of one or more commodities may be sufficient to influence world price and equilibrium conditions. Thus, the impact of any changes in domestic investment strategy can be measured only by linking these exports to one or more commodity models reflecting world market conditions. This would be accomplished using the following macroeconomic system as an example.

$$
\begin{aligned}
C_t &= c(Y_t) \\
V_t &= v(Y_t, R_t) \\
Y_t &= C_t + V_t + E_t - M_t \\
F_t &= M_t - E_t \\
S_t &= Y_t - C_t
\end{aligned}
\qquad (70)
$$

Definition of variables:

C = Consumption expenditure
Y = National income
V = Investment
R = Interest rate
E = Exports
M = Imports
S = Savings
F = Net inflow of foreign capital

The impact of commodity exports on the macroeconomy is seen principally through E, which can be disaggregated into noncommodity E^{nc} and commodity E^c components:

$$
E = E_t^{nc} + E_{ct}^{c}
\qquad (71)
$$

The value of commodity exports is determined from the commodity balance considered at the country level:

$$
E_t^c = P_t X_t \text{ where } X_t = Q_t - D_t \pm \Delta I_t
\qquad (72)
$$

Exports can be determined as a residual from the market equilibrium identity in a commodity model, although they also can be estimated from a behavioral relationship.

Of course such a model is weak in its inclusion of the various linkage effects mentioned. More complex models are used in practice that concentrate on the demand, investment, employment, wage and price, fiscal and monetary aspects of the macroeconomy rather than on its two-gap character. Econometric linkage models of this type are just beginning to be developed. As explained by Adams and Roldan (1980), linkage models can assume either that the world commodity market impacts on the dependent economy without intervention or that domestic policy can be used to offset fluctuations on the world commodity markets.

A third approach to combining commodity models and macro models would integrate one of several commodity models with country or area models for the major commodity consuming and producing countries. This idea was originally suggested by Klein (1971), who saw this integration as necessary for improving the explanation of world trade patterns by the Project LINK model. In brief, the economic relationships between the developed and developing countries depend largely on the quantities and prices of commodities in world trade. Exports of commodities from developing countries depend on the income and activity variables of the importing countries. In turn, income and industrial activity in the latter depend on the regular availability of these commodities. Price formation then depends on the world imbalances between supply and demand. Since this process is intrinsically tied to the transmission of business cycles from developed to developing countries, it would be important to incorporate commodity effects into any comprehensive world trade model.

Commodity linkage efforts so far consists of Adams' (1973 and 1978a) grafting of models to the existing LINK structure and of Hicks (1975) integrating of simple income determination relationships with a substantial number of commodity models in SIMLINK.

References

Abe, M. A. (1973) 'Dynamic Microeconomic Models of Production, Investment and Technological Change of the US and Japanese Iron and Steel Industries' in G. Judge and T. Takayama (eds.), *Studies in Economic Planning Over Space and Time*, Amsterdam: North-Holland

Adams, F. G. (1973) 'The Integration of World Primary Commodity Markets into Project Link: The Example of Copper', Paper prepared for the annual meeting of Project Link, Stockholm, September 3–8

— (1975a) 'Applied Econometric Models of the Non-Ferrous Metal Markets: The Case of the Ocean Floor Nodules' in W. Vogely (ed.), *Mineral Materials Modeling*, Baltimore: Johns Hopkins University Press

— (1975b) 'An Interrelated Econometric Modeling System for Fats and Oils Commodities', A study prepared for the United Nations Conference on Trade and Development, Wharton School of Finance and Commerce

— (1978a) 'Primary Commodity Markets in a World Commodity System' in F. G. Adams and S. A. Klein (eds.), *Stabilizing World Commodity Markets*, Lexington: Heath Lexington Books, pp. 83–104

— (1978b) 'Implementation of Commodity Market Theory in Empirical Econometric Models' in F. G. Adams and J. R. Behrman (eds.), *Econometric Modeling of World Commodity Policy*, Lexington: Heath Lexington Books, pp. 47–70

— and Behrman, J. (1976) *Seven Models of Agricultural Commodity Markets*, Cambridge: Ballinger Publishing Co

— and Behrman, J. R. (1978) *Econometric Modeling of World Commodity Policy*, Lexington: Heath Lexington Books

— and Griffin, J. M. (1969) 'An Econometric Model of the US Petroleum Refining Industry' in L. R. Klein (ed.), *Essays in Industrial Economics*, vol. I. Philadelphia: Wharton School of Finance and Commerce

— and Griffin, J. M. (1972) 'An Econometric Linear Programming Model of the US Petroleum Industry', *Journal of the American Statistical Association*, 67: 542–51.

— and Klein, S. A. (1978) *Stabilizing World Commodity Markets*, Lexington: Heath Lexington Books

— and Roldan, R. A. (1980) 'An Econometric Approach to Measuring the Impact of Primary Commodity Price Fluctuations on Economic Development: Coffee and Brazil' in W. C. Labys, M. I. Nadiri and J. Nunez del Arco (eds.), *Commodity Markets and Latin American Development: A Modeling Approach*, New York: National Bureau of Economic Research, pp. 159–84

Adelman, I. and Adelman, F. (1959) 'The Dynamic Properties of the Klein-Goldberger Model', *Econometrica*, 27: 596–625

Aperjis, D. G. (1981) *Oil Markets in the 1980's, OPEC Policy and Economic Development*, Cambridge, MA., Ballinger

Apland, J. D., McCarl, B. A., Thomson, R. L. and Santini, J. (1982) 'A Computer Package for Analysis of International Trade in a Single Commodity', Agricultural Experiment Station Bulletin, Purdue University, West Lafayette, IN

Arzac, E. R. (1976) 'The Stochastic Dynamics of the US Grain Market', Research Paper No. 10, Graduate School of Business, Columbia University

Basile, P. S. (1979) 'The IIASA Set of Energy Models', Working Paper, International Institute for Applied Systems Analysis, Laxenburg

Baughman, M. L. (1974) 'A Model for Energy-Environment Systems Analysis', *Energy Modeling*, London: IPC Science and Technology Press

Bawden, D. L. (1966) 'A Spatial Price Equilibrium Model of International Trade', *Journal of Farm Economics*, 48: 862–74

Behrman, J. R. (1978) 'International Commodity Market Structures and the Theory Underlying International Commodity Market Models' in F. G. Adams and J. R. Behrman (eds.), *Econometric Modeling of World Commodity Policy*, Lexington: Heath Lexington Books, pp. 9–46

Beneson, P. (1974) 'Input-Output Analysis of An Energy Embargo', Report prepared for Electric Power Research Institute, Palo Alto

Bingham, T. H. and Lee, B. S. (1976) 'Estimates of the Interrelationship Between Consumer Expenditures and Natural Resource Consumption', *The XIV Symposium of the Council for the Application of Computers and Mathematics in the Mineral Industry*, University Park

Bishay, F. K. (1974) *Models for Spatial Agricultural Development Planning*, Rotterdam: Rotterdam University Press

Bjarnason, H. F., McGarry, M. J. and Schmitz, A. (1969) 'Converting Price Series of International Commodites to a Common Currency Prior to Estimating National Supply and Demand Equations', *American Journal of Agricultural Economics*, 51: 139–92

Blakeslee, L. L., Heady, E. O. and Framingham, C. F. (1973) *World Food Production, Demand and Trade*, Ames: Iowa State University Press

Brandow, G. E. (1961) *Interrelationships Among Demands for Farm Products and Implications for Control of Market Supply*, Pennsylvania Agricultural Experiment Station Bulletin No. 680, Pennsylvania State University, University Park

Bullard, C. W. (1975) 'An Input-Output Model for Energy Demand Analysis', CAC Report No. 146, Center for Advanced Computation, University of Illinois

Burrows, J. C. (1971a) *Cobalt: An Industry Analysis*, Lexington: Heath Lexington Books

— (1971b) *Tungsten: An Industry Analysis*, Lexington: Heath Lexington Books

Burt, O. R. (1969) 'Control Theory for Agricultural Policy: Methods and Problems in Operational Models', *American Journal of Agricultural Economics*, 51: 394–404

Byerlee, D. and Halter, A. (1974) 'A Macro-Economic Model for Agricultural Sector Analysis', *American Journal of Agricultural Economics*, 56: 520–33

CAES (1974) 'Economic Models for Agricultural Policy Issues', *Proceedings of the Canadian Agricultural Economic Society Workshop*, Ottawa

Charles River Associates. (1978) *Economics and Geology of Mineral Supply*, NSF/CRA, Report No. 327, Boston

— (1980) *World Cobalt Market*, CRA Report No. 356, Boston

Charpentier, J. P. (1974) 'A Review of Energy Models', vols. I and II, RR 74-10, International Institute for Applied Systems Analysis, Laxenburg, Austria

Choucri, N. (1980) 'Interdependence in the World Oil Market: Structure and Process', Working Paper, Massachusetts Institute of Technology, Cambridge

Clark, J. and Church, A. (1981), 'Process Analysis Modeling of the Stainless Steel Industry', Washington, DC: National Academy of Sciences, Committee on Nonfuel Mineral Demand Relationships

Cohen, K. (1960) *A Computer Model of the Shoe, Leather and Hide Sequence*, Englewood Cliffs: Prentice Hall

Common, M. S. and McPherson, P. (1982) 'A Note on Energy Requirements: Calculations Using the 1968 and 1974 UK Input-Output Tables', *Energy Policy*, 10: 42–8

Copithorne, L. W. (1973) 'The Use of Linear Programming in the Economic Analysis of a Metal Industry: The Case of Nickel', Working Paper, Department of Economics, University of Manitoba

Cournot, A. (1838) *Research into the Mathematical Principles of the Theory of Wealth*, translated by Nathaniel T. Bacon, New York: Macmillan

Cremer, J. and Weitzman, M. (1976) 'OPEC and the Monopoly Price of World Oil', *European Economic Review*, 8: 155–64

Crom, R. (1970) 'A Dynamic Price-Output Model of the Beef and Pork Sectors', Technical Bulletin No. 1426, Economic Research Service, US Department of Agriculture, Washington

Dammert, A. (1980) 'Planning Investments in the Copper Sector in Latin America' in W. C. Labys, M. I. Nadiri and J. Nunez del Arco (eds.), *Commodity Markets and Latin American Development: A Modeling Approach*, New York: National Bureau of Economic Research, pp. 65–84

Dartmouth Systems Dynamics Group. (1977) 'FOSSIL I: Introduction to the Model', Dartmouth College, Hanover, NH

Day, R. H. (1963) *Recursive Programming and Production Response*, Amsterdam: North-Holland

— (1973) 'Recursive Programming Models: A Brief Introduction' in G. Judge and T. Takayama (eds.), *Studies in Economic Planning Over Space and Time*, Amsterdam: North Holland

— and Nelson, J. P. (1973) 'A Class of Dynamic Models for Describing and Projecting Industrial Development', *Econometrica*, 2: 155–90

— and Sparling, E. (1977) 'Optimization Models in Agriculture and Resource Economics' in G. G. Judge (ed.), *Quantitative Methods in Agricultural Economics*, vol. 2 in the AAEA Survey of Agricultural Economics Literature, Minneapolis: University of Minnesota Press, pp. 93–127

— and Tabb, W. K. (1972) 'A Dynamic Microeconomic Model of the US Coal Mining Industry', SSRI Research Paper, University of Wisconsin

Dean, G. W. and Collins, N. R. (1967) 'World Trade in Fresh Oranges: An Analysis of the Effects of European Economic Community Tariff Policies', Giannini Foundation Monograph No. 18, University of California, Davis

Desai, M. (1966) 'An Econometric Model of the World Tin Economy', *Econometrica*, 34: 105-34

Driehuis, W. (ed.) (1976) *Primary Commodity Prices: Analysis and Forecasting*, Rotterdam: Rotterdam University Press

Duloy, J. H. and Norton, R. D. (1974) 'Prices and Incomes in Linear Programming Models', Mimeographed, Development Research Center, IBRD, Washington, DC

Eckbo, P. L., Jacoby, H. D. and Smith, J. L. (1978) 'Oil Supply Forecasting: A Disaggregated Process Approach', *Bell Journal of Economics*, 9: 218-38

Energy Information Administration. *Documentation of the Project Independence Evaluation System*, vols, I-IV, Department of Energy, Washington, DC, 1979

Energy Modeling. (1974) A special *Energy Policy* publication, London: IPC Science and Technology Press Ltd

Enke, S. (1951) 'Equilibrium Among Spatially Separated Markets: Solution by Electric Analog', *Econometrica*, 19: 40-7

Epps, M. L. (1975) 'A Simulation of the World Coffee Economy' in W. C. Labys (ed.), *Quantitative Models of Commodity Markets*, Cambridge: Ballinger Publishing Co, pp. 107-38.

Ezekiel, M. (1938) 'The Cobweb Theorem', *Quarterly Journal of Economics*, 52: 255-80

Ferrari, T. J. (1978) *Elements of System-Dynamics Simulation*, New York: John Wiley

Foote, R. J. (1958) *Analytical Tools for Studying Demand and Price Structure*, USDA Agricultural Handbook, Washington, DC

Forrester, J. W. (1965) *Industrial Dynamics*, Cambridge: The MIT Press

Fox, K. A. (1953a) *The Analysis of Demand for Farm Products*, Technical Bulletin No. 1081. USDA, Washington, DC

— (1953b) 'A Spatial Equilibrium Model of the Livestock Feed Economy', *Econometrica*, 21: 546-66

— and Tauber, R. C. (1955) 'Spatial Equilibrium Models of the Livestock Feed Economy', *American Economic Review*, 45: 584-608

Fritsch, B., Condon, R. and Saugy, B. (1977) 'The Use of Input-Output Techniques in an Energy Related Model' in G. Bruckmann (ed.), *Input-Output Approaches in Global Modeling*, New York: Pergamon Press

Gilbert, R. (1978) 'Dominant Firm Pricing Policy in a Market for an Exhaustible Resource', *Bell Journal of Economics*, 9: 385-95

— and Goldman, S. (1978) 'Potential Competition and the Monopoly Price of an Exhaustible Resource', *Journal of Economic Theory*

Grennes, T. R., Johnson, P. R. and Thursby, M. (1978) *The Economics of World Grain Trade*, New York: Praeger Publishers

Griffin, J. M. (1976) 'Energy Input-Output Modeling Problems and Prospects', EPRI Report No. EA-298, Electric Power Research Institute, Palo Alto

Guedry, L. L. (1973) 'An Application of a Multi Commodity Transportation Model to the US Food Grain Economy' in G. Judge and T. Takayama (eds.), *Studies in Economic Planning Over Time and Space*, Amsterdam: North Holland Publishing Co

Haavelmo, T. (1943) 'The Statistical Implications of a System of Simultaneous Equations', *Econometrica*, 11: 1-12

Haidacher, R. C., Kite, R. C. and Matthews, J. L. (1975) 'Application of a Planning Decision Model for Surplus Commodity Removal Programs' in

W. C. Labys (ed.), *Quantitative Models of Commodity Markets*, Cambridge: Ballinger Publishing Co

Halter, A. N., Hayenga, M. L. and Manetsch, T. J. (1971) 'Simulating a Developing Agricultural Economy: Methodology and Planning Capability' in M. D. Intriligator (ed.), *Frontiers of Quantitative Economics*, Amsterdam: North Holland, pp. 228–58

Heady, E. O. and Srivasta, U. K. (1975) *Spatial Sector Programming Models in Agriculture*, Ames: Iowa State University Press

Heien, D. (1976) 'Price Determination Processes for Agricultural Sector Models', Paper Presented at the Annual Meetings of the American Economic Association, Atlantic City, NJ

Henderson, J. M. (1959) 'The Utilization of Agricultural Land: A Theoretical and Empirical Enquiry', *Review of Economics and Statistics*, 41: 242–60

Herrara, A. O. and Scolnik, H. D. (1976) 'Catastrophe or New Society: A Latin American World Model', International Development Research Center, Ottawa, 1976

Hicks, N. L. (1975) 'The SIMLINK Model of Trade and Growth for the Developing World', Staff Working Paper No. 220, World Bank, Washington, DC

Higgins, C. I. (1969) 'An Econometric Description of the US Steel Industry' in L. R. Klein (ed.), *Essays in Industrial Economics – Vol. II*, Philadelphia: Wharton School of Finance and Commerce

Hildreth, C. and Jarrett, F. J. (1955) *A Statistical Study of Livestock Production and Marketing*, New York: John Wiley and Sons

Hitch, C. J. (ed.) (1977) 'Modeling Energy-Economy Interactions: Five Approaches', Research Paper No. R-5, Resources for the Future, Washington, DC

Hnyilicza, E. and Pindyck, R. (1976) 'Pricing Policies for a Two-Part Exhaustible Resource Cartel: The Case of OPEC', *European Economic Review*, 8: 136–54

Hogan, W. H. and Weyant, J. P. (1980) 'Combined Energy Models', Discussion Paper E80-02, Kennedy School of Government, Harvard University, Cambridge

Holder, Jr., S. H., Shaw, D. L., and Snyder, J. C. (1971) 'A Systems Model of the US Rice Industry', Technical Bulletin No. 1453, Economic Research Service. USDA, Washington, DC

Holland, F. D. and Pratt, J.E. (1980) 'MESS: A FORTRAN Program for Numerical Solution of Single Commodity Multi-Market Equilibrium Problems with Nonlinear Supply and Demand Functions and Flow Distortions', Agricultural Experiment Station Bulletin No. 296, Purdue University, West Lafayette, Ind

Hotelling, H. (1931) 'The Economics of Exhaustible Resources', *Journal of Political Economy*

Houck, J. P., Ryan, M. E. and Subotnik, A. (1972) *Soybeans and Their Products: Markets, Models and Policy*, Minneapolis: University of Minnesota Press

Howrey, P. and Witherell, W. H. (1968) 'Stochastic Properties of a Model of the International Wool Market', Econometric Research Program Memorandum No. 101, Princeton University

Hudson, E. A. and Jorgenson, D. W. (1976) 'Tax Policy and Energy Conservation' in D. Jorgenson (ed.), *Econometric Studies of US Energy Policy*, Amsterdam: North Holland, pp. 7–90

Hughes, B. B. and Mesarovic, M. D. (1978) 'Analysis of the WAES Scenarios Using the World Integrated Model', *Energy Policy*, 129–39

— Mesarovic, M. and Pestel, E. (1974) 'Energy Models: Resources, Demand and Supply', Multilevel Regionalized World Modeling Project, Case Western Reserve University, Cleveland

Japan, Ministry of Agriculture and Forestry. (1974) *The World Food Supply Demand and Projections of Agriculture Products for 1980 and 1985*, Tokyo: Association of Agricultural and Forestry Statistics

Johnson, S. R. and Rausser, G. C. (1977) 'Systems Analysis and Simulation: A Survey of Applications in Agricultural and Resource Economics' in G. G. Judge *et al*. (eds.), *A Survey of Agricultural Economics Literature*, vol 2. Quantitative Methods in Agricultural Economics, Minneapolis: University of Minnesota Press, pp. 157-304

Jorgenson, D. W. (1976) *Econometric Studies of US Energy Policy*, Amsterdam: North Holland

Judge, G. G. and Takayama, T. (eds.) (1973) *Studies in Economic Planning Over Space and Time*, Amsterdam: North Holland

— and Wallace, T. D. (1959) *Spatial Price Equilibrium Analyses of the Livestock Economy*, Technical Bulletin TD-78, Department of Agricultural Economics, Oklahoma State University

Katarack, F. E., King, T. B., and Clark, J. P. (1980) 'Analysis of the Supply and Demand for Stainless Steel in the US', *Materials and Society*, 4: 427-33

Kendrick, D. (1967) *Programming Investment in the Process Industries: An Approach to Sectoral Planning*, Cambridge: MIT Press

— and Stoutjesdijk, A. (1978) *The Planning of Industrial Investment Programs: A Methodology*, vol. I in the Series, The Planning of Investment Programs, A. Meeraus and A. Stoutjesdijk (eds.), Baltimore: John Hopkins University Press for the World Bank

Kennedy, M. L. (1974) 'An Economic Model of the World Oil Market', *Bell Journal of Economics and Management Science*, 5: 540-77

Kim, H. K., Goreux, L. M. and Kendrick, D. (1975) 'Feedback Control Rule for Cocoa Market Stabilization' in W. C. Labys (ed.), *Quantitative Models of Commodity Markets*, Cambridge: Ballinger Publishing Co

King, G. A. (1974) 'Econometric Models of the Agricultural Sector', Paper presented at the Annual Meetings of the American Economic Association, San Francisco.

King, R. A. and Foo-Shiung Ho. (1965) 'Reactive Programming: A Market Simulating Spatial Equilibrium Algorithm', Economics Special Report, Department of Economics, North Carolina State University at Raleigh

Klein, L. R. (1971) 'Some Notes on the Introduction of Commodity Models into Project LINK', Mimeographed, LINK Working Paper

— (1978) 'Potentials of Econometrics for Commodity Stabilization Policy Analysis' in F. G. Adams and S. A. Klein (eds.), *Stabilizing World Commodity Markets*, Lexington: Heath Lexington Books, pp. 105-16.

Koopmans, T. C. and Hood, W. C. (1953) 'The Estimation of Simultaneous Linear Economic Relationships' in W. C. Hood and T. C. Koopmans (ed.), *Studies in Econometric Method*, New York: John Wiley and Sons

Kopp, R. J. and Smith, V. K. (1980) 'Measuring Factor Substitution with Neoclassical Models: An Experimental Evaluation', *Bell Journal of Economics*, 11: 631-58

Kost, W. E. (1975) 'Trade Flows in the Grain-Livestock Economy of the EEC' in W. Labys (ed.), *Quantitative Models of Commodity Markets*, Cambridge: Ballinger Publishing Co

Kovisars, L. (1975) 'Copper Trade Flow Model', SRI Project MED 3742-74, Stanford Research Institute, Stanford

— (1976) 'World Production Consumption and Trade in Zinc: A LP Model', Working Paper, Stanford Research Institute

Krallman, H. (1979) 'Methodological and Practical Aspects of the Linkage of Systems Dynamics and Input-Output', Paper presented at the Workshop on Commodity Market Modeling, Applied Economic Association of France, Paris

Krueger, P. K. (October 1976) 'Modeling Futures Requirements for Metals and

Minerals', *Proceedings of the XIV Symposium of the Council for the Application of Computers and Mathematics in the Minerals Industries*, University Park, PA

Kuenne, R. E. (1980) 'Modeling the OPEC Cartel with Crippled Optimization Techniques', Paper Presented at the Conference on World and World Region Energy Studies, International Congress of Arts and Sciences, Harvard University, June 16

Labys, W. C. (1973) *Dynamic Commodity Models: Specification, Estimation and Simulation*, Lexington: Heath Lexington Books

— (ed.) (1975) *Quantitative Models of Commodity Markets*, Cambridge: Ballinger Publishing Co

— (1977) 'Mineral Commodity Modeling: The State of the Art' in *Proceedings of the Minerals Economics Symposium on Mineral Policies in Transition*, Council of Economics of the AIME, Washington, DC, pp. 80–106

— (1978) 'Commodity Markets and Models: The Range of Experience' in F. G. Adams (ed.), *Stabilizing World Commodity Markets: Analysis, Practice and Policy*, Lexington: Heath Lexington Books

— (1980a) 'A General Disequilibrium Model of Commodity Market Adjustments', NSF Working Paper, Department of Mineral, Energy and Resource Economics, West Virginia University

— (1980b) 'Interactions Between the Resource Commodity Sector, The Developing Economy and the Environment', Resource Memorandum No. 60, UNCTAD, Geneva

— and Yang, C. W. (1980) 'A Quadratic Programming Model of the Applachian Steam Coal Market', *Energy Economics*, 2: 86–95

— Nadiri, M. I. and del Arco, J. Nunez (1980) *Commodity Markets and Latin American Development: A Modeling Approach*, New York: National Bureau of Economic Research/Ballinger

— (1982) 'A Critical Review of International Energy Modeling Methodologies', Energy Laboratory Working Paper No. MIT-EL 82-034WP, Massachusetts Institute of Technology, Cambridge, MA

Lapido, O. O. (1973) 'General Systems Analysis and Simulation Approach: A Preliminary Application to Nigerian Fisheries', Unpublished PhD dissertation, Michigan State University

Leontief, W., Carter, A. P. and Petri, P. A. (1977) *The Future of the World Economy*, New York: Oxford University Press

Lewis, T. and Schmalensee, R. (1979) 'Cartel and Oligopoly Pricing of Nonrenewable Natural Resources' in P. T. Liu (ed.), *Dynamic Optimization and Applications to Economics*, New York: Plenum Press

Libbin, J. D. and Boehlji, M. D. 'Interregional Structure of the US Coal Industry', *American Journal of Agricultural Economics*, (1977): 456–66

Limaye, D. R. (1974) *Energy Policy Evaluation*, Lexington: Heath Lexington Books

Linneman, H. (1976) 'MOIRA: A Model of International Relations in Agriculture – The Energy Sector', Working Paper, Institute for Economical Social Research, Free University, Amsterdam

Loury, G. (1981) 'A Theory of 'Oil'igopoly: Cournot Equilibrium in Exhaustible Resource Markets with Fixed Supplies', *Bell Journal of Economics*

Macavoy, P. W. and Pindyck, R. S. (1975) *The Economics of the Natural Gas Shortage*, Amsterdam: North Holland

Mackrakis, M. S. (ed.) (1974) *Energy*, Cambridge: MIT Press

Manetsch, T. J., Hayenga, M. L. and Halter, A. R. (1968) 'A Simulation Model of the Nigerian Beef Industry', Mimeographed, Michigan State University, East Lansing

Mariano, S. (1978) 'Commodity Market Modeling: Methodological issues and Control Theory Applications' in F. G. Adams and J. R. Behrman (eds.), *Econometric Modeling of World Commodity Policy*, Lexington: Heath Lexington Books, pp. 71–98.

Martin, N. R. Jr. (1972) 'Stepped Product Demand and Factor Supply Functions in Linear Programming Analyses', *American Journal of Agricultural Economics*, 54: 116–120

Martin, L. and Zwart, A. (1975) 'A Spatial and Temporal Model of the North American Pork Sector for the Evaluation of Policy Alternatives', *American Journal of Agricultural Economics*, 57: 55–66

Meadows, D. L. (1970) *Dynamics of Commodity Production Cycles*, Cambridge: Wright-Allen Press

Meeraus, A. *et al.* (1975) 'Regional Investment Planning, The Case of the South-East Asian Fertilizer Industry', Washington, DC: The World Bank

Meinken, K. W. (1953) 'The Demand and Price Structure of Oats, Barley and Soybeans', Technical Bulletin No. 1080, USDA, Washington, DC

Mikesell, R.F. (1979) *The World Copper Industry*, Baltimore: Johns Hopkins University Press for RFF

Moore, H. L. (1919) 'Empirical Laws of Supply and Demand and the Flexibility of Prices', *Political Science Quarterly*, 34: 546–67

Moore, R., Elassar, S. and Lessley, B. V. (1972) 'Least-Cost World Trade Patterns for Grains and Meats', Agricultural Experiment Station Miscellaneous Publication No. 796, University of Maryland, College Park

Naill, R. F., Mass, N. J., Randers, J. and Simpson, M. K. (1973) 'Dynamic Modeling as a Tool for Managerial Planning: A Case Study of the US Hog Industry', Mimeographed, Thayer School of Engineering, Dartmouth College, Hanover

Nash, T. F. (1953) 'Two-Person Cooperative Games', *Econometrica*, 21

National Academy of Sciences (NAS) (1982) *Mineral Demand Modeling*, A Report prepared by the Committee on Nonfuel Mineral-Demand Relationships of the Board on Mineral and Energy Resources-National Research Council, Washington, DC: National Academy Press

Naylor, T. H. (1971) *Computer Simulation Experiments with Models of Economic Systems*, New York: John Wiley & Sons

— Wallace, W. H. and Sasser, W. C. (1967) 'An Econometric Model Of the Textile Industry in the US', *Review of Economics and Statistics*, 50: 13–22

Nelson, J. P. (1971) 'An Interregional Recursive Programs Model of Production Investment, and Technological Change', *Journal of Regional Science*, 11: 33–47

Nerlove, M. (1956) 'Estimates of the Elasticities of Supply of Selected Agricultural Commodities', *Journal of Farm Economics*, 37: 286–301

Nguyen, H. D. (1977) 'World Food Projection Models and Short Run World Trade and Reserve Policy Evaluations', PhD Dissertation, University of Illinois, Urbana

Pant, S. P. and Takayama, T. (1973) 'An Investigation of Agricultural Planning Models: A Case Study of India's Food Economy' in G. Judge and T. Takayama (eds.), *Studies in Economic Planning Over Space and Time*, Amsterdam: North Holland

Perlman, L. and Allingham, M. (1975) 'Econometric Supply-Demand Models' in W. Vogely (ed.) *Mineral Materials Modeling*, Baltimore: Johns Hopkins University Press

Pindyck, R. S. (1978) 'Gains to Producers from the Carelization of Exhaustible Resources', *Review of Economics and Statistics*, 60: 238–51

Polito, J., McCarl, B. A., and Morin, T. L. (1980) 'Solution of Spatial Equilibrium Problems with Bender's Decomposition', *Management Science*, 26: 593–605

Quance, L., and Mesarovic, M. (1980) 'US Agriculture in an Interdependent World: Closing the Gap Between Analytical Systems and Changing Reality', *Agricultural Economics Research*, 32: 51-3

Quirk, T. and Smith, V. (1969) 'Dynamic Economic Models of Fishing' in *Proceedings of the H. R. McMillan Fisheries Economics Symposium*', A. Scott (ed.), Vancouver: University of British Columbia

Radhi, A. M. (1979) 'An Economic Model of the World Nitrogen Fertilizer Market', PhD Dissertation, Purdue University, West Lafayette, Ind

Raulerson, R. C. and Langham, M. R. (1970) 'Evaluating Supply Control Policies for Frozen Concentrated Orange Juice with an Industrial Dynamics Model', *American Journal of Agricultural Economics*, 52: 197-208

Rausser, G. C. (ed.) (1980) *New Directions in Econometric Modeling and Forecasting in US Agriculture*, New York: Elsevier North Holland

— and Freebairn, J. W. (1974) 'Approximate Adaptive Control Solutions to US Beef Trade Policy', *Annals of Economic and Social Measurement*, 3: 177-204

— and Hochman, E. (1979) 'Government Farm Programs and Commodity Interactions: A Simulation Analysis', *American Journal of Agricultural Economics*, 54: 578-90

Reutlinger, S. (1976) 'A Simulation Model for Evaluating World-wide Buffer Stocks of Wheat', *American Journal of Agricultural Economics*, 58: 1-12

Ridker, R. G. and Watson, W. D. (1980) *To Choose A Future*, Baltimore, MD: The John Hopkins University Press

Roberts, F. S. (ed.) (1976) *Energy: Mathematics and Models*, Philadelphia: Society for Industrial and Applied Mathematics

Rojko, A. S. and Schwartz, M. W. (1976) 'Modeling the World Grain-Oilseeds-Livestock Economy to Assess World Food Prospects', *Agricultural Economics Research*, 28: 89-98

Roop, J. M. and Zeitner, R. H. (1976) 'Agricultural Activity and the General Economy: Some Marco Model Experiments', Presented at the Annual Meetings of the American Economic Association, Atlantic City

Russell, C. S. and Vaughan, W. J. (1976) *Steel Production: Processes, Products, and Residuals*, Baltimore: Johns Hopkins University Press

Salant, S. W. (1976) 'Exhaustible Resources and Industrial Structure: A Nash-Cournot Approach to the World Oil Market', *Journal of Political Economy*, 84: 1079-94

— (1979) 'Staving off the Backstop: Dynamic Limit-Pricing with a Kinked Demand Curve', in *The Production and Pricing of Energy Resources*, Advances in the Economics of Energy Resources, vol. 2 edited by Robert S. Pindyck, Greenwich, Conn.: JAI Press

— (1980) 'Imperfect Competition in the International Energy Market', *Operations Research*, 29

Samuelson, P. A. (1952) 'Spatial Price Equilibrium and Linear Programming', *American Economic Review*, 42: 283-303

Schinzinger, R. (1974) 'Integer Programming Solutions to Problems in Electric Energy Systems', in D. R. Limaye, (ed.), *Energy Policy Evaluation*, Lexington, MA: Heath Lexington Books

Schmitz, A. and Bawden, D. (1973) *World Wheat Economy: An Empirical Analysis*, Giannini Foundation Monograph No. 32, University of California at Berkely

Schrader, L. F. and King, G. A. (1962) 'Regional Location of Beef Cattle Feeding', *Journal of Farm Economics*, 44: 64-81

Schultz, H. (1938) *The Theory and Measurement of Demand*, Chicago: University of Chicago Press

Searl, M. F. (ed.) (1973) *Energy Modeling*, Working Paper EN.1, Washington, DC: Resources for the Future

Segura, E. L. (1973) *An Econometric Study of the Fish Meal Industry*, FAO Fisheries Technical Paper No. 199, FIEF/T119 (En.), Food and Agricultural Organization of the United Nations, Rome

Simpson, J. R. (1980) 'Input-Output Modeling and Its Implications for Commodity Planning in Latin America' in W. Labys, M. Nadiri and J. Nunez del Arco (eds.), *Commodity Markets and Latin American Development: A Modeling Approach*, New York: National Bureau of Economic Research

Singh, I. J. and Ahn, C. Y. (1972) *A Dynamic Model of Agricultural Development In Southern Brazil: Some Retrospective Policy Simulations* (1960-70), Occasional Paper No. 113, Department of Agricultural Economics and Rural Sociology, Ohio State University, Colombus, OH

Smithson, C. W. (1979) 'World Mineral Markets: An Econometric and Simulation Analysis', Mineral Policy Background Paper No. 8, Canadian Ministry of Natural Resources, Ottawa

Sparrow, F. and Soyster, A. (1980) 'Process Models of Minerals Industries', Proceedings of the Council of Economics of the AIME, New York: AIME, pp. 93-101

Steele, J. L. (1971) *The Use of Econometric Models by Federal Regulatory Agencies*, Lexington, MA: Heath Lexington Books

Strongman, J. E., Killingsworth, W. R. and Cummings, W. E. (1976) 'The Dynamics of the International Copper System', *The XIV Symposium of the Council for the Applications of Computers and Mathematics in the Mineral Industry*, University Park, PA

Suits, D. (1955) 'An Econometric Model of the Watermelon Market', *Journal of Farm Economics*, 37: 237-51

Takayama, T. (1975) 'World Food and Energy Modeling: A Market Oriented Approach', Mimeographed, Department of Economics, University of Illinois, Urbana-Champaign

— and Hashimoto, H. (1976) 'Dynamic Market-Oriented World Food Projection and Planning Model and Their Empirical Results for the 1970-1974 World Food Situation', World Food Protection Project Report No. 2, Department of Agricultural Economics, University of Illinois, Urbana

— and Judge, G. G. (1964) 'Equilibrium Among Spatially Separated Market: A Reformation', *Econometrica*, 32: 510-24

— — (1971) *Spatial and Temporal Price and Equilibrium Models*. Amsterdam: North-Holland Publishing Co

— Judge, G. G. and Guise, J. W. B. (1971) 'Optimal Control Formulation of Spatial-Temporal Price Equilibrium Models', Mimeographed, Department of Economics, University of Illinois

— and Liu, C. L. (1975) 'Projection of International Trade in Farm Products I: Wheat', *Illinois Agricultural Economics*, 15: 1-7

— and Onishi, H. (1976) 'Spatial and Intertemporal price Equilibrium Models and Optimal Control Theory', Mimeographed, Department of Economics, University of Illinois, Urbana

Thompson, R. L. (1981) 'A Survey of Recent US Developments in International Agriculture Models', BLAN 21, Economic Research Service, US Department of Agriculture, Washington, DC

Tinbergen, J. (1939) Statistical Testing of Business Cycle Theories. League of Nations, Economists' Intelligence Service, Geneva

Tinsley, C. R. (1976) 'Computer Application of Non-Ferrous Econometric Models from the Raw Materials Consumer Perspective', *The XIV Symposium of the Council for the Application of Computers and Mathematics in the Mineral Industries*, University Park, PA

Tramel, T. E. and Seale, A. D. Jr. (1959) 'Reactive Programming of Supply and

Demand Relations – Applications to Fresh Vegetables', *Journal of Farm Economics*, 41: 102-22

Tsurumi, H. (1976) 'Demand for Steel Products in Japan: A Suboptimization Approach', Mimeographed, Department of Economics, Rutgers University

Tsao, C. S. and Day, R. H. 'A Process Analysis Model of the US Steel Industry', *Management Science*, 17 (1971): 588-608

Ulph, R. (1980) 'Exhaustible Resources and Cartels: An Intertemporal Nash-Cournot Model', *Canadian Journal of Economics*, 25: 645-58

— and Folie, M. (1978) 'Gains and Losses to Producers for Cartelisation of an Exhaustible Resource', CRES Working Paper R/WP26, Australian National University, Canberra

US Department of Agriculture (1970) *Proceedings of a Workshop on Systems Research in the Livestock Industries*, Washington DC: Economic Research Service

— (1974) *The World Food Situation and Prospects to 1985*, Washington, DC: USA Foreign Agricultural Economic Report, Economic Research Service, No. 98

US Department of Commerce (1979) *The Detailed Input-output Structure of the US Economy: 1972*, Washington, DC: Government Printing Office

Vogely, W. A. (ed.) (1975) *Mineral Materials Modeling*, RFF Working Paper EN-5, Baltimore: Johns Hopkins University Press

von Stackelberg, H. (1952) *The Theory of Market Economy*, Oxford: Oxford University Press

Waelbroeck, J. L. (ed.) 1976) *The Model of Project LINK*, Amsterdam: North Holland

Wang, Kung Lee, and Kokat, R. G. (1967) *An Inter-Industry Structure of the US Mining Industries*, IC 8338, United States Bureau of Mines, Washington, DC

Warner, D. L. (1979) 'An Econometric Model of the World Wheat Economy', PhD Dissertation, Princeton University, Princeton, NJ

Weymar, H. (1968) *Dynamics of the World Cocoa Market*, Cambridge: The MIT Press

Whitacre, R. C. and Schmidt, S. C. (1980) 'Analysis of a World Grain Reserve Plan Under a New International Wheat Agreement', *North Central Journal of Agricultural Economics*, 2: 83-95

Williams, G. W. (1977) 'Economic Structure of the Brazilian Soybean Industry – A Prototype Model', MS thesis, Purdue University, West Lafayette, IN

Witherall, W. H. (1967) *Dynamics of the International Wool Market: An Econometric Analysis*, Econometric Research Program, Memorandum No. 91, Princeton University

Wold, H. and Jureen, L. (1953) *Demand Analysis: A Study in Econometrics*, New York: John Wiley and Sons

Wolstenholme, E. F. (1979) 'A System Dynamic Approach to an Analysis of Factors Affecting Growth and Stability in International Mineral Industries', Working Paper, University of Bradford

Working, E. J. (1927) 'What Do Statistical Demand Curves Show?' *Quarterly Journal of Economics*, 41: 212-35

World Bank. (1981) *World Bank Commodity Models*, vol. 1, World Bank Staff Commodity Working Paper No. 6, World Bank, Washington, DC

Yaron, D. (1967) 'Incorporation of Income Effects into Mathematical Programming Models', *Metroeconomica*, 19: 141-60.

Zusman, P. (1962) 'Econometric Analysis of the Market for California Early Potatoes', *Hilgardia*, 33: 539-668

— Melamed, A. and Katzir, A. (1973) 'Spatial Analysis of EEC Trade Policies in the Market for Winter Oranges' in G. Judge and T. Takayama (eds.), *Studies in Market Planning Over Time and Space*, Amsterdam: North Holland Publishing Co

3 VALIDATION OF COMMODITY MODELS

This chapter is concerned with the process of validating and judging the performance of commodity models. One of the most important aspects of applying commodity models is that policy makers or other users have confidence in a model's ability to analyze policy or to forecast. This also implies that at some stage in the modeling process, the model selected has been compared and preferred to other alternative models. Both of these considerations depend on the application of appropriate validation methods and techniques.

The Validation Problem

Although the validation of commodity models has been practised for some time, no validation tests have been specifically designed for this purpose. Rather the commodity model builder can call upon a variety of generally available validation tests such as that discussed, for example, in the National Bureau of Economic Research (1975). The particular applicability of certain of these tests to econometric commodity models has been reviewed by Labys (1973). Later the discussion extended to a much wider group of models (Labys, 1982). Johnson and Rausser (1977) employed a similar approach in explaining the validation of agricultural systems models. And McCarl and Spreen (1980) have addressed the case of validating mathematical programming forms of agricultural sector models. The most recent attempts at commodity model validation have taken place within the context of energy modeling. These consist of studies by the MIT (1979) Model Assessment Group including Wood (1979), by Gass (1979), by Weisbin, Peelle and Loebl (1981), and by Labys (1982).

The approaches taken to validation in these and other recent modeling studies can be categorized into two groups. First, they have concentrated on the general process of examining model performance. This has been termed model *evaluation* or *assessment*. Second, they have dealt more specifically with the significance of model parameters and the accuracy of model forecasts. This has been termed model *validation*.

The role of model validation in the general model assessment process can best be understood by examining the four elements that constitute

the assessment process of the MIT (1979) Model Assessment Group:
(1) *Review of the Literature* — Evaluates the model's structure based
on published materials. It discusses the model's objectives, structure,
and principal results and evaluates the appropriateness of the structure
for what it was designed to do. (2) *Overview Model Assessment* — Surveys unpublished technical documentation. An overview assessment
can be expected to (a) evaluate the empirical content of the model;
(b) discuss the model's limitations with regard to its structure; and
(c) identify the critical points (critical points are elements that may
significantly influence the model's behavior and that could be questioned by other experts). An overview evaluation does not answer
many of the questions that it raises. (3) *Independent Audit* — Evaluates
the model's validity, applicability, and performance through data derived from experiments run with the model. The audit report uses the
experimental data with the information developed in the earlier steps
of the evaluation to provide a statement about the model's validity.
(4) *In-depth Assessment* — Generates data by hands-on operation of the
model and makes identification of errors between documentation and
implementation easier.

These four elements are actually four levels of model evaluation,
which are best viewed as different stages in a comprehensive model
evaluation process; these stages should be considered interactive and
complementary. However, every model evaluation will not require all
four stages. In the case of model validation, this has been mentioned
as occurring within stage (3), but it can be employed at any of the
other stages. For the present purpose of judging the performance of
commodity models, we deal only with the specific process of model
validation.

Validation and Modeling Methodologies

Model *validation* can be defined as a test of whether a model is an
adequate representation of the elements and relationships of the reference systems that are important to experiments planned with the model.
In short, validation refers to the correspondence of the model to the
underlying processes being modeled. Important to validation are: (1)
the statistical significance of the parameter configuration of the structure, (2) the correspondence of *ex post* and *ex ante* estimated values of
the model's variables to actual data, and (3) the sensitivity of the model
to discriminate among policy outcomes which might be compared.

An important aspect of model validation is that there is a relation between the degree of model validity and the methodology chosen as well as between the nature of the validation techniques and the methodology chosen. Regarding the first of these, modeling methodologies vary in their costs as well as in their scope and accuracy. As stated by Chambers, Mullick and Smith (1971, p. 46), the policy maker 'must fix the level of inaccuracy he can tolerate — in other words, decide how his decision will vary, depending on the range and accuracy of the forecast'. This allows him to trade-off cost against the value of accuracy in choosing the modeling methodology.

Figure 3.1: Balancing Cost of Forecasting Versus Cost of Inaccuracy

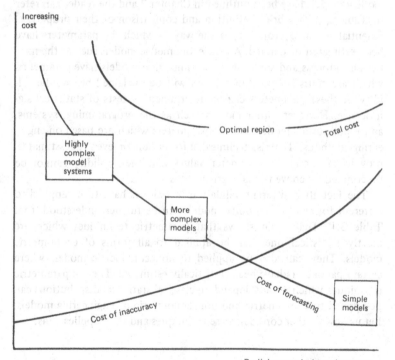

Figure 3.1 shows how cost and accuracy are likely to vary and graphs this against the corresponding cost of the model's errors, given some general assumptions. The figure intends to show that ideally the policy maker must hope to weigh the cost of a more accurate (expensive) model against that of a less accurate (inexpensive) model or a different

modeling methodology. The most sophisticated model that can be economically justified is one that falls in the region where the sum of the two costs is minimal. There may be some debate as to the extent that this approach might apply to the vast array of commodity models already in existence. There are also a host of other questions such as whether a more complex or disaggregated model structure is necessarily more accurate than a simpler highly aggregated structure. But the figure does demonstrate some guidelines for determining a desired level of validity.

The second interface between validation and modeling methodology concerns the specific nature of the statistical or mathematical validation techniques to be used. The methodologies that can be applied to commodity models have been outlined in Chapter 2 and the reader can refer to Table 2.2 for a brief definition and comparison of their properties. Essential to these properties is the way in which the parameters have been estimated or derived. All the econometric models such as the market and process and some of the optimization models have parameters which are statistically estimated. As will be explained below, the validity of these parameters can be determined by tests of statistical significance. However, other models such as the programming, systems, and input-output models feature parameters which are based on engineering methods. That is, technical information or even 'guesstimates' provide the basis for parameter values and their validity cannot be determined by conventional statistical tests.

The fact that different validation techniques have to be applied to different forms of commodity models can be further understood from Table 3.1. That table shows that parametric techniques which are mostly statistical ones can be applied to all forms of econometric models. They can also be applied to noneconometric models where certain parameters have been statistically estimated. The nonparametric techniques which do not depend on classical statistical distributions can be applied to econometric and noneconometric or engineering models. Let us now further consider these techniques and their applications.

Validation Techniques Defined

The approach commonly taken in defining the above validation techniques or criteria is to separate the structure of the model from the observation or data points generated by computer simulations with the model.[1] In the first case, criteria are presented applicable primarily to

Table 3.1: Commodity Modeling Methodologies and the Range of Validation Techniques

Commodity Modeling Methodologies	Parametric Techniques						Nonparametric Techniques						
	Model Selection	Sensitivity Analysis	Coefficient Tests	Goodness of Fit	Specifications Tests	Pseudo Forecasts	Single Point Criteria	Interval Criteria	Error-Cost Analysis	Turning Point Analysis	Comparative Errors	Spectral Analysis	Sensitivity Analysis
Econometric													
Market Model	X	X	X	X	X	X	X	X	X	X	X	X	X
Process Model	X	X	X	X	X	X	X	X	X	X	X	X	X
Optimization Model	X	X	X	X	X	X	X	X	X	X	X	X	X
Input-Output				X				X	X				
Programming													
Linear Programming		X						X			X		X
Quadratic Programming	X	X	X	X	X					X	X		X
Recursive Programming		X									X		X
Integer Programming	X	X					X		X	X	X		X
Systems													
System Dynamics	X	X	X	X		X	X	X		X	X	X	X
System Simulation	X	X	X	X	X	X	X	X		X	X	X	X

models where the coefficients of the structural equations have been estimated statistically. Because it is nearly impossible to validate 'guesstimates' of coefficients used in engineering and system types of models, these criteria are mostly applicable to models employing regression (econometric) equations. In the second case, the performance of the model is determined on the basis of the generated values of the model's variables by comparing the values to their corresponding actual or assumed values. Generated values are assumed to be the result of a sequence of computer simulation exercises usually employing numerical methods. In this section a number of validation techniques, both parametric and nonparametric, are presented to deal with both forms of validation. More detailed information on these techniques can be found in sources such as Labys (1973), NBER (1975), Pindyck and Rubinfeld (1976), and Zellner (1979).

Parametric Techniques

Model Selection. This form of test is directed to the problem of selecting between alternative functional representations of an economic relation. These relations normally are defined as a single equation or regression

$$Y = X\beta + u \tag{1}$$

which is part of a complete econometric model system such as that defined in Chapter 2.

$$\Gamma Y + B_1 Y_{-1} + B_2 X = U \tag{2}$$

Significance of Coefficients. The basis for selecting among individual regressions is to examine the statistical properties of the coefficients β where a particular equation specification is assumed or given. Values for the coefficients are normally estimated based on single-equation or multiple-equation estimation methods such as OLS, 2SLS or FIML. Hypothesis tests of the coefficients are normally based on the use of the t distribution.

Goodness-of-Fit. In econometric models, goodness-of-fit statistics such as the coefficient of determination, the standard error of the estimates, and chi-square or F statistics are normally computed for each equation. These statistics normally measure the proportion of the variance of Y explained by the linear influence of X. One can also perform an 'analysis of variance' or F-test for the regression as a whole or for particular variables within the regression.

Specifications Error Tests. The appropriateness of a relation or a variable within it can also be evaluated using specifications error tests. Among those suggested are the omitted variable test, functional form test, simultaneous equation test, heteroscedasticity test, and the chi-square goodness-of-fit test for normality.

Pseudo Forecasts. It is possible to examine deviations of forecast $\hat{Y}_t$ from actual values Y_t generated from econometric models with parametric methods. Here the model builder should have available an additional set of observations on each of the independent and dependent variables of the model. These data can be considered as being 'saved' for comparison purposes but are too few in number to permit re-estimation of the model. Thus the model is used to generate a set of forecasts which can be compared to the known or saved values.

Sensitivity Analysis. It is also important to observe the sensitivity of model solutions to variations in the parameters of the model. In the case of econometric models, parameters can simply be varied systematically and variations in the solutions evaluated in terms of deviations from a base solution. A more careful analysis would involve statistical experimental design methods, an approach which is not yet fully developed.

In the case of input-output and programming models, there generally are mechanical relations between model parameters (or exogenous variables) and optimal solutions, i.e., the Leontief inverse for the input-output approach and the Kuhn-Tucker theorems for the mathematical programming technique. Consequently, the validity of the models to a large extent depends on the sensitivity of the models, defined as variations of the optimal solutions once the system is slightly perturbed.

Nonparametric Techniques

Single Point Criteria. The techniques which have been applied traditionally to measure the forecast error between actual and estimated or simulated observations are single point criteria, such as the mean absolute percentage error and the mean squared error

$$\text{MAPE} = \frac{1}{n} \sum_{t=1}^{n} \frac{|Y_t - \hat{Y}_t|}{Y_t} \times 100\% \tag{3}$$

$$\text{MSE} = \frac{1}{n} \sum_{t=1}^{n} (Y_t - \hat{Y}_t)^2 \tag{4}$$

where Y_t = actual observation values and $\hat{Y}_t$ = forecast or estimated values. These tests can also be made in the context of the 'pseudo forecasts' discussed earlier. Similarly useful is the Theil inequality or U coefficient, which derives from a regression of actual on forecast values and which can also provide information as to sources of error.

Interval Criteria. If the modeler is more interested in predicting an interval or range of values, then the test of confidence intervals could be developed based on the mentioned 't' distribution and applied for this purpose.

Error-Cost Analysis. While the above criteria probably are the most practical for evaluating performance with a historical sample or a small post-sample data set, they fail to define the surrounding probabilistic conditions in a way which would be useful with a large post-sample data set. There are two ways to improve this situation. First, an informative forecast could accompany the point forecasts based on some mathematical statement regarding the probability distributions surrounding these forecasts. This amounts to an interval forecast in which the point forecast is now presented along with an appropriate confidence interval. Second, a decision forecast could be prepared which recommends that the forecast be accepted in relation to some alternative consequence.

Turning Point Errors. A major characterization of a model's performance is its ability to explain the turning points of fluctuations in values of the endogenous variables. There are a number of descriptive variables or statistics which can be used to describe turning point errors. Most often they pertain to the number of turning points missed, the number of turning points falsely predicted, the number of under and over predictions, rank correlations of predicted and actual changes, and various tests of randomness in prediction.

Comparative Errors. Validation also can take the form of comparing the forecast errors obtained from the equation of interest to the forecast errors achieved from a naive or statistical equation or from judgmental or other noneconometric forecasts. As discussed in Labys and Granger (1970) and Zellner (1979), naive and statistical equations can provide a rigorous standard for most commodity forecast comparisons, especially when using short run data. As a starting point one could begin by comparing forecasts from an equation to forecasts generated by naive methods such as 'no change', where literally no change takes place in the endogenous variables from one period to the next, $\hat{Y}_t = Y_{t-1}$, or 'same change', where the endogenous variables will continue to change in the same direction and by the same magnitude as the previous change $\hat{Y}_t - Y_{t-1} = Y_{t-1} - Y_{t-2}$. Expressed in levels, it becomes a weighted sum $\hat{Y}_t = 2Y_{t-1} - Y_{t-2}$. Such comparisons are made for each endogenous variable in the overall model. A more adequate approach would be to generate the alternative forecasts using Box-Jenkins or autoregressive integrated moving average (ARIMA) equations.

Spectral Analysis. This technique involves the transformation of time series observations from the time domain to the frequency domain. One can then compare frequency components in the actual and estimated series or alternatively one can examine the correlation of these frequency components using cross-spectral analysis. Several advantages have been cited in using spectral techniques for commodity model validation. First, the information content of spectral analysis is greater than that of the sample means and sample variances associated with point error measures. Second, spectral analysis overcomes the problems of analyzing data that are highly autocorrelated, a phenomenon which invalidates the applicability of classical statistical criteria. Thirdly, examining the spectrum of the simulated series yields information about the dynamic behavior of a model that cannot be obtained in forecast error measures. Finally, spectral analysis permits the construction of confidence bands so that alternative policy decisions can be evaluated by comparing the spectra of the estimated data that conform to the respective alternatives.

In terms of applicability, the spectral approach is most useful for linear or (linearized) nonlinear models which are stochastic and econometrically derived. It also works equally well over the sample or post-sample period, the only reservation for an application being that the output data are of sufficient length and are convertible to a non-stationary form. Among the principal variants of this approach are (1) comparisons of power spectra for estimated and sample data series, (2) spectral serial correlation tests of structural or reduced form sample disturbances and (3) cross-spectral statistics of the relationships between estimated and actual sample values. Among applications of this technique, Howrey and Witherell (1968) applied a 'spectrum matrix' approach to a model of the wool market; and Naylor, Wertz and Wonnacott (1969) employed spectral statistics to analyze the estimated paths of a model of the textile industry.

Sensitivity Analysis. One drawback with sensitivity analysis based on parametric techniques is that it is costly. A substantial number of stochastic solutions of the model are necessary, normally employing numerical methods. Such tests normally have been suggested for the case of dynamic econometric models of a linear or nonlinear type. In the case of the spatial equilibrium models, notably linear and quadratic programming models, the stochastic programming approach has been occasionally employed in the linear case. In the non-linear or quadratic case Labys and Yang (1979), and Yang (1980) show that the response surfaces of regional production, consumption and interregional flow are piecewise linear, whereas the value of objective function is piecewise quadratic. Hence, within a given set of basic variables in the simplex tables, the sensitivity of a model is entirely predictable. The advantage of this technique lies in the fact that once the response interval is known, a modeler can forecast the decision variables without resimulating his model.

Validating the Methodologies

The above validation criteria can be applied to the various modeling methodologies under a number of different circumstances. To some extent, the range of possible applications has already been presented in Table 3.1. In deciding when to use parametric as compared to nonparametric techniques, some of the factors discussed earlier can now be put into focus.

A first consideration is the accuracy of a model in terms of the commodity market or system that it attempts to represent. We can thus judge the specification and content of the model according to:

(1) Identification of relevant policy instruments useful for the model's intended application; and
(2) Selection of appropriate hypotheses to test, based on the underlying economic theory.

A second consideration is that most commodity models described in Chapter 3 are time dependent. It is thus appropriate to dichotomize the application of the above criteria according to those relevant for the sample period of model estimation as compared to the post sample period of model forecasting. The validation criteria that are applicable to the sample period are mostly the parametric ones that are concerned with model structure and parameter estimation.

(1) Model selection
(2) Coefficient tests
(3) Goodness-of-fit tests
(4) Specification tests
(5) Sensitivity analysis

The other validation criteria that are applicable to the sample period are more concerned with measuring the accuracy of a model's simulated values to the corresponding actual values of observations. To a certain extent, these criteria which are mostly nonparametric are even more effective in the post sample or forecast period. It is here that a model's ability to function is most important, because it extends the model's capabilities into the domain of future inference. The criteria deemed most useful for this purpose include:

(1) Pseudo forecasts
(2) Single point criteria
(3) Interval criteria
(4) Error-cost analysis
(5) Turning point analysis
(6) Comparative errors
(7) Spectral analysis
(8) Sensitivity analysis

We now turn to a discussion of the relevance of these criteria for the modeling methodologies of interest. Since the relevance of these criteria are less for the noneconometric methodologies, several additional criteria have appropriately been introduced.

Econometric Models

The validation techniques applicable to the validation of econometric models shown in Table 3.1 are both parametric and nonparametric techniques. Examples of useful parametric criteria listed above include model selection, coefficient tests, goodness-of-fit and pseudo forecasts. Nonparametric criteria include single point criteria, interval criteria, error-cost analysis, turning point analysis, and comparative errors. In short, the full-battery of criteria are applicable to econometric models and encompass all of the considerations mentioned above. In examining the documentation for appropriately validated econometric commodity models, one can typically find such criteria that help assess the model's quality and performance.

Input-Output Models

Input-output models can be evaluated in two fronts similar to econometric models: the coefficients employed and the values of the variables generated. However, the principal concern has been with the quality of the technical coefficients which are considered fixed in the short run but do change in the long run. Their variations are related to changing trade patterns as well as to changing technologies. Consider the case of a regional commodity input-output model. If regional output reaches a level of a technological advancement or scale effect that will support local production of its own inputs, the result is a shift from imported to locally-produced inputs that makes the previously used coefficients obsolete (Miernyk, 1972). Even within the framework of fixed coefficients, there are problems as to whether national coefficients are good substitutes for regional coefficients.

Five criteria not previously defined in this chapter are typically used to assess the effectiveness of tested nonsurvey methods of coefficient estimation:

(1) Paelinck and Waelbroeck (1963) plot the frequency distribution of the deviations of $a_{ij}^* - a_{ij}$, where a_{ij} is the national input-output coefficient and a_{ij}^* denotes an estimated technical coefficient.

(2) Isard and Romanoff (1963) used the Leontief index to measure the relative effectiveness of the coefficients. The index of relative change

$$RC_{ij} = |a_{ij} - a_{ij}^*|/\tfrac{1}{2}(a_{ij} + a_{ij}^*) \tag{5}$$

has its value ranging from zero to two. To normalize the index, Isard and Romanoff modified the range of the index from zero to one or

$$S_{ij} = 1 - |a_{ij} - a_{ij}^*|/(a_{ij} + a_{ij}^*). \tag{6}$$

(3) The Chi-square statistic or

$$X_j^2 = \Sigma_1(a_{ij} - a_{ij}^*)^2/a_{ij} \tag{7}$$

has been calculated by Schaffer and Chu (1969) to identify those sectors with statistically significant estimates of the coefficients.

(4) Czamanski and Malizia (1969) use a test of information content. That is, the closer the estimates are, the lower the values of information content will be.

(5) And Schaffer and Chu (1971) employ regression analysis for the comparison of nonsurvey estimated input-output tables. The a_{ij}'s of the survey table are the dependent variables and those of nonsurvey tables are the independent variable. The relative effectiveness of each criterion above has been discussed by Morrison and Smith (1974).

Because of the lack of accurate information upon which these coefficients are often based, these criteria are in many cases difficult to apply. Further information can be found in the sources cited.

Programming Models

The basic validation problem associated with mathematical programming models, even when of moderate size, is the limitation of positive basic commodity flows. It is a well-known result (Gass, 1969; Silberberg, 1970) that both linear and quadratic programming transportation models yield no more than $2n-1$ positive flows. In empirical studies, there can be as many as n^2 possible flows. In attempting to validate these flows where the allocation pattern is meaningful, the normal approach has been to observe the deviation between optimal and observed flows. McCarl and Spreen (1980, p. 95) report on validation tests that involve (1) 'how well the model solution, when specified with the base period data, corresponds to the real situation in the base period; (2) how well the model replicates the base period quantity (a test of whether price equals marginal cost); and (3) how well the model replicates base period quantities with prices fixed at base period actuals'. Such validation data based on deviations, however, require further development. Often the deviation between optimal and observed flows does not convey very meaningful results; each deviation not only explains the errors due to data, estimation, and specification of the model but also those due to imperfect market conditions in the corresponding market or industry.

It is also possible to apply Monte Carlo analysis to a linear programming model, since such a model can always be transformed into a Kuhn-Tucker system of linear equations. Similar to the econometric approach, the probability distribution of the parameters and the error terms (usually normally distributed) are known and, therefore, the confidence interval of the dependent variables (in the case of econometric approach) and the dual-primal variables (in the case of linear programming approach) can be established. However, in the case of the quadratic programming model, the Kuhn-Tucker system is no longer linear with respect to model parameters e.g., transportation costs, slopes and intercepts of regional equations. The only remaining workable statistical criterion in this case is that of factorial design analysis (Yang and Labys, 1982; and Naylor, 1971).

In conclusion, it would appear that sensitivity analysis of the above type based on parametric tests shows promise in application to programming types of commodity models. Where such parametric tests are not applicable, Yang and Labys (1982) have shown that the deterministic response surface can be appropriately applied in the form of model sensitivity analysis. It should also be noted that the size of the model serves as a limitation to validating mathematical programming and input-output models, both analytically and computationally.

Systems Models

Since systems models can combine several methodologies and thus contain coefficients estimated by different techniques, the validation criteria applicable depend on the structure of the model of interest. If a system dynamics model employing econometrically estimated equations is to be validated, then most of the parametric and nonparametric criteria are applicable. If a system simulation model featuring programming methodologies and switches is to be validated, then applying nonparametric criteria to the simulated observations over the sample and post sample period is appropriate. Most validation experiments with systems models have tended to be of the latter type.

Conclusions

Several additional considerations remain in validating the various commodity modeling methodologies. First of all, econometric models of small to medium-scale (size) can be validated relatively easily and the model user should search for or insist upon appropriate validation. One can also pursue the application of the above parametric and nonparametric techniques to the other commodity modeling methodologies.

Secondly, validation is difficult to imagine for large-scale commodity models with many technically determined coefficients such as those including programming methodologies. Perhaps such large scale models should be first justified in terms of the cost-accuracy criteria mentioned earlier. These criteria place pressure on modelers to undertake validation even under the most stringent of conditions. For example, Fromm, Hamilton and Hamilton (1974) point to the possible development of Federal standards for model validation. In that context validation is seen as a means of avoiding or discarding bad models and enhancing the credibility of good ones for policy applications.

Another consideration in dealing with large-scale models should be to examine the internal consistency of a model as well as its consistency with theory. This is particularly important for long-term models where the accuracy of the forecast cannot be judged for many years to come. Also of interest is a comparison of the results of a particular model with the results of other models or of other surveys that purport to measure the same factors. This comparison need not only relate to the level of the variables; it can also embody a sensitivity analysis of the response of the alternative models to similar perturbations. This validation process implies not only validation in the nature of comparative results but also a serious look at the data and documentation to see if variations can be explained reasonably.

Many of these factors have been embodied in the approach of the MIT (1979) Model Assessment Group mentioned earlier: (1) review of the literature, (2) overview model assessment, (3) independent audit, and (4) in-depth assessment. These steps are viewed as interactive and complementary. They involve not only comparing different model runs based on similar data and assumptions but also assessor-modeler relations.

A final important consideration is that no matter how difficult, commodity model validation must be practised. Otherwise, we have no other way of judging and comparing the performance of a model for practical decision making and forecasting.

Notes

1. The remaining materal in this chapter is based on W. C. Labys, 'Measuring the Validity and Performance of Energy Models', *Energy Economics*, 4 (1982): 159-68. It has been reprinted with permission of Butterworth Scientific Limited, Guildford Surrey.

References

Chambers, J. C., Mullick, S. K and Smith, D. D. (1971). 'How to Choose the Right Forecasting Technique', *Harvard Business Review*, 45-74

Czamanski, S. and Malizia, E. E. (1969). 'Applicability and Limitations in the Use of National Input-Output Tables for Regional Studies', *Regional Science*, 23: 65-77

Fromm, G., Hamilton, W. L., and Hamilton, D. E. (1974). 'Federally Supported Mathematical Models, Survey and Analysis', Research Applied to National Needs (RANN), National Science Foundation, Washington, DC

Gass, S. I. (1969). *Linear Programming*, Third Edition, New York: McGraw-Hill

—— (1979) *Validation and Assessment Issues of Energy Models*, Proceedings of a NBS Workshop, US Department of Commerce, Washington, DC

Howrey, E. P. and Witherell, W. H. (1968). 'Stochastic Properties of a Model of the International Wool Market', *Econometric Research Program Memorandum* No. 101, Princeton University, Princeton

Isard, W. and Romanoff, E. E. (1968). 'The Printing and Publishing Industries of Boston SMSA 1963', Technical Paper No. 7, Regional Science Research Institute, Cambridge, MA

Johnson S. R. and Rausser, G. C. (1977). 'Systems Analysis and Simulation: A

Survey of Applications in Agricultural and Resource Economics' in G. Judge and others (eds.), *Quantitative Methods in Agricultural Economics* (vol. 2 of A Survey of Agricultural Economics Literature), Minneapolis: University of Minnesota Press, pp. 157–304

Labys, W. C. (1973). *Dynamic Commodity Models*, Lexington: Heath Lexington Books

— (1982). 'Measuring the Validity and Performance of Energy Models', *Proceedings of the ECE-DOE Conference on Energy Conservation Modeling*, London: Pergamon Press. A similar version also appeared in *Energy Economics* (July, 1982)

— and Granger, C. W. J. (1970). *Speculation, Hedging and Commodity Price Forecasts*, Lexington: Heath Lexington Books

— and Yang, C. W. (1980). 'A Quadratic Programming Model of the Appalachian Steam Coal Market', *Energy Economics*, 2: 86–95

McCarl, B. A. and Spreen, T. H. (1980). 'Price Endogenous Mathematical Programming as a Tool for Sector Analysis', *American Journal of Agricultural Economics*, 62: 87–102

Miernyk, W. H. (1972). 'Regional and Interregional Input-Output Models: A Reappraisal' in B. Chinitz *et al.* (eds.), *Spatial, Regional and Population Economics*, London: Gordon and Breach Science Publishers Ltd, pp. 263–92

MIT Model Assessment Group (1979). *Independent Assessment of Energy Models*, Prepared for the Electric Power Research Institute, Report No. EA-1071, Palo Alto, CA

Morrison, W. I. and Smith, P. (1974). 'Nonsurvey Input-Output Techniques at the Small Area Level: An Evaluation', *Journal of Regional Science*, 14: 1–14

National Bureau of Economic Research (NBER) (1975). 'Conference on Model Formulation, Validation and Improvement', Summary Paper, NBER, Cambridge, MA

Naylor, T. H. (ed.) (1971). *Computer Simulation Experiments with Models of Economic Systems*, New York: John Wiley and Sons

— Wertz, K. and Wonnacott, T. (1969). 'Spectral Analysis of Data Generated by Simulation Experiments with Econometric Models', *Econometrica*, 37: 333–52

Paelinck, J. and Waelbroeck, J. (1963). 'Etude empirique sur l'évolution des coefficients input-output', *Economic Appliquée*, 16: 81–111

Pindyck, R. S. and Rubinfeld, D. L. (1976). *Econometric Models and Economic Forecasts*, New York: McGraw-Hill

Schaffer, W. and Chu, K. (1971). 'Simulating Regional Interindustry Models for Western States', *Papers and Proceedings of the First Pacific Regional Science Conference*, 1: 123–63

Silberberg, E. (1970). 'A Theory of Spatially Separated Markets', *International Economic Review*, 341–8

Weisbin, C. R., Peelle, R. W. and Loebl, A. S. (1981). 'An Approach to Evaluating Energy-Economy Models', *Energy*, 6: 999–1027

Wood, D. O. (1979). 'Model Assessment and the Policy Research Process: Current Practice and Future Promise' in Saul Gass (ed.), *Proceedings of the DOE/NBS Workshop on Validation and Assessment Issues of Energy Models*, National Bureau of Standards, Washington, DC

Yang, C. W. (1980). 'The Stability of the Interregional Trade Model: The Case of the Takayama-Judge Model' in *Modeling and Simulation*, G. Vogely and H. Mickle (eds.), Pittsburgh: Instrument Society of America

— and Labys, W. C. (1982). 'Sensitivity Analysis of the Quadratic Spatial Equilibrium Model', *Empirical Economics*

Zellner (1979). 'Statistical Analysis of Econometric Models', *Journal of the American Statistical Association*, 74: 628–51

4 COMMODITY MODEL APPLICATIONS: POLICY ANALYSIS AND FORECASTING

Commodity models have been shown to serve three purposes in particular: (1) the replication of market history, (2) the analysis and prediction of the impacts of commodity related policies, and (3) the forecasting of commodity market and industry behavior. The background to these model applications is provided in terms of the needs of economic and commodity planning. A methodological framework is then presented which describes how commodity models are utilized in policy and forecasting exercises. The actual practice of policy analysis based on modeling is described next. The remainder of the chapter centers upon the essential aspects of forecasting with commodity models. These aspects include a review of forecasting approaches, formal model forecasting, assumptions and certainty, forecast reliability, and forecast management.

Role of Models in Economic Planning

The planning perspective developed here concentrates on the role of economic analysis and modeling in the planning procedure. Planning is widespread at all levels of economic activity. Not only do we have ministries of planning and central planning boards, but we also have economic forecasting units and planning research departments. At one extreme, planning may consist of the normal task of any economic unit concerned with the future. Some examples of planners and users of commodity forecasts are corporate managers, marketing organizations, production units, finance and accounting organizations, government budgeters, public managers, and international organizations. At the other extreme, planning consists of preparing a detailed framework for the future economic structure and implementing it through direct or indirect manipulation of government policies. While in the former case market prices play a large role, in the latter they may be subordinate to overall plan goals, e.g. see Pyatt and Thorbecke (1976).

The types of planning associated with commodity markets lies in between these extremes. Most typically it consists of forecasts of the prices, production or exports of commodities; alternatively it focusses on the importance of nonprice factors in allocating scarce resources among competing commodities. Although planning varies considerably among corporations, government agencies or countries, its character depends on considerations such as the degree to which the market mechanism pervades economic decisions or the extent of market imperfections and price distortions and their causes. In the case of commodity markets, market adjustments are often less than perfect if not incomplete, and sometimes in disequilibrium. This makes the planning process difficult and requires that it depend on an appropriate forecasting system.

Although it is difficult to generalize about the nature of corporate institutional, or even national planning processes, the example given in Figure 4.1 provides a starting point. Beginning at the top of the figure and following downwards, the recognition stage views the planner as being confronted with certain policy problems. These problems normally are concerned with relating commodity activity to specific planning targets or national objectives. At the identification stage, a number of alternative decisions or policies are proposed which could help solve these problems.

The most complex stage is the next one, that of evaluating the alternatives. Although most planners have a verbal or mental model of their evaluation process, they seldom are able to quantify it. We do know that it consists of assessing the relative welfare outcomes of alternative policies, each of which is influenced by economic, political, technological and institutional considerations. Economic considerations, for example, might pertain to economic gains resulting from investment in the domestic or export commodity sector. Political considerations might refer to a commodity's importance in terms of bargaining strategies at the contract or trade level. Technological considerations might relate to the level of capital intensiveness to be adopted in the production or extraction of the commodity. And institutional considerations might reflect ecological, sociological or legal factors.

Once the alternatives are examined, planners make decisions hoping the outcome will be acceptable to management. In some cases as shown, the decision may not be acceptable and previously stated problems and alternatives will have to be reconsidered. The entire planning process can thus be described as one requiring feedback to previous stages until an acceptable decision is reached. Once a decision or policy is deemed acceptable, it moves to the implementation stage.

Figure 4.1: Commodity Policy Analysis and Planning

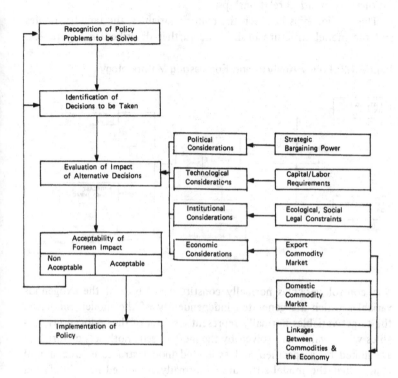

The Methodological Framework

Our first concern is with an appropriate methodological framework which can help planners analyze economic considerations in their evaluation of the impact of alternative commodity policies or decisions. The framework examined depends on the formal models described in Chapter 2. In the present context, a model can be said to embody an hypothesis which involves a relationship between variables and which intends to explain and predict events past, present and future or to describe policies and predict their outcome. For policy purposes, a model distinguishes between target variables which constitute the objectives of economic policy and control variables which are instruments affected by such policies. By systematically varying the levels of the control variables, we can observe the impact of policies on the target variables. In addition to specifying the economic relationship between variables, a model also attempts to incorporate technological, institutional and political relationships.

The relationships between the control variables, the target variables and the model structure utilized are further described in Figure 4.2.

Figure 4.2: Policy Analysis and Forecasting Methodology

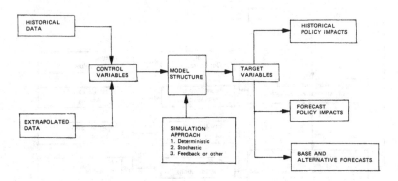

The control variables normally constitute a subset of the exogenous variables which are generated independently of the model. Similarly, the target variables normally represent a subset of the endogenous variables whose values are solved by the model itself. Both sets of variables are linked by a specified and estimated model structure. One should realize that the model structure is normally embodied in a simulation algorithm which provides successive solutions of the model over time and/or space. While such an algorithm typically accepts control variable inputs as given or deterministic, it can also manipulate the control variables by varying them stochastically, for example, with the use of Monte Carlo techniques. Such an approach permits policy and forecasting analysis to be conducted in the context of risk and uncertainty. This approach has been employed, for example, in exploring the impacts of weather variations or of political disruptions on commodity markets. Lastly, the simulation algorithm itself can be modified to handle specific policy modeling needs such as in the case of applying optimal control theory to the commodity system.

Commodity Policy Analysis

The above explanation can be tailored specifically to policy analysis by relating the policy simulation goals to the control variable inputs. If the goal is to determine how a new or changed policy might have affected the target variables in the past, then only the historical values of a particular policy variable need be varied and the simulation conducted. If the goal is to determine how a new or changed policy might affect the target variables in the future, then future values of the particular policy variables must be given. Future or extrapolated values must also be provided for the other exogenous variables in the model. In the case of a spatial non-temporal model, the policy simulation is normally conducted for one period only, either in the past, present or future.

Referring again to Figure 4.1, commodity policies can be directed to either domestic markets or export markets. Domestic commodity policies normally are analyzed using a commodity model which interrelates factors inherent to commodity supply, demand, inventories and prices. One can then demonstrate through simulations of the model how changing policies, for example regarding national incomes, employment or capacity adjustment can influence quantities and prices. This dependence can be described according to how the market might have reacted historically or how it might react in the future. Essential to employing the model is that it be validated employing the methods of Chapter 3, so that planners will have confidence in its explanation of market behavior or in its predictions.

Export commodity policies are analyzed with a similar modeling approach; only now the empirical information relates to the world economy and to world commodity markets. As we shall see in the next chapter, such models have been used to determine the impact of commodity stabilization schemes such as those proposed within UNCTAD. One weakness of this approach is its limitations for explaining the impact of commodity exports on various sectors of the dependent national economy. The type of modeling exercise required, as described in Chapter 2, involves instead linking one or more commodity models with a macro model or an equivalent computational model of the national economy.

Commodity Forecasting

Commodity forecasts either of important market and industry variables or of the impact of policies are essential to the planning exercises of many industries, government agencies, and international organizations.

The crucial element that determines the need for forecasts is the perception that the decision maker holds about the risks associated with the consequences of a decision he makes now. The greater the risk of a potential negative outcome in the future, the greater will be the need for an 'accurate and reliable' forecast that assists in assessing the risks associated with various potential outcomes.[1]

The very fact that 'accurate and reliable' forecasts are often not available – or the fact that decision makers have frequently little confidence in available forecasts – has a decisive impact on the decision making process. The prudent decision maker will tend to opt for a course of action that would minimize his risks. Most decision makers look in such a situation for the 'worst-case scenario' – and the probability of it to occur.[2] Hence, decision makers want not only to know the most likely outcome, but also the worst of all possible outcomes – and frequently the probabilities associated with these outcomes. The forecaster faces here two distinctly different tasks: first, he has to provide a menu of possible outcomes (which is by no means an easy task in a world that grows increasingly more and more complex from day to day), and second he has to attach probabilities to these various outcomes or scenarios. The difficulty for the forecaster is to capture as many relevant variables in his scenario as possible. For example, few economic forecasts before 1972 included an explicit assumption or projection on petroleum prices. This was simply not a 'variable' forecasters were too concerned about. Hence, it is not surprising that few people foresaw the dismal economic performance of the 1970s.[3]

This is also one of the reasons why forecasts based on econometric models have been increasingly disregarded in favor of those derived in the context of 'scenario approaches'. The parameters of most econometric models are derived on the basis of the relationship variables displayed in the past. Not only may the qualitative and quantitative nature of these relationships change in the future, but more importantly, the model may not contain variables that would be relevant then. While the forecaster may be aware that certain variables could, in the future, be important, lack of their 'behavior' in the past may make it difficult to build them into his model. Consider, for example, the difficulty model builders and forecasters have with the 'economic adjustment to the increase in energy prices'. Analysts are aware that these adjustments will take place over long time spans. But since this is such a recent phenomenon, econometric estimation methods are of little help here.

Another factor that influences the behavior of the decision maker is his perception of the reliability of the forecasts. Apart from the fact that it is easier to forecast some events than others, some forecasters tend to enjoy a better 'track record' than others. While most forecasts are forgotten by the time a new forecast is issued, some forecasters (presumably the successful ones) do keep track of their 'hits' and 'misses'. Not only does this provide a basis for the decision maker on which to evaluate the quality of the forecasts presented to him, but (perhaps even more importantly) it gives the forecaster a chance to evaluate past mistakes and to improve his forecasting ability.

Forecasting Approaches

Most traditional approaches to commodity market analysis, such as those described in Chapter 1, have been developed largely for purposes of market forecasting. The characteristics of these approaches together with those of commodity models have been summarized in Table 4.1. The approaches include judgmental, balance sheet, charting, technological, time series, economic regression, commodity models, and interactive computer systems. The importance of these techniques is that they provide a number of alternatives for forecasting commodity markets, depending on the level of detail, research expenditures, and forecast accuracy involved. Since this study concentrates specifically on forecasting with formal models, detailed information on these other techniques should be consulted in other sources. For example, see Ashby (1964), Chambers, Mullich and Smith (1972), Driehuis (1976), Granger (1980), Granger and Newbold (1977), Jiler (1975), Labys and Granger (1970), Makridakis and Wheelwright (1978), and Nelson (1973).

Forecasting with commodity models provides the advantage of possessing an overall view of a market or industry through the interaction of a number of essential economic (and sometimes political) behavioral relationships. Model configuration can be short to long run or spatial. And tradeoffs can be made between required accuracy and modeling costs. Important to the present use of commodity models as well as to the other forecasting techniques is the use of interactive computer systems. These do not constitute a separate forecasting approach but rather a means of facilitating the preparation of forecasts, particularly in the case of commodity models. For example, considerable difficulty was encountered in predicting the recent world-wide inflation and recession, because of a failure to link commodity phenomena and national economic phenomena. As a consequence increased use has been made of computer systems which use macroeconomic forecasts or which integrate models of these two areas. In the United States, forecasts based on such systems are included in the services of several major consulting

Table 4.1: Commodity Market Forecasting Techniques

Technique (Increasing Complexity)	Characteristics	Type of Model	Time Horizon	Costs	Accuracy	Applicability
Judgmental	Critical analysis of available information	Intuitive (Spatial/temporal)	Short to long	Low to high	Medium	Market analysis and forecasting
Balance Sheet	Equilibration of demand + imports ± inventories = supply + exports	Accounting (Spatial/temporal)	Short to long	Low	Medium to high	Market analysis and forecasting
Charting	Uses past price patterns to predict future	Geometric (Temporal)	Short to medium	Low	Medium	Price forecasting only
Technological	Critical and deterministic analysis of technological developments	Statistical and Qualitative (Temporal)	Long to very long	Medium	Medium to high	Forecasting
Time Series	Deterministic analysis of underlying temporal structure of data	Statistical (Temporal)	Short to medium	Low	Low to high	Forecasting
Economic Regression	Deterministic and behavioral analysis of market variables	Causal and Statistical (Spatial/Temporal)	Short to medium	Low to medium	Medium to high	Forecasting
Commodity Models	Behavioral analysis of market variables	Formal modeling methodologies, see Table 2.2 (Spatial/Temporal)	Short to long	Medium to high	High to very high	Market, stability, policy analysis, and forecasting
Interactive Computer Systems	Integration of behavioral commodity models and national economic models	Causal, Statistical Formal (Spatial/Temporal)	Short to long	Medium to high	High to very high	Market, stability, policy analysis, and forecasting

firms. These firms also provide facilities for linking the forecasts to corporate models of individual companies, which leads to a refinement known as corporate commodity modeling.

Formal Model Forecasting

The actual method of commodity model forecasting can be understood by referring again to Figure 4.2. To forecast the target variables for a particular future period, the control and other exogenous variables also have to be forecast into the future. The simulation algorithm, particularly if it is a simultaneous one, will then solve for values of the target variables successively from period to period. Manipulating the control input variables via the simulation algorithm, as described will give the forecast a particular characteristic. Using the 'most likely' values of the input variables will provide the most 'realistic' or 'base' solution forecast. When these input values are not deterministic but are varied stochastically, the forecasts provided can have a variance or confidence range attached to them. When these input values are varied around the base forecast, the forecasts generated are termed 'conditional' and constitute a scenario.

The regular preparation of commodity forecasts requires that the modeling procedure be dealt with in a systematic way, such as that described by Klein and Young (1980, pp. 82-3).

1. The sample period for the model's data should be updated regularly.

2. As structural change is perceived, model specification as well as estimation should be redone.

3. Residuals from each structural equation should be observed for each forecasting exercise. These residuals should be checked for any trends or systematic bias.

4. Where such bias occurs, adjustment factors should be included in the corresponding equations. Or the equations should be newly specified and estimated.

5. Preliminary forecasts should be made to evaluate the consistency of assumptions and adjustments with the forecast solution. This process should be continued until exogenous assumptions and equation adjustments are consistent with the forecast.

6. Present the commodity model forecasts to one or more experts and adjust the forecasts where appropriate to accommodate this external judgment.

7. Revise forecasts as new information becomes available regarding the updating of exogenous assumptions and the data set.

Assumptions and Certainty

Another important aspect of model forecasts is their validity, that is the degree of certainty with which the model describes future events. This depends not only on the technical and behavioral relationships which make up the model, but also on the information and data (the so-called 'assumptions') that are available at the time the forecast is made. For econometric models, these assumptions usually represent forecasts for the control or exogenous variables. Examples of such forecasts for exogenous variables in commodity models include population projections, forecasts of *per capita* incomes, economic growth extrapolations, and price projections for related products and commodities. It is easy to see that errors in the assumptions on which a forecast is built are likely to result in a wrong forecast. Another source of error which can affect forecast quality concerns the model structure, i.e., possible model misspecification. However, the modeler normally strives to remove this form of error before forecasting begins. It is interesting to note, that these two errors — assumption and specification errors — can offset each other in rare, fortunate circumstances. Correct forecasts have been made for the wrong reasons.

Commodity forecasters can sidestep the risk associated with using the 'wrong' assumptions by preparing scenario forecasts.[4] Each scenario using the same model is based on a different set of assumptions or sets of stepwise or incremental values of the control variables. These assumptions can be labelled 'optimistic — realistic — pessimistic' or 'high-medium-low', or in some other way. The purpose of this approach is to provide the decision maker not with the most likely forecast, but with the most likely range of possible forecasts. The 'high' or 'optimistic' scenario describes a future that is based on an optimistic set of assumptions, such as optimal economic policies and the absence of any man-made or natural disasters. It is a future that is attainable, if 'everything works out according to plan'.

Interestingly, most decision makers are more interested in what is usually referred to as the 'worst case scenario'. It is the answer to the question, 'what happens if everything goes wrong'. It is this scenario that provides the basis for contingency plans and 'fallback positions' of corporations and governments. However unpleasant the commodity forecast may be, it becomes an unequally more valuable planning tool for the decision maker than the 'optimistic' or 'realistic' forecasts. Hence, market analysts spend a good deal of their time asking themselves, 'what happens if . . .?'; in other words, drawing up a set of likely, but undesirable or pessimistic assumptions. In forecasting petroleum prices, for example, the most frequently asked questions are, 'how could prices climb or tumble and under what conditions would this happen?'.

The medium or realistic forecast tends to represent the most likely outcome — at least, in the opinion of the commodity forecaster. It is not uncommon that the analyst is asked to attach probabilities or a likelihood to his forecasts. This information is of equal importance to the decision maker as is the content of the various scenarios. If the likelihood of the 'pessimistic' scenario is low and the cost of the realization of contingency plans is high, the decision maker may find that 'he can live with the risk' and decide not to take any contingency action. Although statistical methods exist that make it possible to compute the probability of a set of related events, the application of these methods in econometric models has been limited to that of supply contingency analysis. Hence, most forecasters use either computational short cuts or rely on their judgment when they attach probabilities to their forecast scenarios.

Scenarios need not necessarily be associated with 'optimistic' and 'pessimistic' assumptions. Sometimes forecasters will prepare scenarios based on sets of assumptions that are free from the implied value judgment of an 'optimistic' or a 'pessimistic' outcome. Considering that buyers always prefer low to high prices and sellers the opposite, the concepts of 'optimistic' and 'pessimistic' assumptions are not unambiguous. Since the primary concern of the forecaster is to stake out the range within which future events will occur, a good deal of his efforts are directed towards identifying sets of assumptions that would accomplish the task. The task the forecaster faces consists of two parts: one, he needs to identify all those factors that could influence the variables he intends to forecast; and second, he has to attach values (and probabilities) to these variables.[5] While the former attempts to answer the question, 'Did I take all relevant factors into consideration,' the latter looks for the likely weights of these factors in the future. Consider, for example, the so-called second oil price shock that occurred in 1979. Few analysts (that publish their forecasts) predicted this second jump in oil prices, which was, to a large extent, triggered by the revolution in Iran. The departure of the Shah was a factor few forecasters had built into their models.

Forecast Reliability

The forecaster faces three important questions: 'Do my forecasts conform to conventional wisdom' (or, are the projections vastly different from what everybody else projects); 'Am I presenting a picture of the future that is internally consistent;' and finally 'How do these projections differ from my previous projections?'. In addition, most organizations continuously monitor and evaluate forecast performance. Not only does the credibility of a forecast depend on the 'track record', that is the quality of past forecasts, but a continuous monitoring system points out areas in commodity analysis that need to be strengthened.

The preparation of market forecasts in an organization usually goes through a series of more or less well-defined steps, whose primary purpose is, in essence, to assure that the forecasts conform to current conventional wisdom, are internally consistent and that deviations from previous forecasts are explained. In some organizations it is the responsibility of the forecaster to consider these steps; in others, each stage is clearly identified in the organization of the forecasting process.

Conventional Wisdom. Most commodity market forecasters — whether they use formal models or rely on their judgment in making forecasts — develop over time a sense of the direction markets will take. Of course, this sense will only develop for short term forecasts. It is for this period that forecasts can be checked, and conclusion can be drawn from past that forecasts can be checked, and conclusions can be drawn from past short term, the possible range within which these markets move is more predictable in the short than in the long term. Although speculation, strikes, and the unexpected introduction of economic policies (e.g., embargoes) can lead to a highly erratic behavior of commodity markets, most of the fundamental market forces (supply, demand, income, inventories, etc.) are either fixed or change slowly in the very short term. Hence, the range of possible market developments in the short term is for most commodity markets narrower and more predictable. Since most forecasters have access to much of the same information as everybody else, short term forecasts tend to cluster around a fairly narrow band.[6] Also, they are revised more frequently, which contributes to this impression of a narrow band of possible outcomes.

In the long term, forecasters lack this 'gut feeling' which is derived from frequent comparisons of forecasts and actual outcomes. What criteria does a forecaster use to judge the 'realism' of his projections? Or what are the arguments he can make to convince his audience about the likelihood he attaches to his forecasts? Several approaches are possible. The forecaster may argue that his forecasts were made with the help of a commodity model, and that the model has passed the tests of validation given in the previous chapter. Hence, there is every reason to believe that the model will also explain the future, assuming, of course, that the assumptions about the exogenous variables are 'realistic'. While this line of argument may convince some, others may still feel uncomfortable with forecasts that are well beyond, say, historical averages. Many forecasters look at 'historical trends' of key market variables or relationships of variables (e.g., inventories in relation to demand and relative prices) for some guidance. After all, few commodity markets undergo drastic changes. In addition to historical trends and relationships most forecasters tend to comapre their forecasts with those made by others. It is difficult to criticise a forecast that is well in the 'ball park' of forecasts prepared and hopefully published by other organizations. Somehow these historical relationships and other forecasts form what is frequently referred to as 'conventional wisdom', which becomes an informal standard against which commodity forecasters can gauge their own predictions.

Consistency. One of the most important criteria for the evaluation of a market forecast is its 'internal consistency'. This means that statements about likely developments of prices, demand, supplies, etc. have to be consistent with each other *and* in line with past experience, i.e., past market behavior and established economic theories.[7] If a forecaster, for example, projects that the demand for any commodity is likely to outpace its expected available supplies, then economic theory (as well as experience) would suggest that the price for this commodity is likely to rise — and *vice versa*. This type of consistency check is frequently disregarded in forecasts that are not based on commodity models. These models assure also that the projected subtotals, for example, of regional demands or supplies add up to the correct world total.

Increasingly market analysts provide not only global forecasts, say for next year's global wheat harvest, but they indicate also projected supplies for major producing countries. The difference between the global forecast and the sum total of the forecasts for specific countries is the implied forecast for all those producers not included in the sample, usually refered to as the 'rest of the world'. A careful check is necessary that this 'implied forecast for the rest of the world' is well in line with past experience and current knowlege about investment plans, plantings, yield, etc. An econometric commodity model, if it does not explicitly include behavioral equations for the group of countries comprised under the 'rest of the world', does not provide any more information than a forecast based solely on judgment.[8]

One way to assure this type of consistency is to prepare forecasts for all countries. This is usually referred to as the 'bottom-up' approach.[9] Although this approach requires quite a bit more information (on a country-by-country basis), it assures the desired 'accounting consistency' since all countries are accounted for. However, it is important to keep in mind that the sum totals of the individual country forecasts do not necessarily yield a consistent global picture. The total of all country exports may, for example, exceed the corresponding sum of all imports. Hence, the 'bottom-up' approach requires some kind of mechanism (which need not necessarily be truly mechanical, but could also be based on the analyst's best judgment) to assure global consistency.

The markets of many primary commodities are closely related. Their products either compete with each other (e.g. fats and oils, most metals), or complement each other, that is, they are used jointly together (e.g. grains and high-protein meals). Hence, different market forecasts have to be consistent with one other. To the extent that commodity models are used, the relationships among related commodities can be explicitly taken into consideration, either by linking existing models for individual markets into a multicommodity market model or by introducing the prices of related commodity markets as exogenous variables into the model. The first approach 'endogenizes' the existing relationships between two or more commodities, and hence the model generates prices for the related commodities simultaneously. The second approach uses price forecasts of related commodities as any other assumption (e.g. economic growth). The prices of these commodities then become just an additional market force.

If formal commodity models are not available, as would be the case in making judgmental forecasts, commodity forecasters tend to rely on past averages or trends in price ratios to assure this multi-market consistency. Most of this discussion about the consistency of forecasts may appear pedantic. However, it is important to keep in mind that the acceptance of a forecast (e.g. by management or a wider audience) depends to a large extent on the credibility of the forecaster. By definition, forecasts cannot be verified but by actual observation. In the case of long term forecasts this may be five, ten or twenty years from now. By this time the original forecast on which, say, investment or other business decisions were based may be long forgotten. Of course, in the case of short-term forecasts, validation is much easier and the credibility of the forecaster depends largely on his track record. Whatever his track record might be, if the forecast contains inconsistencies it is almost certain that it will be ignored. The implication is that the forecaster is either unfamiliar with the peculiarities of a specific market and his underlying model misspecified or simply 'sloppy workmanship', neither of which helps in the marketing of forecasts.

Continuity. The markets for primary commodities as for other products undergo changes continually. New producers or buyers emerge; new trading patterns replace established ones; new government regulations change trade patterns; or new technologies or processing techniques alter the structure of demand or supply, etc. All these factors lead to structural changes in the market or a change in the market forces that determine commodity prices. In addition, commodity forecasters are faced with continuous changes in the so-called 'assumptions' or the over-all economic environment in which primary commodities are imbedded. These changes force the forecaster to update or revise his forecasts usually at regular intervals.[10]

Most forecasters are reluctant to change their estimates, particularly long term ones, drastically. If there is not a significant change in the market structure, major revisions of long-term forecasts tend to shed an unfavorable light on the abilities of the forecaster. After all, the basic economic structure of a market and hence the fundamental market forces tend to change only slowly over time. Substantial revisions of long-term forecasts indicate, therefore, either a significant change in the market structure, such as the changes in international oil markets that occurred during the early 1970s, changes in the long-term assumptions, or simply the fact that the analyst either overlooked an important force in the market or misjudged its 'weight'. Since few analysts, if any, would like to be accused of this type of negligence, most of them change their long-term forecasts only in response to a revision of the assumptions or a major change in the market structure.

In preparing long-term forecasts, even with the help of formal models, the judgment of most forecasters will be influenced by recent market developments. A gloomy short-term outlook often results in downward revisions of long-term forecasts, and *vice versa*.

Unlike revisions of long term forecasts which usually reflect changes in 'the underlying trends' of assumptions or in the structure of the market, revisions of short-term forecasts tend to mirror rapidly changing market conditions. Information about unusual weather conditions, labor unrest, changes in government policies (e.g. embargo, changes in exchange rates etc.,) will send short term forecasters back to their models. Hence, revisions of short-term forecasts tend to be greater and more frequent than those of the long term.[11]

Forecast Management

Proper management of forecasting demands that all revisions, those of short as well as those of long term forecasts, can be explained by the forecaster in qualitative (what factors did change) and quantitative (how did these changes affect the forecasts) terms. This analysis of forecast revisions will not only enhance the credibility of the forecaster, it represents also a learning experience and thus adds to his knowledge about the market.

Forecast management also requires that information be accumulated regarding a forecaster's 'track record'. How often has he or she been correct in the past? Or, in other words, how accurate were past forecasts? While many forecasters might prefer to forget their past forecasts (of course, only those which were far off the mark), a growing number of organizations have implemented a systematic analysis of the forecasting performances of their staff. The primary purpose is not, as one might assume, some form of personal performance evaluation, but rather an attempt to systematically 'learn from past errors' and to uncover weak spots in market analysis and forecasting. This kind of analysis might find that a particular forecasting technique yielded better results or led to a consistent error (bias) in the forecasts; it might also reveal to what extent the assumptions on which the forecasts were based or 'unforeseen events' (e.g., a revolution in a major producing country, a drastic change in the weather) were responsible for errors. Obviously, this kind of analysis can only be carried out for short-term forecasts, unless a long series of long-term forecasts is available.[12]

What are the criteria for a 'good' forecast? Obviously, most users would want forecasts that are consistently 'on the mark'. Current forecasting techniques make this an unattainable goal for most commodity markets, and many forecasters regard themselves as successful if their predictions come close to actual market conditions or if they were able to correctly predict 'turning points'.[13] These points are of great importance in the short-term, particularly in the timing of buying or selling decisions. For medium-term and long-term forecasts, most analysts will attempt to capture the long-term cyclical behavior of markets as well as their trends.[14] Of course many of the validation techniques in addition to turning-point analysis described in the previous chapter are appropriate for analyzing forecast performance.

A final aspect of forecast management is the need for modelers to maintain a particular commodity model as well as its data base. Too often other pressing needs will cause a model to be put on a 'shelf' and its underlying data support system to be curtailed. Commodity models regularly require updating, including changes in specification and estimation. Commodity data sets are also best maintained with regular updating. Neglecting either of these activities is likely to make commodity modeling more expensive than it need be.

Notes

1. Of course, this statement will be true only if the decision maker intends to minimize risks. A gambler who in a roulette game decides to put all his chips on one number is obviously not in need of a forecast.

2. It is a widespread practice among economic forecasters to provide either a 'range' in their forecasts or a 'high' and a 'low case'. Since few forecasters attach probabilities to their high and low cases, the arithmetic average of these two cases is frequently taken by decision makers as the most likely outcome.

3. It is interesting to observe that in the late 1970s many macroeconometric models began to include a wider range of energy and other primary commodity prices as influences on the determination of the wholesale price deflator.

4. Some model builders test the 'robustness' of their models by feeding it highly unlikely assumptions, that is they use values for the exogenous variables that are far outside the range of values observed in the past.

5. The emergence of a factor that may significantly influence the forecasts, but has not been important in the past, may force the forecaster to revise or expand his model.

6. However, this does not mean that short-term forecasts are either more often correct than long-term forecasts or are easier to prepare. What it means is that on the basis of nearly identical information and similar experience with a market, most forecasters will come up with a similar answer.

7. In rare instances where a drastic change in the market structure occurred, past market behavior may no longer be a relevant 'standard' against which projections may be checked. The changes that occurred in international oil markets since the early 1970s serve to some extent as an example.

8. However, econometric models usually assure that definitional equalities are maintained such as global exports equal global imports, or technical relationships where supply is based on product yields and extraction rates, or the relationship between the price of a raw material, its joint products and the cost of processing.

9. See p. 22.

10. Most companies or government organizations have regular forecasting cycles. Usually starting with the availability of the economic growth forecasts, analysts begin to prepare their market forecasts. Some organizations alter the economic growth forecasts on the basis of changes in the assumed market forecasts. While the economic growth of industrial countries is hardly affected by changes in the markets for non-oil primary commodities, the growth performances of some developing countries depend to a large extent on the value of their primary commodity exports. Several attempts have been made to link changes in primary commodity markets to the pattern of economic growth in industrial and developing countries, e.g. see the World Bank (1975) SIMLINK model.

11. As information about markets becomes more widely and quickly available in increasing detail – through improvements in electronic transmission and

computers – market forecasters are under pressure to reflect this in their revisions of short-term forecasts. Hence, the management of market information becomes an important element in the preparation and revision cycle of short-term forecasts. Additional market intelligence, if used appropriately, is likely to improve forecasts and hence the track record of the forecaster.

12. Such a series of long-term forecasts would consist, for example, of 10 and 20 year forecasts prepared annually beginning, say, in 1950. By 1982, it would be possible to analyze 22 ten year and 12 twenty year forecasts.

13. See p. 110.

14. Knowledge about the behaviour of cycles is an important factor in investment decisions of perennial tree crops, mining operations, etc.

References

Ashby, W. W. (1964) 'On Forecasting Commodity Prices by the Balance Sheet Approach', *Journal of Farm Economics*, 46: 633–43

Chambers, J. C., Mullich, S. K., and Smith, D. D. (1972) 'How to Choose the Right Forecasting Technique', *Harvard Business Review*, 49: 45–74

Driehuis, W. (ed.) (1976) *Primary Commodity Prices: Analysis and Forecasting*, Rotterdam: Rotterdam University Press

Granger, C. W. J. (1980) *Forecasting in Business and Economics*, New York: Academic Press

— and Newbold, P. (1977) *Forecasting Economic Time Series*, New York: Academic Press

Jiler, H. (ed.) (1975) *Forecasting Commodity Prices*, New York: Commodity Research Bureau

Klein, L. R. and Young, R. M. (1980) *An Introduction to Econometric Forecasting and Econometric Forecasting Models*, Lexington: Heath Lexington Books

Labys, W. C. and Granger, C. W. J. (1970) *Speculation, Hedging and Commodity Price Forecasts*, Lexington: Health Lexington Books

Makridakis, S. and Wheelwright, S. (1978) *Interactive Forecasting*, San Francisco: Holden Day

Nelson, C. R. (1973) *Applied Time Series Analysis for Managerial Forecasting*, San Francisco: Holden Day

Pyatt, G. and Thorbecke, E. (1976) *Planning Techniques for a Better Future*, Geneva: International Labor Office

World Bank. (1975) 'The SIMLINK Model of Trade and Growth for the Developing World', Staff Working Paper No. 220, World Bank, Washington, DC

5 COMMODITY MODEL APPLICATIONS: MARKET STABILIZATION ANALYSIS

This chapter presents the basic modeling approaches and modeling issues involved in analyzing policies for commodity market stabilization.[1] This is a major aspect of commodity model applications stimulated by Keynes' historical proposal that commodity market stabilization could contribute to the growth of world trade and economic development (see Jalwardena, 1976). More recently, this model application has been stimulated by proposals within the United Nations calling for the creation of an 'Integrated Program for Commodities' to stabilize commodity prices. One strand of the Program has been the commendation that international commodity agreements should be formulated for eighteen commodities. International buffer stocks were viewed as suitable control mechanisms for the ten 'core' commodities. It was envisaged that such schemes would benefit both developing countries whose export earnings would be stabilized as well as industrialized countries whose import expenditures would be stabilized.

The presentation of stabilization modeling in this chapter has been organized to include approaches which can be classified as theoretical, empirical and econometric models. As in other taxonomies of this type, the task of classification is difficult and some overlap exists between the studies selected for these different groupings. Some other studies which review stabilization analysis include Adams and Klein (1978), Bigman and Reutlinger (1978), Blandford and Lee (1978), Just and Hallam (1978), Newberry and Stiglitz (1981), and Turnovsky (1978). After presenting the three modeling approaches, the chapter concludes with a discussion of future model applications and analysis.

Theoretical Models

The theoretical literature on commodity price stabilization has been long occupied with buffer stock analysis. The beginnings of this literature are normally traced to Waugh (1944) who employed social surplus analysis with linear demand and supply curves. To Waugh, buffer stock intervention represented an attempt to stabilize price fluctuations caused by shifts in supply. When such shifts occur, a buffer stock manager who bought a commodity at low prices and sold it at high prices could increase expected producers' surplus by a greater amount than it would reduce consumers' surplus. Oi (1961) extended this work by introducing shifts in demand. He found that complete price stabilization would increase consumers' surplus by a greater amount than it would reduce producers' surplus. Massell (1969) drawing upon the work of Waugh and Oi presented a combined supply-demand approach, showing that the surplus outcome depended on whether the price variance approaches zero for demand function shifts, as compared to supply function shifts.

Implied in the WOM[2] framework is that producers and consumers appear to gain more from price stabilization, where price fluctuations result primarily from shifts in their particular market function. There should also be an overall increase in total social surplus and compensation of losers by gainers, thus leading to a preference for price stability. The more recent literature has represented modifications of this framework, both to correct its deficiencies and to extend it. These modifications have included treatments of surplus in a trade-earnings context, nonlinearities in the supply and demand curves, variations in the form of equation disturbances, risk response and uncertainty, social surplus definitions, partial vs. complete price stabilization, and stabilization of flows rather than prices. References to these studies and their comparative properties appear in Table 5.1.

Among the different contributions which have been made, Hueth and Schmitz (1972) based on the work of Gruebel (1964) have recognized the possibility that surplus may change where consumers or producers are identified separately from either importing or exporting nations. They conclude that the expected surplus for all parties would be reduced by price stabilization where the supply or demand functions remain stable. However, the expected surplus of the party whose shifting functions caused the price fluctuations would increase by a larger amount.

The WOM framework has also suffered from the assumption of linearity in the supply and demand curves. Turnovsky (1978), Just and Hallam (1978) and Sarris and Taylor (1978) have developed methods for determining the size and distribution of gains from price stabilization. Their results generally imply that the benefits of price stabilization for producers and consumers depend on the nonlinearities of the functional forms of the demand and supply curves rather than just the source of the instability.

Also omitted in the WOM framework has been a consideration of

Table 5.1: Theoretical and Related Empirical Price Stabilization Studies[a]

Authors	Commodities	Extensions of the Basic Framework								
		Non-linearities	Disturbance Form	Risk Response	Surplus	Partial Stabilization	Export Earnings	Optimization	Simulation	Other Policies
Bigman, Reutlinger	Grains	No	No	No	Yes	Yes	Yes	No	Yes	Yes
Brook, Grilli, Waelbroeck	Core[b]	Yes	Yes	No	Yes	No	Yes	No	No	Yes
Brown	General	Yes	No	No	No	Yes	Yes	No	Yes	Yes
Duloy	Wool	No	No	No	No	Yes	No	No	Yes	No
Gardner	Wheat	No	Yes	No	No	Yes	No	Yes	Yes	Yes
Glismann, Stecher	General	No	No	No	No	Yes	Yes	No	No	No
Goreux	General	No	No	No	Yes	Yes	No	Yes	Yes	No
Hueth, Schmitz	General	No	No	No	No	No	No	No	No	Yes
Maizels	General	No	No	No	No	Yes	Yes	No	No	Yes
Mo	General	No	No	No	No	Yes	No	Yes	No	No
Newberry, Stiglitz	Cocoa, Coffee, Cotton, Jute, Rubber, Sugar	Yes	Yes	Yes	Yes	Yes	Yes	No	Yes	Yes
Nguyen	General	No	Yes	No	No	Yes	Yes	No	No	No
Sarris, Taylor	Wheat, Feedgrains	Yes	No	No	Yes	Yes	No	No	Yes	No
Subotnik, Houck	Agricultural	No	No	No	Yes	No	No	No	No	Yes
Turnovsky	General	Yes	Yes	No	Yes	Yes	No	No	No	No

Notes: a. See references for sources. Omitted are studies prior to 1970 related to Waugh-Oi-Massel Framework.
b. Coffee, cocoa, tea, sugar, cotton, jute, sisal, rubber, tin and copper.

the form in which random or stochastic equation disturbances are introduced. The mentioned works of Massell (1969) and Hueth and Schmitz (1972) have been based on the use of additive disturbances in the supply and demand equations. Turnovsky (1976) has argued that the outcome of their work is highly sensitive to the form of disturbances employed. In particular, he has shown that multiplicative disturbances in demand are more plausible than additive ones. Just and Hallam (1978) have further shown that domestic consumers gain from stabilization of domestic supply disturbances (with multiplicative disturbances and domestic supply relatively elastic to demand) which is contrary to the results of Hueth and Schmitz (1972), based on additive disturbances.

Risk response analysis also has been absent in the theoretical approaches. As prices become stabilized, risk-responsive producers may adjust their rates of output. Just and Hallam (1978) suggest that by excluding risk estimates, gains from stabilization may be seriously biased downward and optimal stabilization decisions may be wrong ones. Impacts of risk analysis have also been evaluated in a major study by Newberry and Stiglitz (1977). They conclude that omissions of risk in the past may have led to an underestimate of costs and an overestimate of benefits, particularly benefits falling upon consumers.

Uncertainty also has been excluded; the WOM framework assumes that the demand and supply relations depend on actual or known market prices. As emphasized by Turnovsky (1978), such an assumption is unrealistic, because most production decisions are made before the actual price is known. Taking this into account through the use, for example, of adaptive or rational expectations will affect the social surplus outcome.

Also questioned has been the definition of social surplus or welfare impacts employed. Just and Hallam (1978) have argued for improvements in defining as well as in applying the concepts of consumers' and producers' surplus. In particular, producers' surplus should include consideration of input prices and consumers' surplus should include recognition of final product prices. Newberry and Stiglitz (1977) also have attempted to improve the definition by showing the impact of risk, income variability, and differences between consumer and producer prices.

Another weakness has been the dependence on the unrealistic theoretical assumption that a buffer stock scheme should stabilize prices completely. Price stabilization more accurately is seen as requiring partial stabilization rather than a fixed or complete stabilization. This opens a range of possibilities regarding the exact degree of stabilization needed to produce particular outcomes. Studies by Maizels (1978) and Nguyen (1978) have addressed this issue, showing how partial as compared to complete stabilization affects the earnings of commodity exporting nations. They also demonstrate how critical the choice of price elasticities is to the outcome. While there appears to be agreement that price stabilization stabilizes earnings if market instability is dominated by demand variation, the same policies may destabilize earnings if instability is dominated by supply variation, depending on the values of the demand and supply elasticities.

Finally, Bigman and Reutlinger (1978) question that the social value or welfare gains from buffer stock operations should be based on consumers' and producers' surplus alone. They argue that the primary objective of such stocking policy should be to ensure a regular flow of supplies to consumers and to overcome critical supply deficiencies. The expected outcome of stabilization analysis should be regarded as an insurance premium paid by market participants to assure commodity supplies. This same idea appears in a work by Konandreas and Schmitz (1976).

The advantage of the theoretical WOM framework together with its more recent modifications has been that a definitive answer to the question of the impact of price stabilization can be offered, subject to a particular set of assumptions. As can be seen in the recent modifications, the assumptions underlying the theory which have proven wanting are numerous. This implies that a number of complex factors have to be interrelated in deriving the stabilization outcome for a particular situation. As always, this makes theoretical analysis less clear and more complex to execute. For example, complications such as applying multiple objectives to a buffer stock operation cannot easily be accommodated. As a consequence, a number of basically theoretical studies also have employed empirical observations or data to test or to demonstrate certain hypotheses. This can also be seen as an attempt to provide a more realistic framework within which stabilization policies can be evaluated.

Empirical Models

Empirical stabilization models have used commodity data to fix parameters and to evaluate outcomes of the theoretical stabilization models. They have not gone as far as to employ commodity models of an econometric nature. A good example of an empirical stabilization model is that of Brook, Grilli, and Waelbroeck (1977). Studying issues related to the UNCTAD Integrated Program, the authors have investigated the income and pure welfare gains of exporters (and importers) of some 17 primary commodities considered suitable for inclusion in the Integrated Program. Most of their work has been based on simple model assumptions: linear demand and supply relations, no adjustment lags, additive stochastic disturbances, no storage costs, and complete price stabilization about known trends.

Their findings have shown that developing countries who act as net exporters would experience income gains from stabilization for only a few agricultural commodities: cocoa, coffee, wool and jute. As net importers, these countries would only gain in the case of wheat. For metals and minerals, the developing countries who act as exporters would not experience an increase in income and the resulting balance between pure welfare gains and income losses is uncertain. One other conclusion of the authors has been that analysis of the benefits of price stabilization should include factors other than just income and pure welfare gains.

Although the authors did not intend to introduce more stringent assumptions, critics have suggested that changing one or more of their assumptions would change their empirical results significantly. For example, Maizels (1978, p. 3) comments as follows: 'Price stabilization by means of buffer stocks is shown to be desirable only for those commodity markets subject to demand instability; and, in the case of markets subject to supply instability, only for those commodities with low elasticities of both demand and supply. For other commodity markets, their conclusion would appear to be that price stabilization should be avoided for fear of destabilizing export earnings.' A major criticism of the assumptions underlying their results is that complete price stabilization has never been considered in international commodity agreements. Using partial stabilization which implies a price range, Maizels has found that export losses for a large group of commodities would only be marginal, while the revenues themselves would not be more unstable, even for commodities with a high supply elasticity. He further found that analyses of this type should include additional policies such as export controls and that gains to developing countries have to be measured by more than income and welfare transfers.

This need for partial price stabilization has also been stressed in other empirical studies. The results obtained also appear to be highly dependent on the stochastic nature of the supply and demand functions. For example, Nguyen (1978) has employed a model with stable demand but random shifts in supply as well as partial price stabilization to test the outcome of the Brook, Grilli and Waelbroeck study. He accepts the result that a buffer stock scheme will always stabilize earnings for markets subject mainly to demand fluctuations. But the results of his model show that earnings will be destabilized for markets subject to supply fluctuations, where demands are elastic. Where they are inelastic, earnings are more stabilized with partial stabilization, while the long term level of earnings would not be affected.

Newberry and Stiglitz (1977) have also criticized the deficiencies of past theoretical and empirical studies, showing the need to introduce risk analysis and to improve the definition of social surplus. Their empirical findings relate to six of the UNCTAD 'core' commodities: cocoa, coffee, cotton, jute, rubber, and sugar.[3] They have found that the benefits of income transfer through price stabilization are marginal, but that greater benefits could be obtained from direct income stabilization. Jute and sugar are shown to experience some gains from price stabilization, but cocoa, cotton, rubber and coffee offer lower returns.

Several other studies have concentrated on using representative but not actual data and on employing computer simulation techniques. For example, Brown (1975) has developed a format for analyzing export earnings, producer profits, and price stabilization effects of various stabilization policies in addition to buffer stocks. These include export taxes, buffer funds and export quotas. He also expanded his assumptions to include nonlinear demand and supply functions as well as dynamic or 'period' analysis. Goreux (1978) has criticized the empirical (and econometric) studies for not selecting the stocking rules according to an optimization procedure. He has attempted to correct this deficiency by employing a dynamic optimizing simulation technique which includes stochastic supply and demand shifts as well as partial price stabilization.

His two major criteria for evaluating the outcome of stabilization are the coefficient of price variation and the present value of the financial profit or loss of the buffer stock agency. Costs of storage and operation are now included in the analysis. Based on assumed values of elasticities and other parameters, Goreux's results have shown that partial price stabilization of a limited nature can be obtained at low cost, while increased price stabilization can cause costs to rise rapidly. He also discovered that the outcome of buffer stock analyses are highly sensitive to the values of the parameters used. Similar findings have been reported by Gardner (1978). He also found that the derivation of optimal stocking policies requires using probability distributions for the included as well as for the stochastic variables.

A final empirical model of interest is that of Bigman and Reutlinger (1978) who consider quantity stabilization to be more important than price stabilization particularly for food commodities. They have conducted empirical simulations (related to the wheat market) to analyze benefits from the stocking operations based on stabilization of consumption as well as of prices and incomes. Trade policy alternatives are also introduced as essential to stabilization analysis. Their results suggest that the stabilizing effects of buffer stocks are reduced as trade policy moves progressively from that of a 'closed' to an 'open' economy. Opening a country to trade in itself also tends to have stabilizing effects.

The advantage of these empirical models has been that they have helped to expand the usefulness of the theoretical models by making them more realistic. They have also provided a starting point to determine what to expect from the stabilization of different commodity markets. With the exception of one or two studies, nonetheless, they have helped only minimally with the testing of the more stringent model revisions suggested in the above section. The results obtained also have been too general, pertaining mostly to groups of commodities (e.g., those falling into certain elasticity ranges) rather than to individual ones. This deficiency has been particularly severe, because it is well known that the characteristics of individual commodity markets differ considerably. This applies not only to structural properties but also to related policy influences and to sudden shocks such as climatic changes. As a consequence, studies of stabilization have also employed econometric commodity models which have the potential of including more complete market information.

Econometric Models

The econometric commodity modeling studies of interest are those of a conventional microeconomic nature, with all elasticities and parameters appropriately estimated. Because of the importance of this approach, we consider it in this section as well as in the next one. Altogether the following modeling configurations are examined: (1) single commodity studies, (2) multiple commodity studies such as those dealing with UNCTAD 'core' commodities, (3) single commodity-single country studies, and (4) multiple commodity-multiple country studies.

Listing and comparison of the properties of the more important of these studies appear in Table 5.2.

One of the earliest stabilization studies employing a single commodity model including buffer stocks is that of Desai (1966). Supply

Table 5.2: Econometric Modeling Studies of Commodity Price Stabilization[a]

Authors	Commodities	Stochastic Simulation		Economic Gains/Losses		Country Earnings
		Past	Future	Financial[b]	Surplus	Impact
Adams	Copper	No	Yes	No	No	Yes
Behrman	Coffee, cocoa, tea, jute, rubber, sisal, wheat, rice, wool, bauxite, tin, copper, iron ore	No	No	No	No	No
Blond	Wheat	No	No	No	Yes	Yes
Bhaskar, et al.	Copper	No	No	Yes	No	No
Chaipravat	Rice	Yes	Yes	No	No	Yes
CRA	Copper	No	No	Yes	No	No
Cuddy (UNCTAD/L.2)	Core[c]	Yes	Yes	Yes	No	No
Dalton	Wool	No	No	Yes	No	No
Desai	Tin	Yes	Yes	No	No	No
Edwards, Parikh	Coffee	No	Yes	Yes	No	Yes
Just, Hallam	Wheat	Yes	No	No	Yes	No
Kim, et al.	Cocoa	Yes	Yes	Yes	No	No
Kanbur	Rice	No	No	Yes	No	No
Kofi	Cocoa	Yes	No	Yes	No	Yes
Konandreas	Grains	No	No	No	No	Yes
Labys	Jute	Yes	No	Yes	Yes	No
Labys	Lauric Oil	Yes	No	Yes	No	Yes
Phillips	Cocoa	No	No	No	No	No
Reutlinger	Wheat	No	Yes	Yes	Yes	Yes
Smith	Copper	No	No	Yes	No	No
Smith, Schink	Tin	No	No	No	No	No
Spearman, Labys	Copper	No	No	Yes	Yes	Yes
Walker, Sharples	Wheat	Yes	Yes	No	No	No
Zwart, Meilke	Wheat	No	No	Yes	Yes	Yes

Notes: a. See references for sources.
b. Financial costs of buffer stock operation as compared to producers' and consumers' surplus.
c. Coffee, cocoa, tea, sugar, cotton, sisal, rubber, tin and copper.

and demand equations have been embodied in an econometric model of the tin market, including price and stock adjustments. Not only did the study feature simulations of buffer stock levels including stochastic shocks but changes in producers' revenues were also computed. The advantage of including stochastic shocks for demand as well as for supply is obviously to incorporate the random disturbances which so typically characterize commodity market behavior. This single modeling approach to buffer stock simulation has been applied extensively. Among examples of such studies are those of Kofi (1972) for cocoa, Labys (1971 and 1973) for lauric oils, Smith (1975) for copper, Smith and Schink (1976) for tin, and Chaipravat (1978) for rice.

A major theoretical and econometric deficiency of these earlier studies has been their neglect of optimization in stocking rules together with appropriate optimization techniques. While some of the studies have searched for levels of stock holding and price stabilization that maximized the benefits from stabilization, the feedback was external rather than internal to the system. More correctly, Kim, Goreux and Kendrick (1975) have employed a stochastic feedback control rule to optimize the management of a buffer stock operation including export controls for the cocoa market. A slightly different approach is that of Gustafson (1958) and of Dalton (1976) based on dynamic programming. In addition to examining tradeoffs between the degree of stabilization and the size of the buffer stock, both of these studies have examined financial implications for the buffer stock agency. Other possibilities for employing control theory have recently been suggested by Klein (1978) and by Mariano (1978).

Another problem with many of the econometric models is that they have failed to include simulation or computation of the welfare gains to be made from stabilization. To correct this deficiency, Reutlinger (1975) proposed a method of computing gains and losses accruing to producers and consumers as well as to any buffer stock agency. Although only a rudimentary wheat model was used in the simulation analysis, he did compute future gains and losses under probabilistic conditions. A recent application of this method is that of Labys (1979) who analyzed gains and losses from the operation of an international buffer stock for jute. Sarris and Taylor (1978), however, have pointed to the difficulties of determining who will gain or lose from price stabilization based on a conventional commodity model. In their simulation study concerning wheat and feedgrains, they show the importance of considering the nonlinearity of demand, the types of restriction found in international markets, and the intricacies of explaining supply response.

With the announcement of the proposed 'UNCTAD Integrated Program' which would feature interaction between buffer stocks for different commodities, interest in multiple-commodity modeling studies of buffer stock stabilization grew quickly. Some of these studies have been conducted to determine financial costs, capital requirements and welfare gains from simultaneously operating buffer stocks for the ten 'core' commodities as well as several on the periphery. Behrman (1978) has employed simple nonlinear eight-equation models (i.e., supply and demand relations for developing, developed, and centrally planned economics, a price-inventory relation, and an ex-post identity between appearance and disappearance) using nonstochastic simulations to compute gross revenue gains across commodities over the recent historical period. Cuddy in his UNCTAD (1976) study also used simple commodity models but went beyond the historical analysis of Behrman to produce forecasts of buffer stock impact. He also used Monte Carlo methods to capture potential variations in supply due to natural, social or political upheavals.

Econometric studies attempting to link single commodity-single country models for buffer stock analysis have been fewer. Chaipravat (1975) has simulated buffer stock impact by linking a rice model to his model of the Thai economy and Roldan (1978) has similarly linked a coffee model to a model of the Brazilian economy.

Adams (1978) is known for his attempt to link multiple commodity-multiple country models in his extension of the LINK model to include a number of commodity models. This he has termed COMLINK. The only reported stabilization analysis has been an attempt to determine the impact on world trade, income and payments of a copper stockpiling program.

Applying Stabilization Models

What this chapter has demonstrated thus far is that the modeling analysis of commodity price stabilization schemes requires considerable effort on the part of the model builder and the model user. While many suggestions have been made as to what a modeling analysis should include to be more correct from the view of economic theory, not enough has been said as to the usefulness of commodity models in this regard. The various econometric modeling studies which have been performed certainly have contributed to our understanding of the efficacy of buffer stock operations for particular commodities. In this remaining section, we discuss some more recent attempts in this area and make suggestions as to what an appropriate modeling analysis should include.

As a starting point, one important issue is that the results obtained from the studies are fairly sensitive to the characteristics of the buffer stock mechanism itself. This would explain some of the wide differences obtained among researchers in analyzing welfare effects for the same commodity, e.g. copper. Evidence supporting this view can be found in studies by CRA (1977) and by Goreux (1978); both found that the costs of stock operation escalate rapidly as the degree of price stabilization increases. The CRA study also found that a tight price range might even increase price instability and that prices rise very sharply once stocks become low or are exhausted.

Almost all of the modeling studies have been of a partial equilibrium nature. However, there would appear to be real gains from moving towards a general equilibrium approach. To begin with, interactions between buffer stock operations and the major economies involved will provide a better description of producer and consumer impacts than will simplistic surplus analysis. This point is well made in the mentioned work of Adams (1978). Where studies deal with the UNCTAD 'core' or a greater number of commodities, there is a need to interrelate the corresponding commodity models or alternatively to construct multi-commodity models. As shown by Labys (1976), the correlation between commodity prices is not as one would expect and the analysis of any multiple stocking mechanism must take commodity interactions into account.

The correct functional specification of econometric relations to be included in the model as well as the overall choice of relations is also important. Sarris and Taylor (1978) have shown that welfare gains to producers and consumers might be miscalculated if this step is not seriously considered. For example, they point out that demand in cereal markets probably becomes more inelastic as prices rise. Overall commodity market response might also change if the model is operated in a world of stabilized prices. Here problems enter not only of the correct formulation of price expectations but also of variations in producer response. The actual types of demand, supply and price equations to be included change somewhat in markets which are noncompetitive in nature or which contain certain structural rigidities. For this reason, Sarris and Taylor have also attempted to isolate domestic commodity behavior from international commodity behavior.

There is also the question of specifying the nature of private as well as public stockholding in a commodity market, including interactions between the two. At present very little exploration has taken place as to how expectations underlying market behavior would be affected by buffer stock operations. A study performed for the US Commission of Supplies and Shortages (1976) attempts to show the impact of price stabilization on speculative stockholding, but only at an elementary level. Another exception is a study conducted by Mo (1976) within the US Bureau of Mines, which attempts to examine the impact of counter-stocking on stabilization.

Another important issue is that most of the models built to analyze the benefits of price stabilization assume risk neutrality. In this respect Newberry and Stiglitz (1981) reject the traditional buffer stock approach that prices should be kept within a specified bandwidth. Rather they show that with a complete set of futures and risk markets, an efficient stocking rule can, in the absence of economies of storage, be supported by competitive speculation. The approach taken is to develop a stocking rule based on the conditions of a competitive market economy. They then show what intervention policies need to be introduced when market efficiency is reduced by deviations from the competitive case. Their analysis is based on the case where agents have developed an optimal stockpiling policy which provides greater consumer and producer benefits than that possible by following bandwidth policy.

Extending the dynamic analysis of stabilization studies is also important. Not much research has taken place recently using techniques such as spectral analysis to determine the underlying generating processes of price and inventory variables. Such an analysis might improve the formulation of a dynamic buffer stock mechanism in which price variance and trends are interrelated. Also possible in this context is analyzing the role of futures' markets in price stabilization schemes. This relation could be clarified by conducting cross-spectral analyses of the type employed by Labys and Granger (1970).

Often associated with dynamic considerations are stochastic processes and their simulation using Monte Carlo Methods. A number of the received studies restrict their welfare analysis to a particular historical time span. But the historical record is usually so short or so dated that it tells us little of the future. It is obvious that the preferred approach would be to base the analysis on a more complete representation of plausible patterns of market stocks in future periods. As an example, this can draw attention to problems of successive years of stock accumulations or decumulations.

The use of Monte Carlo methods is also helpful for investigating partial stabilization schemes which do not aim to eliminate price variation completely. While one might desire a high level of price stability, a buffer stock might be exhausted before this was possible or storage capacity exceeded. Cuddy in his UNCTAD (1976) study used a frequency distribution of stocking requirements for each commodity to obtain a stated probability of success of maintaining prices within a range of so many percent around the stated floor and ceiling prices. The use of these methods can also help to examine the impact of the form of random disturbances in equations in determining the outcome of stabilization analysis. Blandford and Lee (1978) show that this can be done not only by including stocks reflecting uncertainty regarding climate but also by including the probability distributions associated with the empirical variability of certain variables.

In conclusion, it would appear that many fruitful commodity model applications could take place in analyzing commodity market stabilization. The more recent developments mentioned in this section should provide a starting point for further modeling efforts.

Notes

1. The chapter represents a revision of W. C. Labys, 'Commodity Price Stabilization Models: A Review and Appraisal', *Journal of Policy Modeling*, 2 (1980): 121–36. It has been reprinted here with permission of the Society of Policy Modeling and of Elsevier North Holland, New York.
2. The term 'WOM framework' is employed here to refer to the Waugh-Oi-Massell methodology.
3. The 'core' commodities include coffee, cocoa, tea, sugar, cotton, jute, sisal, rubber, tin and copper.

References

Adams, F. G. and Klein, S. A. (eds.) (1978) *Stabilizing World Commodity Markets*, Lexington: Heath Lexington Books
— (1978) 'Primary Commodity Markets in a World Model System' in F. G. Adams and S. A. Klein (eds.), *Stabilizing World Commodity Markets*, Lexington: Heath Lexington Books, pp. 83–104
Behrman, J. R. (1978) 'International Commodity Agreements An Evaluation of the UNCTAD Integrated Program for Commodities' in F. G. Adams and S. A. Klein (eds.), *Stabilizing World Commodity Markets*, Lexington: Heath Lexington Books, pp. 295–321
Bhaskar, K. N., Gilbert, C. L. and Perlman, R. A. (1978) 'Stabilization of the International Copper Market', *Resources Policy*, 4: 13–24
Bigman, D. and Reutlinger, S. (1977) 'Food Price and Supply Stabilization Policies: National Buffer Stock and Trade Policies', Working Paper, World Bank, Washington, DC

Blandford, D. and Lee, S. (1978) 'Quantitative Evaluation of Stabilization Policies in International Commodity Markets', Working Paper, Department of Agricultural Economics, Cornell University

Blond, D. L. (1978) 'Controlling US Domestic Prices of Internationally Traded Agricultural Products Under Conditions of Growing Worldwide Scarcity', Working Paper, UNCTAD, Geneva

Brook, E. M., Grilli, E. R. and Waelbroeck, J. (1977) *Commodity Price Stabilization and the Developing Countries: The Problem of Choice*, World Bank Staff Working Paper 262, Washington, DC: The World Bank

Brown, C. P. (1975) *Primary Commodity Control*, Kuala Lumpur: Oxford University Press

Chaipravat, O. (1975) 'Aggregate Structures of Production and Domestic Demand for Rice', Paper No. 4, Bank of Thailand

— (1978) 'International Rice Buffer Stock Operations: A Simulation Study' in F. G. Adams and S. A. Klein (eds.), *Stabilizing World Commodity Markets*, Lexington: Heath Lexington Books, pp. 63-82

Charles River Associates. (CRA) (1977) 'The Feasibility of Copper Price Stabilization Using a Buffer Stock and Supply Restrictions from 1953 to 1976', TD/B/IPC/COPPER/AC/L.42, UNCTAD, Geneva

Dalton, M. E. (1978) 'Dynamic Stockholding Policies for Stabilizing the Wool Market', *Quarterly Review of Agricultural Economics*, 29: 179-92

Desai, M. (1966) 'An Econometric Model of the World Tin Economy, 1948-1961', *Econometrica*, 34: 105-34

Duloy, J. H. (1965) 'On the Variance Effects of a Buffer Stock Scheme: A Simulation Study of a Floor Price Plan for Wool', *Australian Economic Papers*, 4: 79-92

Edwards, R. and Parikh, A. (1976) 'A Stochastic Policy Model of the World Coffee Economy', *American Journal of Agricultural Economics*, 58: 152-60

Gardner, B. L. (1978) 'Robust Stabilization Policies for International Commodity Agreements', Presented at the Annual Meetings of the American Economic Association, Chicago

Glismann, H. H. and Stecher, B. (1977) 'Commodity Arrangements and Stabilization Schemes: Prospects for Improving the International Distribution of Income', Working Paper, University of Kiel

Goreux, L. M. (1978) 'Optimal Rule of Buffer Stock Intervention', Mimeograph Research Department, International Monetary Fund, Washington, DC

Gruebel, H. G. (1964) 'Foreign Exchange and Price Stabilization Schemes', *American Economic Review*, 54: 387-95

Gustafson, R. I. (1958) *Carryover Levels for Grains*, Technical Bulletin No. 1178, US Department of Agriculture, Washington, DC

Heuth, D. and Schmitz, A. (1971) 'International Trade in Intermediate and Final Goods', *Quarterly Journal of Economics*, 86: 351-65

Jalwardena, L. (1974) J. M. Keynes report on 'The International Control of Raw Materials', *Journal of International Economics*, 4: 299-315

Just, R. E. and Hallam, J. A. (1978) 'Functional Flexibility in Analysis of Commodity Price Stabilization Policy', Working Paper, Giannini Foundation of Agricultural Economics, University of California at Berkeley

Kanbur, M. G. (1978) 'Price Stabilization of Rice: Buffer stock Model', Paper presented at the Second World Congress of the Econometric Society, Cambridge

Kim, H. K., Goreux, L. M. and Kendrick, D. (1975) 'Feedback Control Rule for Cocoa Market Stabilization' in W. C. Labys (ed.), *Quantitative Models of Commodity Markets*, Cambridge: Ballinger Publishing Co

Klein, L. R. (1978) 'Potentials of Econometrics for Commodity Stabilization Analysis' in F. G. Adams, and S. A. Klein (eds.), *Stabilizing World Commodity Markets*, Lexington: Heath Lexington Books, pp. 105-16

Kofi, T. A. (1972) 'International Commodity Agreements and Export Earnings: Simulation of the 1968 Draft International Cocoa Agreement', *Food Research Institute Studies*, 11

Konandreas, P. A. and Schmitz, A. (1976) 'Welfare Implications of Grain Price Stabilization: Some Empirical Evidence for the US', Working Paper, Food Policy Research Institute, Washington, DC

Labys, W. C. (1971) 'Feasibility of Operating a Supply Stabilization Scheme for the Lauric Oils Market: Returns, Costs and Financing', UNCTAD/CD/Misc. 41, United Nations, Geneva

—— (1973) *Dynamic Commodity Models: Specification Estimation and Simulation*, Lexington: Heath Lexington Books

—— (1979) 'Simulation Analysis of an International Buffer Stock for Jute', *Journal of Development Studies*

—— (1980) 'Commodity Price Stabilization Models: A Review and Appraisal', *Journal of Policy Modeling*, 2: 121-36

—— and Granger, C. W. J. (1970) *Speculation, Hedging and Commodity Price Forecasts*, Lexington: Heath Lexington Books

—— and Perrin, Y. (1976) 'Multivariate Analysis of Price Aspects of Commodity Stabilization Schemes', *Weltwirtschaftliches Archives*, 122: 556-64

Maizels, A. (1978) 'Commodity Market Stabilization and the Exports of Developing Countries', Working Paper, UNCTAD, Geneva

Mariano, R. S. (1978) 'Commodity Market Modeling: Methodological Issues and Control Theory Application' in F. G. Adams and J. R. Behrman (eds.), *Econometric Modeling of World Commodity Policy*, Lexington: Heath Lexington Books

Massell, B. F. (1969) 'Price Stabilization and Welfare', *Quarterly Journal of Economics*, 83: 285-97

Mo, W. Y. (1976) 'A Mathematical Model for the Determination of an Optimal Stockpile to Counteract Foreign, Induced Commodity Actions', The XIV Symposium on the Application of Computers in the Mineral Industry, Pennsylvania State

Newberry, D. M. and Stiglitz, J. E. (1977) 'The Economic Impact of Price Stabilization', Report submitted to the Agency for International Development, Washington, DC

—— —— (1981) *The Theory of Commodity Price Stabilization*, London: Oxford University Press

Nguyen, D. T. (1978) 'The Effects of Partial Price Stabilization on Export Earnings Instability and Level', Seminar on the North-South Negotiating Process in Commodities and Money, Oxford

Oi, W. W. (1961) 'The Desirability of Price Stabilization Under Pure Competition', *Econometrica*, 29: 58-64

Phillips, A. W. 'Analysis of the Operation of a Buffer Stock for Cocoa', Working Paper, UNCTAD, Geneva, 1967

Reutlinger, S. (1976) 'A Simulation Model for Evaluating Worldwide Buffer Stocks for Wheat', *American Journal of Agricultural Economics*, 58: 1-12

Roldan, R. 'The Coffee Sector in Brazil: Modeling the Interaction Between a Commodity Producing Sector and the Rest of the Economy', Paper presented at the Conference on Commodity Markets, Models and Policies in Latin America, Lima, 1978

Sarris, A. H. and Taylor, L. (1978) 'Buffer Stock Analysis for Agricultural Products: Theoretical Murk or Empirical Resolution' in F. G. Adams and S. Klein (eds.), *Stabilizing World Commodity Markets*, Lexington: Heath Lexington Books, pp. 149-60

Smith, G. W. (1975) 'An Economic Evaluation of International Buffer Stocks for Copper', Working Paper, US Treasury, Washington, DC
— and Schink, G. R. (1976) 'The International Tin Agreement: A Reassessment', *Economic Journal*
Spearman, J. and Labys, W. C. (1977) 'Simulation Analysis of a Buffer Stock for Copper with Implications for the US Economy', Working Paper, College of Mineral and Energy Resources, West Virginia University
Subotnik, A. and Houck, J. P. (1976) 'Welfare Implications of Stabilizing Consumption and Production', *American Journal of Agricultural Economics*, 58: 13–20
Turnovsky, S. J. (1976) 'The Distribution of Welfare Gains from Price Stabilization: The Case of Multiplicative Disturbances', *International Economic Review*, 17: 133–48
— (1978) 'The Distribution of Welfare Gains from Price Stabilization: A Survey of Some Theoretical Issues' in F. G. Adams and S. A. Klein (eds.), *Stabilizing World Commodity Markets*, Lexington: Heath Lexington Books, pp. 119–48
United Nations Conference on Trade and Development (UNCTAD). (1976) 'Consideration of Issues Relating to the Establishment and Operation of a Common Fund, Financial Requirements', TD/B/IPC/CF/L.2, Geneva
United States National Commission on Supplies and Shortages. (1976) *Studies on Economic Stockpiling*, Washington: Government Printing Office
Walker, R. L. and Sharples, J. A. (1977) 'Stabilizing the International Wheat Market with a US Buffer Stock' in *Contributed Papers Read at the 16th International Conference of Agricultural Economists*, Oxford: Oxford Institute of Agricultural Economics
Waugh, F. V. (1944) 'Does the Consumer Benefit from Price Instability?' *Quarterly Journal of Economics*, 58: 602–14
Zwart, A. and Meilke, K. (1976) 'Economic Implications of International Grain Reserves', Discussion Paper No. 1. School of Agricultural Economics, University of Guelph

6 FUTURE MODEL DEVELOPMENTS AND APPLICATIONS

In this final chapter, we examine new directions that commodity modeling can take. Some of these directions have already been mentioned in earlier chapters and will be integrated here to provide more careful prescriptions for the future. Most important is the realization that commodity modeling has made great strides in reducing the uncertainty that surrounds decision making in commodity forecasting and policy applications. Nonetheless, further research is needed to close the gap between the complexities of commodity markets and the simplistic nature of models used to describe them. This chapter thus focuses on: (1) future theoretical developments, (2) future improvements in application, (3) some remaining challenges, and (4) conclusions.

Future Theoretical Developments

Needed improvements in the theoretical aspects of commodity modeling are presented according to the steps of the modeling method: specification, estimation and simulation.

Specification

Supply. Recent major supply improvements have centered upon the producer formulation of price expectations and risk. Agricultural commodity models, particularly those dealing with perennial crops, have included supply relations featuring profit expectations for new acreage planted, acreage removed, and yields. More recently the conventional adaptive expectations and geometric lag models have been expanded to incorporate quadratic lag terms indicative of risk. Concepts of expected prices and yields which now include the subjective evaluation of mean values of gross returns as well as the variance of these returns are likely to receive increased modeling applications.

Mineral commodity models suffer mostly from their inability to model the combined long- and short-run adjustments needed to link reserves and supply. Mineral supply is concerned with a complex conversion process which embodies a number of sequential stages: geology and mineral occurrence, exploration and discovery, development of

mineral deposits, mineral extraction and depletion, and mineral benefici-
ation and processing. Dynamic considerations also involve feedback
relationships dealing with scrap and recyclable materials. The consumer
goods which utilize metals are durable so that metal may be reclaimed
as scrap. The supply side of a model should thus include secondary
supply in addition to primary supply. And this involves consideration
of fixed coefficients in the production process as well as of price mar-
gins which influence the decision to recycle scrap.

The most crucial need for model development rests on the linkage of
geological and economic characteristics of reserves which are normally
longer run phenomena with the shorter run supply relationships pres-
ently embodied in commodity models. In brief, mineral resources are
exhaustible and these relationships must take into account increasing
resource costs. Regarding possibilities for model improvement, introducing the geostatistical and probabilistic structure of resource base
models should be useful for specifying exploration investment relationships which would then be linked to supply response.

Demand. The improvements needed on the demand side of minerals'
models stem from the fact that mineral demands are based on the markets of final demand. The markets of the former are more immediately
derived from the markets for intermediate goods. Since the demand for
the mineral is derived from the use of material in the production of
other goods, one must understand intimately the engineering production processes of both producers and users. To explain demand, we
have two choices. Demand can be derived from an explicit production
function for the final commodity with one or more minerals as inputs or
from a consumer demand relationship such as that of Hicks – Lancaster
type. The first implies a conventional demand relationship, while the
second depends on some fixed coefficient input-output structure. Incorporating either into a model depends on the nature of the substitution process between a selected mineral and its competitors in a
particular end-use.

In addition to disaggregation of mineral demands by end-use, any
explanation of this demand should involve dynamic considerations.
Changes in the rate of substitution normally are a function of the relative rates of change in the prices of rival materials as well as a function
of engineering production functions. In improving the explanation of
technical change in models, we need to make more use of diffusion and
rate of adoption relationships, thus accounting for the dynamics of
technological change.

Also important to demand analysis is the measuring of elasticities of substitution or the modeling of substitution patterns *per se*. There appear to be three ways that the modeling of intercommodity substitution can be improved. The first of these would deal with aggregate production functions which would treat primary commodities as a single factor of production and would focus on the extent to which they can be replaced by other factors, such as labor, capital and energy. A second approach typically employed in econometric commodity models does attempt to measure intercommodity substitution by focussing on relative price adjustments such as through the use of the prices of competitive commodities. The third type of approach encompasses case studies of commodity substitution, in particular end uses based on a market share approach.

Prices. Specification of price relationships has received the least attention in market models, since values of price variables can easily be generated from the simulated structural form of the model. However, spectral analysis can decipher cycles found in commodity prices and thus improve the formulation of price relationships. This can sometimes be done through the use of time series or unobservable component equations such as ARIMA. With respect to price relationships embedded in market models, it is important to distinguish between stock as compared to flow specifications.

Price determination in most models is based on the assumption of competitive market adjustment. Yet some degree of noncompetitive behavior reflecting an imperfect market structure is present in many commodity markets. Buyers and sellers of a commodity can display various degrees of noncompetitive behavior such that, for example, a monopsonist faces an oligopolist or an oligopsonist faces a monopolist. There is a need then to structure models of certain commodities to reflect bargaining power among the exchange groups as much as conventional economic determinants.

There are other factors affecting prices which are also typically neglected. As a consequence of the difficulties of collecting inventory data, stock-flow adjustments and subsequent disequilibrium adjustments are severely neglected in modeling. Also omitted are speculation and hedging which affect spot and contract prices particularly in the short run, e.g. the role of LME prices in setting tin and copper contract prices. And the impact of inflation and exchange rates are often omitted from price determination in international models. Further research on these factors is likely to lead to modeling improvements.

Model Adjustments and Solution. A major problem in assembling the above components into a market structure is the mentioned prevalence of noncompetitive market structures. This means that some of the components have to be adjusted; the actual simulation mechanism also has to be changed. Another perhaps more serious problem is that the general equilibrium framework normally posed does not explain how prices and quantities are actually determined in commodity markets. In short the explicit disequilibrium characteristics of these markets have been neglected. Our models have been 'dynamized' in the sense of yielding the dynamic paths of the endogenous variables which correspond to some short run equilibrium position, but these positions are not necessarily in agreement with the associated steady state path. A market equilibrium solution is implied but trading takes place only at equilibrium prices.

To explore the stated disequilibrium characteristics, we must explain movements between the steady state or long run equilibrium positions. If the exogenous variables are constant and the market is stable, then the equilibrium will be static. Differences between long run positions can then be explained by persistent departures from equilibrium, as reflected in increments or decrements in stocks. After a change in some exogenous variable, recognition lags, implementation lags and uncertainty reduce the possibilities for immediate adjustments toward equilibrium. The corresponding model should thus feature partial expectations, adaptive expectations or some other form of adjustment mechanism to explain these delays. Some authors have suggested that disequilibrium of this type can best be modeled using continuous adjustment systems. Of the advantages offered, the continuous description of price movements is deemed preferable when trading takes place at prices outside of equilibrium. In addition, decision periods which would distinguish between short and long run equilibria also become less important; in fact, the generated prices trace the path to long run equilibrium.

A further implication of disequilibrium relates to model estimation. With the absence of equilibrium conditions, the *ex ante* consumption and production quantities cannot generally be equated to the observed flow quantities traded in the market. Other information has to be introduced to help determine the nature of the consumption and production equations as well as any included price equation. Recently, appropriate estimating methods have been developed to deal with these problems and these methods could be employed in future modeling efforts.

Estimation

There now exist a number of estimation procedures based on maximum likelihood and fixed point algorithms which permit us to handle previously difficult problems such as dealing with simultaneous equation systems with autocorrelated disturbances or equation systems structured in differential equations. These are further embodied in computer software which enables the estimated model to be solved and verified using stochastic or non-stochastic simulation.

Though these developments satisfy a number of requirements of commodity model builders, other estimation needs relate to the problem of incorporating prior information obtained from sources outside the basic sample employed for system estimation. For example, initial beliefs represented by prior probabilities can be combined with information in data by means of Bayes theorem to yield posterior probabilities relating to parameters by hypotheses of interest. There are also other ways of introducing prior information. Mixed estimation methods known from some time can be helpful. Here we refer to the need to incorporate into a model the exact value of a parameter, to establish an exact relationship between two or more parameters, to introduce an unbiased estimate of a parameter, or to utilize information regarding the range of values of some parameters.

A related problem is that of estimating price and income elasticities of demand and price elasticities of supply. Some recent work suggests that incorporation of prior information obtained from sources outside the sample period can improve elasticity measurement notably. For example, means and variances as well as probability distributions of price elasticities for various commodities can be obtained from existing studies. Fairly complete information of this type has been available for the more important commodities, while for others it can be obtained by aggregating commodities into groups with similar behavior such as beverages or non-ferrous metals. Taking a Bayesian viewpoint, one can combine these prior probabilities with sample information to obtain posterior probabilities relating to parameters of interest. For example, it is now possible to use a Bayesian limited-information estimating procedure which incorporates prior information to measure elasticities imbedded in a commodity market model.

Simulation and Control

Policy simulation analysis has been applied extensively as a means of assessing the welfare impact of commodity policies. Here the target or dependent variables entering the welfare function of the policy maker are determined by conducting successive simulations based on a set of exogenous variables or instruments, which reflect alternative policies that he can control. One possibility for improving simulation analysis of commodity models is to conduct the simulation as a problem in experimental design. The object is to learn more about the model being investigated by examining the surface generated by the endogenous variables in response to changes in levels of the instruments or factors. Some mention of these including design analysis for validation purposes was mentioned in Chapter 3.

These experiments can be organized in several ways. The most well known of these is data analysis, consisting of regression analysis and analysis of variance. The latter can be in the form of F-tests, multiple ranking, spectral analysis, or multiple comparisons. Exploratory experiments where the relationships between the instruments or factors can be found include full and fractional factorial analysis, rotatable designs, and response surface designs. The design experiments which have proven most popular thus far have been randomizations. Including stochastic disturbances in commodity simulation experiments can help to evaluate policies where climate influences production or else to validate a model where its cyclical or stability properties are of interest.

Although optimal control theory is closely tied to simulation analysis, we consider it separately because of its considerable potential for improving the application of commodity models. The varied mathematical approaches available suggest a number of opportunities for conducting commodity control experiments. Modelers can utilize the 'certainty equivalence principle', which can be incorporated with concepts of dynamic programming to solve problems classified under linear-quadratic-stochastic feedback control. Or they might consider the maximum principle of Pontryagin. This makes optimal control solutions possible for problems of planning optimal growth, where nonlinear dynamics and nonquadratic criteria are involved. Other approaches as developed by control engineers include the Kalman filter and other state and parameter estimation schemes. Finally, there is the adaptive control approach whereby initial uncertainties about the parameters or functions within a system are reduced or eliminated as it moves forward in time. If we assume that a prior probability distribution function having a finite variance can be specified for the uncertain coefficients and variables, then the control problem becomes one whereby the 'decision maker' learns about the parameters of the probability distribution function for the uncertain elements of the control situation as the process evolves.

Finally, control theory is highly suitable for analyzing problems related to commodity stabilization schemes and policies, as outlined in Chapter 5. One can analyze agricultural stabilization problems which arise from agricultural commodities with lagged supply response and opportunities for storage. The optimality problem then becomes one of choosing controls for the buffer stock, export tax and other variables so as to maximize the given objective function.

Future Improvements in Application

An area of recent model development concerns methods of adjusting models so that they can cope with problems of structural change and instability in commodity markets. There is no doubt that many of the events that are responsible for economic upheavals and commodity instability simply cannot be predicted. But from this we cannot conclude that nothing can be done in face of such difficulties to improve the applicability of commodity models.

Updating Model Parameters

A problem often responsible for poor forecasting performance in international commodity models is that structural adjustments in the underlying markets result in changes in the values of model parameters (as distinct from changes in model specification). These changes can arise from adjustments in the response of economic decision units such as shifts in technology or in tastes and preferences. Similarly, they can stem from the approximations used in forming macro-relationships. Here changes in the relative importance of groups constituting the weights of such a relation can upset a given weighting pattern and hence the assigned parameter values.

One approach taken to counteract these difficulties has been to assume that the estimation process will improve as more information is added. Models can then be solved using time-varying parameter methods such as those which might combine Bayesian estimation strategies with adaptive control theory. Other approaches to the time-varying parameter problem include systematic (non-random) variation methods and random-coefficient methods.

Including Monetary Factors

Another problem of international models has been their frequent omission of monetary factors, namely inflation and exchange rates. The accepted procedure for incorporating the influence of inflation in a commodity model has been to deflate commodity prices by an index reflecting movements in the general price level. Such an index as represented by the gross national product deflator or the wholesale price index should be well constructed and predictable. However, one can argue that the price index should be included directly into a given commodity price relationship. This implies that commodity prices do not vary in a one to one fashion with the general price level but only in proportion. Yet a full determination of the influence of the general price level would require examining inflationary and recessionary factors that shift demand as well as supply. On the demand side, inflation can force portfolio managers to switch from monetary to physical or more tangible assets such as commodities, and changes in income distribution can lead to a shift in patterns of commodity consumption. Nonetheless, these phenomena cannot be easily modeled, nor can the impact of inflation and recession on supply be easily specified.

A greater possibility exists for including the impact of exchange rate changes, since the latter can be introduced directly in demand, supply, or trade equations (leaving aside commodity feedback effects on the economy). These equations typically feature national price series and hence national currencies. Equilibrium model solutions can be obtained by converting the price series to a common currency prior to estimation. If one prefers estimating the equations in national currencies, it is then necessary to convert the equations to a common currency by multiplying the price parameter by the assumed exchange rate.

Integrating Speculative Phenomena

Speculative and futures market activity which normally increase during periods of economic uncertainty also constitute an important commodity influence. The possibility for modeling interactions between futures markets and physical markets stems from two prevalent notions: that futures markets accommodate the intertemporal allocation of commodities, and that they also provide a forward pricing function. Both of these are consistent with the supply of storage theory whereby inventory coverage provides a link between futures prices and spot prices. With respect to empirical studies confirming this relation, it has been shown that the forward pricing function is more evident for markets with inventories of an annually continuous rather than of a discontinuous nature, e.g., wheat versus potatoes.

One typical way for a model to include futures market activity is by introducing the futures price of contracts for future delivery into the price equation. The futures price would preferably be endogenous, being determined by adjustments in the corresponding futures market. Such adjustments center upon speculative and hedging activity, for example, as can be measured by net long speculative commitments and net short hedging commitments for contracts for future delivery. Such considerations are likely to be of increased interest in commodity modeling.

Introducing Climatic Effects

The inclusion of climatic effects into commodity models is an often stated panacea for coping with poor forecasting performance. But when national and international stocks of agricultural commodities are extremely low, no buffers exist which can help to mitigate the wide price fluctuations caused by changes in climate. Econometric developments which can serve as a basis for introducing climatic effects into commodity models are few. While recent studies of patterns of fresh water supply and demand deal with long run analysis, the performance of short run models depends more on the use of weighted precipitation and temperature indices. In this regard, a major difficulty in relating weather and commodity activity is that discrepancies exist between weather data tabulated for places and economic data aggregated by regions. However, some progress has taken place in incorporating climatic variations in modeling techniques such as linear programming and input-output. Long-term weather forecasts might also be employed to update model predictions. While such improvements might help a model perform better during abnormal weather periods, one might also want to experiment with incorporating effects of episodic events such as typhoons, tornados, or droughts based on probabilistic functions which represent the likelihood of their occurrence.

Market Structures

The nature of the market structure underlying commodity models can be competitive or noncompetitive. One attempt to study the impact of market structure as well as bargaining power and price formation on model performance has employed a structural framework as a basis for analyzing noncompetitive distortions. Distortions of this type can possibly be handled in future modeling efforts by endogenizing the following influences: (1) national government policies which directly or indirectly influence world prices, (2) international intermediaries such as multinational firms which exercise market power, (3) recognition that major actors in international markets may have different objective functions, and (4) provision for feedback between pricing outcomes and market structural change. Given the present state-of-the-art, this might be accomplished by modifying existing modeling theories or by developing alternatives ones.

The possibilities of modeling noncompetitive market structures have appeared from time to time and several of these developments have been reviewed in Chapter 2. It should be possible in future modeling efforts to deal with markets featuring monopoly, duopoloy, or oligopoly. More elaborate kinds of cartel behavior are likely to require some form of differential game theory, based on Nash-Cournot or von Stackelberg underpinnings.

Endogenizing Political Influences

Another obvious aspect of international commodity modeling is the extent to which commodity behavior is dependent upon political decisions. Commodity markets involving some degree of government intervention normally are modeled by including some policy variables or policy instruments through which policy is implemented. Such variables normally are specified as exogenous. Although government intervention can relate to decisions taken concerning monetary factors, decisions analyzed in international models typically relate to trade and production policies. These can include fixed import duty, ad valorem import duty, variable import levy, fixed export subsidy, fixed import quota, percentage import quota, bilateral quantity agreement, and domestic price support or acreage allotment.

A more recent approach would consider government intervention which has continued for a sufficiently long time that it exhibits certain regularities. This behavior can be described analytically and integrated into a commodity model, the government or policy variables now becoming endogenous. Among the theories available for explaining this behavior, the political regularities can be regarded as manifestations of optimizing behavior on the part of policymakers. Applications of this approach have recently appeared and offer promise for future modeling efforts.

Linking Models

What the previous two sections reveal is the need to relate commodity models to the broader economic environment. During the recent period, errors in macroforecasting as well as micro or commodity forecasting have occurred because of a failure to link these two areas. Possible model couplings which could perform this function have already been mentioned in Chapter 2. Future interest, however, centers around the interactions between national economies and commodity markets. Through the linking of national models and commodity models, commodity behavior can be analyzed in a wider context and its role in trade and development better assessed.

One further possibility is to integrate the determinants of demand and supply embodied in a conventional macroeconomic model with the determinants of industry or commodity demand and supply reflected in input-output analysis. This approach is suitable for modeling energy as well as agricultural commodity behavior. For example, one can combine a linear expenditure system with sectoral input-output analysis as well as commodity models to explain supply.

Finally, econometric/biological/technological models are just beginning to receive attention for those commodities whose behavior is highly interrelated with biological or geological systems. These models would integrate a micro-econometric market structure with a set of mathematical equations or programming models describing biological or geological relationships. Improvements in modeling most likely to take place relate to the supply side. A marine production system could be introduced, where maximum substainable yields are described using a logistic decreasing returns function which combines factors of logistic growth of the biomass of, say, fish with a relationship describing decreasing returns from effort.

Several other examples also could be of interest to readers. An industrial production system could be incorporated where the relationship between commodity inputs and product outputs is described using a linear program, cost minimization being assumed. An energy production system could be modeled such as that involving oil or gas wells where geological, engineering, and production factors must be interrelated. Also to be included in a system of this type might be relationships linking costs of pollution and of environmental quality as well as of energy conservation. Agricultural production systems would also lend themselves to this approach. Animal production system could include relationships describing breeding, nutrition, feed, and disease control. As for crop production, probabilistic functions can be introduced which represent the likelihood of variations in climatic conditions.

Some Remaining Challenges

Applications of commodity models resemble those of econometric models in general: explaining market behavior or reconstructing history;

searching for optimal policy decisions related, for example, to growth, stabilization and market organization; and forecasting and planning. Up to now, commodity studies have been concerned with policy problems relating to markets, trade, industry, price forecasting, location and distribution, commodity agreements and stabilization, and regulatory proceedings. These are likely to expand in a number of ways.

A first consideration involves the structuring of models to deal with multicommodity phenomena, principally because of the need to decipher the complex nature of complementarities and substitutabilities among commodities. A multicommodity model is also a convenient approach for obtaining aggregate and individual forecasts for a group of highly interrelated commodities. Examples of this can be found in the present study.

One would also like to determine the influence of financial and speculative factors on commodity markets. Most recently, there have been several modest attempts to examine the commodity impacts of inflation and devaluations. Speculation and hedging effects, having also received only limited empirical study, will be researched at greater lengths in the future.

One possible area of application to be developed relates to the role that commodities could play in improving the international economic order. In particular, recent crises have underscored the necessity of considering commodity modeling from a global viewpoint. Models should examine not only world balances, deficits and surpluses of strategic commodities, but also the possibilities of accumulating buffer or security stockpiles. Here, studying the distribution of commodities between the northern and southern hemispheres or between the developed and the developing countries would be highly useful. There is also the need to show the extent to which commodity stabilization programs might affect income distribution in the related developing countries.

Concerning challenges in modeling theory, there is a need to better explain stock and price behavior in market and other forms of models. Some relevant questions are: What is the role of stocks in market disequilibrium? Are decisions made on a stock or flow basis? And what is that particular nature of the decision structure in commodity stockholding that is to be embodied in theory? Other than the supply of storage theory or one or two applications of the theory of optimal portfolio adjustment, we have no theory which deals with stock and price formation specifically in commodity markets.

Developments in model linkage have been mentioned, but there are many problems remaining in model linkage and integration. Not much work has taken place regarding the construction of multi-commodity models. Such models should be built for commodity markets where partial analysis embodied in a single commodity model is a weak assumption, i.e. the need to link copper with aluminum, feedgrains with livestock and meat, and soybeans with other oilseeds and fats. Integration of commodity models into national models is also of interest. For example, one can combine final product demand, the corresponding industry input-output network, and commodity market models which reflect the supply of inputs. There is also the need to develop the foreign trade sectors of such models, particularly to evaluate the commodity impact of factors such as inflation and fluctuating exchange rates.

The accurate forecasting of commodity prices and quantities remains a problem. The economic structure underlying commodity markets can change more rapidly than that of national economies. Particularly in the last decade, inflation, devaluations, and several petroleum crises have caused the underlying structures to change in a way that has adversely influenced the forecasting capabilities of corresponding models. Our attention to the forecasting performance of commodity models also has lagged behind that of macro models. Principally, we need to know more about the functioning of commodity models on a continuous basis. This, in turn, could lead to a better identification of factors influencing forecast performance and, hence, to the discovery of more fruitful forecasting approaches.

Conclusions

There are obviously other aspects of commodity modeling to be dealt with and a host of additional research problems to be solved. When one combines the separate areas of agricultural models, energy models and mineral models, the conclusion must be that commodity modeling is a much larger field than what is normally envisioned. The aim of this study has been to introduce the reader to this wide and growing area of research and its potential usefulness. We hope that this has been accomplished.

7 COMMODITY MODELS BIBLIOGRAPHY

This bibliography represents an attempt to compile a listing of commodity models currently or previously constructed. It includes a wide range of commodities and a wide range of methodologies. Some eighty commodities are featured; they are among the most important traded on national and international markets. There are also special commodity categories, such as for electricity, multicommodity, metal scrap, and refuse and wastes models. Among the methodologies employed are econometric market models, econometric process models, interindustry models, spatial equilibrium models, recursive programming models, integer programming models, system dynamics models, and general systems models. A special characteristic in selecting models is that most models include both demand and supply aspects of price determination. Econometric studies of demand or supply *per se* are too numerous to list. However, because new models are being constructed, the list obviously contains omissions and the authors apologize for those models excluded.

Aluminum

Adams, F. G. 'Applied Econometric Modeling of Non-Ferrous Metals Markets: The Case of Ocean Floor Nodules' in W. Vogely (ed.), *Mineral Materials Modeling*, RFF Working Paper EN-5, Washington, DC, 1975

Brown, M., Dammert, A., Meeraus, A., and Stoutjesdijk, A. 'Worldwide Investment Analysis: Case of Aluminum', Working Paper, World Bank, Washington, DC, 1981

Burrows, J. 'Analysis and Model Simulations of the Non-Ferrous Metal Markets: Aluminum', Special Report, Cambridge: Charles River Associates, 1972

Dorr, A. 'International Trade in the Primary Aluminum Industry', PhD thesis, Pennsylvania State University, 1975

Earl, Paul H. 'A Forecasting Methodology for Aluminum Prices', Preprint 79-107, Society of Mining Engineers of the AIME, 1979

Hibbard, W. R. Jr., Soyster, A. L., and Kelly, M. A. 'An Engineering/Econometric Model of the US Aluminum Industry', Working Paper, Virginia Polytechnic Institute and State University, Blacksburg, 1979

Hojman, D. E. 'An Econometric Model of the International Bauxite-Aluminum Economy', *Resources Policy*, 7 (1981): 87-102

Rasche, R. H. 'Forecasts and Simulations with an Econometric Model of the

Aluminum Market', Special Report, Wharton Economic Forecasting Associates, Philadelphia, 1970

Schlager, K. J. 'A Systems Analysis of the Copper and Aluminum Industries: An Industrial Dynamics Study', MS thesis, Massachusetts Institute of Technology, 1961

Slade, M. 'An Econometric Model of the Domestic Copper and Aluminum Industries: The Effects of Higher Energy and Declining Ore Quality on Metal Substitution and Recycling', PhD thesis, George Washington University, 1979

Smithson, C. W., Anders, G., Gramm, W. P. and Maurice, S. C. 'Aluminum Model' in C. W. Smithson *et al.*, *World Mineral Markets: An Econometric and Simulation Analysis*, Ontario: Canadian Ministry of Natural Resources, 1979

Apples

Fuchs, H. W. 'An Interregional Intertemporal Activity Analysis Model of the US Apple Industry', PhD thesis, University of Connecticut, 1973

Marzouk, M. S. 'An Econometric Analysis of the Supply and Marketing of Apples in Nova Scotia', *Canadian Journal of Agricultural Economics*, 20 (1972)

Piggott, R. R. 'A Farm Level Econometric Model of the US Apple Industry: Applications to Forecasting and Analyzing Policy Issues', PhD thesis, Cornell University, 1973

Apricots

Eryilmaz, A. 'An Econometric Analysis of the California Apricot Industry', PhD thesis, California, Davis, 1979

Asparagus

Grossman, E. C. 'National and State Level Econometric Models of the US Asparagus Industry, 1948–1969', PhD thesis, Rutgers University, 1973

Matthews, J. L. 'Price Determination and Supply Adjustments in the United States and California Asparagus Economies', PhD thesis, University of California, Berkeley, 1966

Bananas

Aggrey-Mensah, W. 'A Study of the Sydney Banana Market and of Potential Benefits to Producers of Supply Control', PhD thesis, University of New England, Australia, 1970

Guise, J. W. B. and Aggrey-Mensah, W. 'An Evaluation of Policy Alternatives Facing Australian Banana Producers' in G. Judge and T. Takayama (eds.), *Studies in Economic Planning Over Space and Time*, Amsterdam: North-Holland Publishing Co., 1973

Beef

Australian Bureau of Agricultural Economics. 'An Econometric Model of the US Beef Market', Beef Research Report No. 20, Canberra: Australian Government Publishing Service, 1977

Freebairn, J. W. and Rausser, G. 'Effects of Changes in the Level of US Beef Imports', *American Journal of Agricultural Economics*, 57 (1975): 676-88

Goodwin, J. W. and Crow, J. R. *The Interregional Structure of the American Beef Industry in 1975 and 1980*, Bulletin No. B-708, Oklahoma Agricultural Experiment Station, Stillwater, 1973

Haack, R., Martin, L. J. and Macauley, T. G. 'A Forecasting Model for the Canadian and US Beef Sectors' in *Commodity Forecasting Models for Canadian Agriculture*, vol. II, Agriculture Canada, Ottawa, 1978, pp. 29-61.

Hunt, R. D. 'The Contrasted Effects of Quota, Autarky, and Free Trade Policies on US Beef Production and Prices', PhD thesis, University of Minnesota, 1972

Kohout, J. C. 'A Price and Allocation Model for the Beef Economy in Argentina', PhD thesis, University of Illinois, 1968

Kulshreshtha, S. N. and Wilson, A. G. 'An Open Econometric Model of the Canadian Beef Cattle Sector', *American Journal of Agricultural Economics*, 54 (February, 1972): 84-91

Langemeier, L. and Thompson, R. G. 'Demand, Supply, Price Relationships for the Beef Sector, Post W.W.II Period', *Journal of Farm Economics*, 49 (1967): 169-83

Lattimore, R. G. 'Econometric Study of the Brazilian Beef Sector', PhD thesis, Purdue University, 1974

Lattimore, R. G. and Schuh, G. E. 'Un Modelo de Politica Para La Industria Brasilena de Ganado Vacuno', (A Policy Model of the Brazilian Beef Cattle Economy,) *Cuadernos de Economia*, 39 (1976): 51-75

Mack, F. G. 'The Impact of Transfer Cost and Trade Policies on International Trade in Beef, 1967-1980', PhD thesis, Texas A & M University, 1973

Manetsch, T. J., Hayenga, M. L. and Halter, A. R. 'A Simulation Model of the Nigerian Beef Industry', Mimeographed, Michigan State University, East Lansing, 1968

McGarry, J. J. 'The World Beef Industry', PhD thesis, University of Wisconsin, 1968

McGuann, J. M. 'Microeconomic Analysis of Opportunities for Increasing Beef Production: The Pampean Area, Argentina', PhD thesis, Texas A & M University, 1973

Morris, J. L. 'An Economic Analysis of Cyclical Variations in the US Beef Industry', PhD thesis, Cornell University, 1979

Otrera, W. R. 'An Econometric Model for Analyzing Argentine Beef Export Potentials', PhD thesis, Texas A & M University, 1966

Posada, A. 'A Simulation Analysis of Policies for Northern Colombian Beef Cattle Industry', PhD thesis, Michigan State University, 1974

Ryan, T. J. 'Commodity Price Determination and Transmission: An Analysis of the Farm-Retail Pricing of US Beef', PhD thesis, University of Minnesota, 1979

Simpson, J. R. 'International Trade in Beef and Economic Development of Selected Latin American Countries', PhD thesis, Texas A & M University, 1974

Sohn, H. K. 'A Spatial Equilibrium Model of the Beef Industry in the US' PhD thesis, University of Hawaii, 1970

Throsby, C. D. 'Quarterly Econometric Model of the Australian Beef Industry', *Economic Record* (June, 1974)

Unger, Samuel G. 'Simultaneous Equations Systems Estimation: An Application to the Cattle-Beef Sector', PhD thesis, Michigan State University, 1966

Viaene, J. 'An Econometric Study and Projection of the Beef Cattle Market in Belgium Using a Recursive Model', Fakulteit van de Landbouweetenschappen, Rijksuniversiteit, Ghent, Belgium, 1974

See also Cattle, Livestock, Meat.

Brussel Sprouts

French, B. C. and Matsumoto, M. *An Analysis of Price and Supply Relationships in the US Brussel Sprouts Industry*, Giannini Foundation, Research Report No. 308, California Agricultural Experiment Station, Berkeley, 1970

Broilers

Brown, L. C. 'An Economic Analysis of the Bolivian Poultry Industry', PhD thesis, University of Maryland, 1974

Burga, G. S. 'Considerations on Development and the Poultry Industry in Peru', PhD thesis, Michigan State, 1971

Fisher, M. 'A Sector Model – The Poultry Industry of the US', *Econometrica*, 26 (1958): 37–66

Holliday, D. C. 'An Analysis of the Economic Relationships in the Canadian Broiler Industry' in *Commodity Forecasting Models for Canadian Agriculture*, vol. II, Agriculture Canada, Ottawa, 1978, pp. 61–86

Lee, T. C. and Seaver, S. V. *A Positive Spatial Equilibrium Model of Broiler Markets: A Simultaneous Equation Approach*, Storrs Agricultural Experiment Station Bulletin No. 417, University of Connecticut, Storrs, 1972

Meadows, D. L. *Dynamics of Commodity Production Cycles*, Cambridge: Wright-Allen Press, 1970

Shapouri, H. 'The Supply and Demand for the US Livestock and Broiler Sectors', PhD thesis, Washington State University, 1979

Cattle

Blakely, P. K. 'A Quarterly Feeder Cattle Price Forecasting Model with Application Towards the Development of a Futures Market Strategy', PhD thesis, Virginia Polytechnic Institute and State University, 1977

Carvello, L. 'An Econometric Model of the US Cattle Industry', PhD thesis, University of Chicago, 1973

Davis, J. T. 'An Economic Analysis of Quarterly Demand and Supply Relationships for Feeder Cattle in the United States', PhD thesis, University of Tennesee, 1974

Hayanga, M. L. and Hacklander, D. 'Monthly Supply-Demand Relationships for Feed Cattle and Hogs', *American Journal of Agricultural Economics*, 52 (1970): 535–44

Jarvis, L. S. 'Cattle as Capital Goods and Ranchers as Portfolio Managers: An Application to the Argentine Cattle Sector', *Journal of Political Economy*, 82 (1974): 489–520

May, R. D. 'A Systems Model of the Cattle Economy: A Guyana Application', PhD thesis, Purdue University, 1975

Miller, S. F. and Halter, A. N. 'Systems Simulation in a Practical Policy-Making Setting: the Venezuelan Cattle Industry', *American Journal of Agricultural Economics*, 55 (1973): 420–32

Mueller, C. 'Factors Affecting the Development of Cattle Industry in Central Brazil', PhD thesis, Purdue University, 1972

Nores, Gustavo A. 'Structure of the Argentine Beef Cattle Industry – A Short Run Model, 1960–1970', PhD thesis, Purdue University, 1972

Posada, A. 'A Simulation Analysis of Policies for the Northern Columbia Beef Cattle Industry', PhD thesis, Michigan State University, 1974

Smith, J. N. 'A Dynamic Model of the Cattle Industry of Argentina', PhD thesis, University of Maryland, 1968

Spreen, T. A. 'An Application of Capital Theory in a Recursive Linear Programming Model of the Cattle Subsector of Guyana', PhD thesis, Purdue University, 1977

Yver, R E. 'The Investment Behavior and the Supply Response of the Cattle Industry in Argentina', PhD thesis, University of Chicago, 1971

Zulberti, Carlos Alberto. 'Supply Response in the Cattle Industry: The Argentine Case', PhD thesis, Massachusetts Institute of Technology, 1969

— 'The Feasibility of Beef Cattle Feed Lots in Argentina: Methodology of Economic Evaluation', PhD thesis, Cornell University, 1974

See also **Beef, Feedgrains, Hogs, Meat**

Cement

Assis, C. 'A Mixed Integer Programming Model for the Brazilian Cement Industry', PhD thesis, Johns Hopkins University, 1977

Chromite

Charles River Associates, Inc. 'Economic Analysis of the Chromium Industry', Prepared for Property Management and Disposal Service, Washington: General Services Administration, 1970

Wharton Econometric Forecasting Associates. Existing In-House Model, Wharton School of Finance and Commerce, 1975

Coal

Ando, F. 'A Satellite Model for Coal', Existing In-House Model, Wharton Econometric Forecasting Associates, Philadelphia, 1976

Dunbar, F. C. and Mehring, J. L. 'Regional Coal Price Forecasting Model', Cambridge: Charles River Associates, 1977

Henderson, J. M. *The Efficiency of the Coal Industry: An Application of Linear Programming*, Cambridge: Harvard University Press, 1958

Labys, W. C. Paik, S., and Liebenthal, A. M. 'An Econometric Simulation Model of the US Market for Steam Coal', *Energy Economics*, 1 (1979): 19–26

— and Yang, C. W. 'A Quadratic Programming Model of the Appalachian Coal Market', *Energy Economics*, 2 (1980): 86–95

— and Shahrockh, F. 'A Dynamic Forecasting Model of the US Coal Market', Working Paper, COMER, West Virginia University, 1980

Libbin, J. D. and Boehji, M. D. 'Interregional Structure of the US Coal Industry', *American Journal of Agricultural Economics*, (1977): 456–66

Schlottmann. 'Environmental Regulation and the Allocation of Coal: A Regional Analysis', PhD thesis, Washington University, 1975

Tabb, W. K. 'A Recursive Programming Model of Resource Allocation and Technological Change in the US Bituminous Coal Industry', PhD thesis, University of Wisconsin, 1968

US Federal Energy Administration. *Project Independence Report*, Washington, DC: USGPO, 1974

— 'The National Coal Model: Description and Documentation', (ICF. Inc.), Washington, DC: NTIS, 1976

Cobalt

Adams, F. 'The Impact of Cobalt Production from the Ocean Floor: A Review of Present Empirical Knowledge and Preliminary Appraisal', A study prepared for the United Nations Conference on Trade and Development, Wharton School of Finance, Philadelphia, 1972

Burrows, J. C. *Cobalt: An Industry Analysis*, Lexington, MA: D. C. Heath and Co, 1971

Dybalski, G. 'An Economic Model of the Cobalt Market', *The XIV Symposium of the Council for the Application of Computers and Mathematics in the Minerals Industry*, University Park, PA, 1976

Gupta, Poonam, 'An Economic Model of the World Cobalt Industry', *Kiel Working Paper*, No. 129, Institute fur weltwiertsdraft an der Universetat Kiel, 1981

Cocoa

Adams, F. G. and Behrman, J. R. *Econometric Models of World Agricultural Commodity Markets*, (One of eight models) Cambridge: Ballinger Publishing Co, 1976

Chang, K. 'A Simulation Policy Analysis of the Western Nigeria Cocoa Industry', PhD thesis, Michigan State University, 1973

Goreux, L. M. 'Price Stabilization Policies in World Markets for Primary Commodities: An Application to Cocoa', Mimeographed, International Bank for Reconstruction and Development, Washington, DC, 1972

Kim, H. K., Goreux, L. and Kendrick, D. 'Feedback Control Rule for Cocoa

Market Stabilization' in W. C. Labys (ed.), *Quantitative Models of Commodity Markets*, Cambridge: Ballinger Publishing Co., 1975

Kofi, Tetteh A. 'International Commodity Agreements and Export Earnings: Simulation of the 1968 Draft International Cocoa Agreement', *Food Research Institute Studies*, 11 (1972)

Mathis, K. *An Economic Simulation Model of the Cocoa Industry of the Dominican Republic*, International Program Information Report 69-2, Department of Agricultural Economics and Sociology, Texas A & M University, 1969

Melo, F. H. 'An Analysis of the World Cocoa Economy in 1980', PhD thesis, North Carolina State University, Raleigh, 1973

Ogawa, K. 'An Econometric Evaluation of Price Stabilization in the World Cocoa Market', Working Paper, Economic Research Unit, University of Pennsylvania, Philadelphia, 1981

Weymar, F. Helmut. *The Dynamics of the World Cocoa Market*, Cambridge, MA: The MIT Press, 1968

Coffee

Adams, F. G. and Behrman, J. R. *Econometric Models of World Agricultural Commodity Markets*, (One of eight models) Cambridge: Ballinger Publishing Co, 1976

Bacha, E. L. 'An Econometric Model for the World Coffee Market: The Impact of Brazilian Price Policy', PhD thesis, Yale University, 1968

Brandt, S. A. 'Spatial Analysis of the World Coffee Market: The Brazilian Position', PhD thesis, Ohio State University, 1967

Ford, D. J. 'Coffee Supply, Trade, and Demand: An Econometric Analysis of the World Market, 1930-1969', PhD thesis, University of Pennsylvania, 1977

— 'Commodity Market Modeling and Simulation of Market Intervention: The Case of Coffee', Conference on Stabilizing World Commodity Markets; Analysis, Practice and Policy, Airlie Virginia, March, 1977

Epps, M. L. 'A Simulation of the World Coffee Economy' in W. C. Labys (ed.), *Quantitative Models of Commodity Markets*, Cambridge: Ballinger Publishing Co, 1975

Muller, S. and Labys, W. C. 'Policy Analysis of the ICA Quota Scheme Based on a Model of the World Coffee Market', Internal Report, US Department of State, Washington, DC, 1982

Parikh, A. 'A Model of World Coffee Economy: 1950-1968', *Applied Economics*, 6 (1974): 23-43

de Vries, J. *Structure and Prospects of the World Coffee Economy*, Bank Staff Working Paper No. 208, World Bank, Washington, DC, 1975

Wickens, M. Greenfield, J. and Marshall, G. *A World Coffee Model*, CCP: 71/W.P.R, Food and Agricultural Organization of the United Nations, Rome, 1971

Columbium

Charles River Associates, Inc. 'Economic Analysis of the Columbium Industry', Prepared for Property Management and Disposal Service, Washington: General Services Administration, 1967

Coconuts

Labys, W. C. 'An Econometric Model of the International Coconut Oil Market: Considerations for Policy Analysis', UNCTAD/CD/Misc. 43/Rev. 1, UN Conference on Trade and Development, Geneva, 1971

Librero, Aida R. 'The International Demand for Philippine Coconut Products: An Aggregate Analysis', *The Philippine Economic Journal*, 10 (1971): 1–22

Copper

Adams, F. G. 'The Impact of Copper Production from the Ocean Floor: Application of an Econometric Model', Prepared by the Economics Research Unit, University of Pennsylvania for the United Nations Conference on Trade and Development, Philadelphia, December, 1973

— 'Econometric Model of the World Copper Market', Paper presented at the National Academy of Sciences Workshops on Non-fuel Mineral-Demand Modeling, held at Airlie House, Warrenton, Virginia, June 1–2, 1981

Ballmer, R. W. 'Copper Market Fluctuations: An Industrial Dynamics Study', Unpublished MS thesis, Massachusetts Institute of Technology, 1960

Bonczar, E. 'An Economic Analysis of the Secondary Copper Industry in the US' PhD thesis, Pennsylvania State University, 1977

Burrows, J. 'Analysis and Model Simulations of the Non-Ferrous Metal Markets: Copper', Special Report, Cambridge: Charles River Associates, 1973

Coyle, R. G. 'A Dynamic Model of the Copper Industry – Some Preliminary Results', Ninth International Conference on Computers in the Mineral Industry, 1975

Dammert, A. 'Planning Investments in the Copper Sector in Latin America' in W. Labys, M. Nadiri and J. Nunez del Arco (eds.), *Commodity Markets and Latin American Development: A Modeling Approach*, New York: National Bureau of Economic Research, 1980

Ertek, Tumay. 'World Demand for Copper, 1948–63: An Econometric Study', PhD thesis, University of Wisconsin, 1967

Fisher, F. M., Cootner, P. H. and Baily, M. 'An Econometric Model of the World Copper Industry', *Bell Journal of Economics and Management Science*, 3 (1972): 568–609

Ghosh, S., Gilbert, C. L. and Hughes, A. J. 'A Quarterly Model of the World Copper Industries', Mimeographed, Institute of Economics and Statistics, Oxford University, 1981

— Gilbert, C. L. and Hughes, A. J. 'Optimal Control and Choice of Functional Form: An Application to a Model of the World Copper Industry', *Discussion*

Paper Series 8109/E, Erasmus University, Institute for Economic Research, Rotterdam, 1981

Hartman, R. S., Boxdogan, K. and Nadkarni, R. N. 'The Economic Impact of Environmental Regulations on the US Copper Industry', *The Bell Journal of Economics*, 10 (1979)

Khanna, I. 'Forecasting the Price of Copper', *Business Economist*, 4 (Spring, 1972)

Kovisars, L. 'World Trade Flows in Copper, an LP-Model', Unpublished report, Stanford Research Institute, 1975

— 'Copper Trade Flow Model', *World Minerals Availability*, SRI Project MED 3742-74, 1975

Labys, W. C. 'Annual Model of Disequilibrium Adjustments in the Copper Market', *Materials and Society*, 4 (1980): 153–64

— and Kaboudan, M. A. 'Quarterly Model of Disequilibrium Adjustments in the Copper Market', NSF Working Paper, West Virginia University, 1980

Lasaga, M. *The Copper Industry in the Chilian Economy: An Econometric Analysis*, Lexington, Mass.: Heath Lexington, 1981

Lonoff, Marc. 'A Model of Long-Run Copper Supply Integrating Geology, Engineering and Economics', *Proceedings of the Council of Economics of the AIME*, New York, 1980

Mahalingsivam, Rasiah. 'Market for Canadian Refined Copper: An Econometric Study', PhD thesis, University of Toronto, 1969

Ogawa, K. 'A New Approach to Econometric Modeling: A World Copper Model', NSF Report, Department of Economics, University of Pennsylvania, 1982

Richard, D. 'A Dynamic Model of the World Copper Industry', Working Paper, International Monetary Fund, Washington, DC, 1977

Smith, G. W. 'An Economic Evaluation of International Buffer Stocks for Copper', Working Paper, US Treasury, Washington, DC, 1975

Smithson, C. W., Anders, G., Gramm, W. P. and Maurice, S. C. 'Copper Model' in C. W. Smithson *et al.*, *World Mineral Markets: An Econometric and Simulation Analysis*, Ontario: Canadian Ministry of Natural Resources, 1979

Soyster, A. L. and Hibbard, W. R. Jr. 'An Equilibrium Model for Copper Demand and Supply', *Proceedings of the Council of Economics of the AIME*, New York, 1980

Staloff, S. 'A Stock-Flow Analysis for Copper Markets', PhD thesis, University of Oregon, 1977

Strongman, J. E., Killingsworth, W. R. and Cummings, W. E. 'The Dynamics of the International Copper System', *The XIV Symposium of the Council for the Applications of Computers and Mathematics in the Mineral Industry*, University Park, PA, 1976

Synergy Inc. 'Joint Aluminum/Copper Forecasting and Simulation Model', US Department of Commerce, National Technical Information Center, 1977

Underwood. 'Optimizing Rules for Producer Groups in a Stochastic Market Setting with Applications to the Copper and Tea Markets', PhD thesis, University of Minnesota, 1976

Whitney, J. 'Analysis of Copper Production, Processing and Trade Patterns, 1950–1972', PhD thesis, Pennsylvania State University, 1976

Corn

Hein, D. 'An Econometric Model of the US Corn Economy', Unpublished paper, US Department of Agriculture, Washington, DC, 1980

Penna, J. A. 'Optimal Storage and Export Levels of a Tradeable Product and Their Relationship with Annual Price Variability: The Case of Corn in Brazil', PhD thesis, Purdue University, 1974

Subotnik, A. and Houck, J. P. 'A Quarterly Econometric Model for Corn: A Simultaneous Approach to Cash and Futures Markets', Technical Bulletin No. 318, Agricultural Experiment Station, University of Minnesota, 1979

Thompson, R. L. and Schuh, G. E. 'Trade Policy and Exports: The Case of Maize in Brazil', Working Paper, Department of Agricultural Economics, Purdue University, 1978

Cotton

Adams, F. G. and Behrman, J. R. *Econometric Models of World Agricultural Commodity Markets*, (One of eight models) Cambridge: Ballinger Publishing Co, 1976

Chen, J. 'World Cotton Market, 1953–1965: An Econometric Model with Applications to Economic Policy', Institute fur Mathematische Wirtschaft, University of Bielefeld, Rheda, Germany, May, 1975

Dugay, G. and Hansen, B. 'Demand for American Cotton: An Econometric Disequilibrium Analysis with an Application to Egyptian Cotton', Department of Economics, University of California at Berkeley, 1977

French, M. 'Effects of Commodity Price Stabilization: An Econometric Model of the World Cotton Market', Unpublished PhD dissertation, University of Pennsylvania, 1980

Hakim, O. A. 'The Effects of the US Cotton Policy on the World Market for Extra-Long Staple Cotton', PhD thesis, University of Arizona, 1972

Kolbe, H. and Timm, H. *Die Bestimmungsfaktoren der Preisentwidklung auf dem Welmarkt fur Baumwoole: Eine Okonometrische Modellanalyse*, NR 4, HWWA Institute fur Wirtschaftsforschung, Hamburg, July, 1971

Dairy

Goldman, O. 'A Quarterly Econometric Model of the US Dairy Subsector', PhD thesis, Pennsylvania State University, 1975

Harrington, D. H. and Sah, R. 'A Note on an Econometric Simulation Model for the Canadian Dairy Industry', *Canadian Journal of Agricultural Economics*, proceedings, 1974

Kottke, M. 'Allocation of Milk through Space and Time in a Competitively Mixed Dairy Industry' in G. Judge and T. Takayama (eds.), *Studies on Economic Planning Over Time and Space*, Amsterdam: North Holland Publishing Co, 1973

Louwes, S. L., Boot, J. C. G. and Wage, S. 'A Quadratic Programming Approach to the Problems of the Optimal Use of Milk in the Netherlands', *Journal of Farm Economics*, 45 (1963): 309–17

McDonald, P. O. 'Consumer Demand for Dairy Products in the United States, 1955-1969 – Quarterly Model', PhD thesis, Pennsylvania State University, 1973

Milligan, R. 'An Econometric Model of the California Dairy Industry', PhD thesis, University of California, Davis, 1975

Riley, J. B. *A Reactive Programming Model for the Fluid Milk Industry*, Oklahoma Agricultural Experiment Station Report No. P-697, Oklahoma State University, Stillwater, 1974

— and Blakley, D. 'Impact of Alternative Class I Pricing Systems of Fluid Milk Prices', *American Journal of Agricultural Economics*, 57 (1975): 67-73

Rojko, A. A. *The Demand and Price Structure for Dairy Products*, Technical Bulletin No.1168, United States Department of Agriculture, Washington, DC, 1957

Ruane, J. J. and Hallberg, M. C. *Spatial Equilibrium Analysis for Fluid and Manufacturing Milk in the United States, 1967*, Bulletin No. 783, Pennsylvania Agricultural Experiment Station, University Park, 1972

Salathe, L. 'An Econometric Simulation Model of Wisconsin's Dairy Industry', PhD thesis, University of Wisconsin – Madison, 1974

Stonehouse, D. P., Harrington, D. H. and Sahi, R. K. 'An Econometric Forecasting and Policy Analysis Model of the Canadian Dairy Industry' in *Commodity Forecasting Models*, vol. 1, Agriculture Canada, Ottawa, 1978, pp. 77-102

White, C. V. 'Supply Response and Interregional Competition in the Midwest Dairy Industry: An Econometric Analysis', PhD thesis, Ohio State University, 1973

Wilson, R. R. and Thompson, R. G. 'Demand, Supply, and Price Relationships for the Dairy Sector – Post W.W.II Period', *Journal of Farm Economics*, 49 (May, 1967): 360-71

Eggs

Gerra, M. J. *The Demand and Price Structure for Eggs*, Technical Bulletin 1204, US Department of Agriculture, Washington, DC, 1959

Hartman, D. G. 'The Egg Cycle and the Ability of Recursive Models to Explain It', *American Journal of Agricultural Economics*, 56 (1974): 254-62

Huff, H. B. and Peckett, M. 'A Quarterly Forecast Model of the Canadian Egg Industry' in *Commodity Forecasting Models for Canadian Agriculture*, vol. 1, Agriculture Canada, Ottawa, 1978, pp. 43-60

Judge, G. G. *A Spatial Equilibrium Model for Eggs*, Competitive Position of the Connecticut Poultry Industry, No. 7, Connecticut Agricultural Experiment Station Bulletin No. 318, Storrs, 1956

Kulshrestha, S. N. and Ng, C. F. 'An Econometric Analysis of the Canadian Egg Market', *Canadian Journal of Agriculture Economics*, 25 (1977): 1-13

Roy, S. K. and Johnson, P. N. 'Econometric Models for Quarterly Shell Egg Prices', *American Journal of Agricultural Economics*, 55 (1973): 209-13

Sidhu, D. S. *Demand and Supply of Eggs: An Econometric Analysis*, New Delhi: Chand & Co, 1974

Electricity

Ford, F. A. 'A Dynamic Model of the United States Electric Utility Industry, 1950-2010', PhD thesis, Dartmouth College, 1975

Jenkin, F. P. 'Electricity Supply Models' in *Energy Modeling*, London: IPC Science and Technology Press, 1974

Pachauri, R. K. *The Dynamics of Electrical Energy Supply and Demand*, New York, Praeger Special Studies, 1975

Rolph, E., and Lees, L. 'California's Projected Electrical Energy Demand and Supply', Report presented to the California Assembly, General Research Committee, Environmental Quality Labs, California Institute of Technology, July, 1972

Steigelmann, W. 'Impact of the Energy Crisis on the Future Price of Electricity' in Limaye, D. R. (ed.), *Energy Policy Evaluation*, Lexington: Heath, 1974

Energy[1]

Baughman, M. L. 'A Model for Energy-Environment Systems Analysis', *Energy Modeling*, London: IPC Science and Technology Press, 1974

Charpentier, J. P. 'A Review of Energy Models', IIASA Reports RR-74-10 and RR-75-35, Institute for Advanced Systems Analysis, Luxenburg, 1975

Chilton, C. H. *A National Energy Model*, Battelle Memorial Institute, Columbus, Ohio, 1974

Deam, R. J. *et al.* 'World Energy Model: Descriptions and Results' in *Energy Modeling*, London: IPC Science and Technology Press, 1974

Debanne, J. B. 'A Pollution and Technology Sensitive Model for Energy Supply-Distribution Studies, in *Energy Modeling*, M. F. Searl (ed.), Working Paper EN-1, Resources for the Future, Inc. Washington, DC, 1973, pp. 374–409

Energy Conference Series. *Energy Modeling*, IPC Science and Technology Press, London, 1974

Federal Energy Administration. *An Energy Independence Model of the US Energy Market*, Washington: Federal Energy Administration, 1973 and 1977

Foell, W. K., Mitchell, J. W. and Pappas, J. L. 'The Wisconsin Regional Energy Model: A Dynamic Approach to Regional Energy Analysis', Mimeographed, University of Wisconsin, Madison, 1975

Folk, H. and Hannon, B. 'An Energy, Pollution, and Employment Policy Model' in Macrakis, M. S. (ed.), *Energy*, Cambridge: MIT Press, 1974

Hoffman, K. C. 'A Unified Framework for Energy System Planning' in *Energy Modeling*, London: IPC Science and Technology Press, 1974

Hudson, E. A. and Jorgenson, D. 'US Energy Policy and Economic Growth, 1975-2000'. *Bell Journal of Economics and Management Science*, 5 (1974): 461–514

Hughes, G., Mersarovic, M. and Pestel, E. 'Energy Models: Resources, Demand and Supply', Multilevel Regionalized World Modeling Project, Case Western Reserve University, Cleveland, March, 1974

Hutber, F. W. 'Modeling of Energy Supply and Demand' in *Energy Modeling*, London: IPC Science and Technology Press, 1974

IIASA. *Proceedings of the IIASA Working Seminar on Energy Modeling*, International Institute for Applied Systems Analysis, Luxenburg, 1974

Iliffe, C. E. 'The Systems Approach in Economic Assessment of Nuclear Power' in *Energy Modeling*, London: IPC Science and Technology Press, 1974

Jorgenson, D. W. *Econometric Studies of US Energy Policy*, Amsterdam: North-Holland, 1976

Khazzoom, J. D. 'An Econometric Model of the Demand for Energy in Canada', Paper presented at NSF Conference, 'Energy: Demand, Conservation and Institutional Problems', Massachusetts Institute of Technology, 1973

Kuh, E. and Wood, D. O. *Independent Assessment of Energy Policy Models*, Report No. EA-1071, Electric Power Research Institute, Palo Alto, 1979

Limaye, D. P. 'TERA – The Total Energy Resource Analysis Model', *Gas Magazine*, (November, 1972)

— *Energy Policy Evaluation*, Lexington, Heath Lexington Books, 1974

— and Sharko, J. R. 'Simulation of Energy Market Dynamics' in Limaye, D. R. (ed.), *Energy Policy Evaluation*, Lexington: Heath, 1974

Macrakis, M. S. *Energy*, Cambridge: MIT Press, 1974

Manne, A., Richels, R. G. and Weyant, J. P. 'Energy Policy Modeling: A Survey', *Operations Research*, (1979): 1–36

Morrison, W. E. and Readling, C. L. 'An Energy Model for the US', Bureau of Mines, US Department of the Interior, Information Circular No. 9394, 1968

Pagoulatos, A. 'Major Determinants Affecting the Demand and Supply of Energy Resources in the United States', PhD thesis, Iowa State University, 1975

Roberts, F. S. *Energy: Mathematics and Models*, Proceedings of the SIAMS 1975 Conference, SIAMS, Philadelphia, 1976

Schweizer, P. F., Love, C. G. and Shiles, H. J. 'A Regional Energy Model for Examining New Policy and Technology Changes' in Macrakis, M. S. (ed.), *Energy*, Cambridge: MIT Press, 1974

United Kingdom. *Energy Forecasting Methodology*, Working Paper No. 29, UK Department of Energy, London, 1978

United Nations. 'A Comparative Study of Some National Energy Models', Energy Working Paper No. 2, UN Economic Commission for Europe, Geneva, 1975

— 'Reports on Current Research During the Year 1978 on the Use of Mathematical Methods in Energy Analysis', No. EC.Ad./8/Add. 1, UN Economic and Social Council, Geneva, 1979

— *Proceedings from the Seminar on Energy Conservation Modeling*, UN Economic Commission for Europe, Geneva, 1980

Verleger, Jr., P. K. 'The Relationship Between Energy Demand and Economic Activity' in Macrakis, M. S. (ed.) *Energy*, Cambridge: MIT Press, 1974

US Bureau of Mines. 'An Energy Model for the United States', featuring energy balances for the years 1947 and 1965 and projections and forecasts to the years 1980 and 2000, Report No. IC 8384, US Department of the Interior, Washington, DC, 1968

Whitehed, M. W. and Smith, C. N. 'The World Energy Crisis: Exploring International Politics, Business and Petroleum Flows Through Simulation Gaming' in Limaye, D. R. (ed.), *Energy Policy Evaluation*, Lexington: Heath, 1974

'World Energy Modeling: Part 1, Concepts and Methods' and 'World Energy Modeling: Part 2. Preliminary Results from the Petroleum Natural Gas Model' in *Energy Modeling*, London: IPC Science and Technology Press, 1974

Fats, Oils and Meals

Adams, F. G. 'An Interrelated Econometric Modeling System for Fats and Oils Commodities', A study prepared for the United Nations Conference on Trade and Development, Wharton School of Finance and Commerce, 1975

Al-Zand, Osama, A. 'Olive Oil Trade and Trade Policies in the Mediterranean Region', PhD thesis, University of Minnesota, St. Paul, 1968

Armore, S. J. *The Demand and Price Structure for Food Fats and Oils*, Technical Bulletin No. 1068, Economic Research Service, US Department of Agriculture, Washington, DC, 1953

Drake, A. E. and West, V. I. *Econometric Analysis of the Edible Fats and Oils Economy*, University of Illinois Agricultural Experiment Station Bulletin No. 695, Urbana, 1963

Huang, Chung-Liang. 'An Econometric Study on the Market Structures of the World Demand for High Protein Meals, with Special Emphasis upon the United States Soybean Economy', PhD thesis, Virginia Polytechnic Institute and State University, 1976

Labys, W. C. 'Multicommodity Substitution Patterns in the International Fats and Oils Market', *European Review of Agricultural Economics*, 4 (1975): 75–84

— 'Dynamics of the Lauric Oils Market' in W. C. Labys (ed.), *Quantitative Models of Commodity Markets*, Cambridge: Ballinger Publishing Co, 1975. See also the description of this model in *Dynamic Commodity Models: Specification, Estimation and Simulation*, Lexington, MA: D. C. Heath and Co, 1973

Matthews, J. L. and Womack, A. W. 'An Economic Appraisal of the US Tung Oil Economy', *Southern Journal of Agricultural Economics*, (1970): 161–8

Moe, E. *World Demand and Supply Prospects for Oilseeds and Oilseed Products in 1980*, Foreign Agricultural Economic Report No. 71, US Department of Agriculture, ERS, 1971

Perone-Pacifico, C. and Pieraccini, L. 'A Working Model of the Market for Vegetable Oils', *Rivista di Economia Agraria*, 29 (1974): 523–71

Pollak, P. K. 'Economic Analysis of Oilseed Markets in Thailand', PhD thesis, University of Minnesota, 1974

— 'Prospects and Structure of the World Fats and Oils Economy', Working Paper, World Bank, Washington, DC, 1979

Price, D. W. *Demand and Supply of US Mint Oil*, Bulletin No. 782, Washington Agricultural Experiment Station, Pullman, 1973

Segura, Edilberto Leoncis. 'Econometric Study of the Fish Meal Industry', PhD thesis, Columbia University, 1972

Thiam, T. B. 'The Palm Oil Industry of Malaysia', PhD thesis, North Carolina State University, Raleigh, 1973

US Department of Agriculture. *World Supply and Demand Prospects of Oilseeds and Oilseed Products in 1980 with Emphasis on Trade by the Less Developed Countries*, Washington, DC, Foreign Agriculture Economic Report, No. 71, Economic Research Service, 1971

Fertilizer

Bell, D. M., Henderson, D. R. and Perkins, G. R. *A Simulation Model of the Fertilizer Industry in the United States: With Special Emphasis on Fertilizer Distribution in Michigan*, Agricultural Economics Report No. 189, Department of Agricultural Economics at Michigan State University and Marketing Economics Division, Economic Research Service, US Department of Agriculture, Washington, DC, 1972

Merraus, A., Stoutjeskijk, A. and Weigel, D. 'An Investment Planning Model for the World Fertilizer Industry', Working Paper, World Bank, Washington, DC, 1975

Radhi, A. 'An Econometric Model of the World Nitrogen Fertilizer Market', PhD thesis, Purdue University, 1979

Robertson, T. 'Structure, Performance, and Conduct of the Peruvian Fertilizer Industry and a Linear Programming Analysis for Future Plant Sizes and Location', PhD thesis, Iowa State University, 1968

Fish (Marine Resources)

Bell, F. W. *et al.* 'A World Model of Living Marine Resources' in W. C. Labys (ed.), *Quantitative Models of Commodity Markets*, Cambridge: Ballinger Publishing Co, 1975

Farrell, J. E. and Lampe, H. O. *The New England Fishery Industry: Functional Markets for Tinned Food Fish, I and II*, Agricultural Experiment Station Bulletins Nos. 379 and 380, University of Rhode Island, Kingston, 1965

Lapido, O. O. 'General Systems Analysis and Simulation Approach: A Preliminary Application to Nigerian Fisheries', PhD thesis, Michigan State University, 1973

McGraw, Richard L. 'An Application of Supply Response to Fisheries Economics', Working Paper No. 7901, Department of Economics, the University of New Brunswick, 1979

Segura, E. L. *An Econometric Study of the Fish Meal Industry*, FAO Fisheries Technical Paper No. 119, FIEF/T119(en), Food and Agriculture Organization of the United Nations, Rome, August, 1973

Sun, T. Y. 'Statistical Analysis of the Demand and Price Structure for Selected Shellfish in the US', PhD thesis, University of Maryland, 1974

Wang, Der-Hsiung. 'An Economic Study of the Canadian Salmon Market', PhD thesis, Oregon State University, 1976

Gas (Natural)

Federal Power Commission. 'Natural Gas Supply and Demand: 1971 to 1990', Staff Report No. 2, Bureau of Natural Gas, Federal Power Commission, Washington, DC, 1972

Khazzoom, D. J. 'The FPC Staff's Econometric Model of Natural Gas Supply in the United States', *Bell Journal of Economics and Management Science*, 2 (Spring, 1971): 51–93

Lawrence, A. 'Pricing and Planning in the US Natural Gas Industry: An Econometric and Programming Study', PhD thesis, SUNY-Buffalo, 1973

MacAvoy, P. W. *The Economics of the Natural Gas Shortage 1960-1980*, Amsterdam: North Holland, 1975
— and Pindyck, R. S. 'Alternative Regulatory Policies for Dealing with the Natural Gas Shortage', *Bell Journal of Economics and Management Science*, 3 (1972): 454-98
McLoughlin, G. T. *Mathematical Modeling of Trading Policies for Natural Gas*, National Energy Board, Ottawa, Canada, 1971

Gold

Ichior, Otarii and Lipshutz, L. 'A Model of the World Gold Market', Working Paper, International Monetary Fund, Washington, DC, 1976

Grains

Ahalt, J. and Egbert, A. C. 'The Demand for Feed Concentrates: A Statistical Analysis', *Agricultural Economic Research*, 17 (April, 1965)
Arzac, E. R. 'The Stochastic Dynamics of the US Grain Market', Research Paper No. 10, Graduate School of Business, Columbia University, 1976
— 'Optimal Policies for Controlling the US Grain Market', Research Paper No. 131, Graduate School of Business, Columbia University, 1976
Barreyro, H. 'An Analysis of the Supply of Grains in the Pergamino Region of Argentina: A Dynamic Approach', PhD thesis, Texas A & M University, 1971
Bjarnason, H. F. 'An Economic Analysis of 1980 International Trade in Feed Grains', PhD thesis, University of Wisconsin, 1967
Chen, Carl Chi-Jian 'Quadratic Programming Models of United States Agriculture in 1980 With Alternative Levels of Grain Exports', PhD thesis, Iowa State University, 1975
Chung, C. H. 'Interregional and International Economic Analysis of the World Feed Grain Economy in 1980 with Emphasis on the USNC Region', PhD thesis, University of Wisconsin, 1972
Cochrane, Willard W. and Danin, Yigal. 'Reserve Stock Grain Models and the World, 1975-1985' in *Analysis of Grain Reserves: A Proceeding*, compiled by David J. Eaton and W. Scott Steele, Economic Research Service Report No. 634, Washington, DC: US Department of Agriculture, 1979
Conley, D. M. 'An Analysis of the Domestic and Foreign Distribution of US Heavy Grains Under Alternative Assumptions Regarding Possible Future Supply, Demand, and Transport Costs', PhD thesis, Iowa State University, 1973
Eaton, David J. 'A Systems Analysis of Grain Reserves', Technical Bulletin No. 1611, Washington, DC: US Department of Agriculture, 1979
Foote, R. J., Klein, J. W. and Clough, M. *The Demand and Price Structure for Corn and Total Feed Concentrates*, Technical Bulletin 1061, Washington, DC: US Department of Agriculture, 1952
Grennes, T., Johnson, P. and Thursby, M. *The Economics of the World Grain Trade*, New York: Praeger, 1978
Jolly, R. W. 'An Econometric Analysis of the Grain-Livestock Economy in Canada

with a Special Emphasis on Commercial Agricultural Policy', PhD thesis, University of Minnesota, 1976

King, G. A. *The Demand and Price Structure for By-Product Foods*, Technical Bulletin No. 1183, US Department of Agriculture, Washington, DC, 1958

Kite, R. D. 'An Interregional Analysis of Livestock Use of Selected Food Ingredients', PhD thesis, Purdue University, 1973

Koo, W. 'Linear Programming Models Applied to Interregional Competition of Grain Transportation and Production', PhD thesis, Iowa State University, 1974

Labys, W. C., Luterbacher, U. and Imhoff, M. 'A Model of US Grain Embargo Policy with Implications for the Soviet Union', Working Paper, Center for Empirical Studies, Graduate Institute of International Studies, Geneva, 1980

Leath, M. N. and Blakley, L. V. *An Interregional Analysis of the US Grain Marketing Industry, 1966-67*, Technical Bulletin No. 1444, Economic Research Service, United States Department of Agriculture, Washington, DC, 1971

Meinken, K. W. *The Demand and Price Structure of Oats, Barley and Soybean Grain*, Technical Bulletin No. 1080, United States Department of Agriculture, Washington, DC, 1953

Meilke, K. D. 'The Demand for Animal Feed: An Econometric Analysis', PhD thesis, University of Minnesota, 1973

— and deGorter, H. 'Quarterly Econometric Model of the North American Feed Grain Industry', School of Agricultural Economics and Extension Education, University of Guelph, 1977

— and deGorter, H. 'A Quarterly Econometric Model of the Feed Grain Industry', *Commodity Forecasting Models for Canadian Agriculture*, vol. I. Z. Hassan and H. B. Huff (eds.), No. 78/2, Economics Branch, Agriculture Canada, 1979

Meyers, W. H. 'Long-Run Income Growth and World Grain Demand: An Econometric Analysis', PhD thesis, University of Minnesota, 1977

Pandey, V. K. 'Intertemporal Pricing and Output Allocation of Major Foodgrains in India', PhD thesis, University of Illinois, 1971

Roy, S. K. and Ireland, M. E. 'An Econometric Analysis of the Sorghum Market', *American Journal of Agricultural Economics*, 57 (1975): 513-16.

Shonkwiler, J. S. 'A Semi-Annual Econometric Model of the US Feed Grain-Livestock Economy', PhD thesis, University of Missouri, 1979

Sorenson, F. L. and Hathaway, D. E. *The Grain-Livestock Economy and Trade Patterns of the European Economic Community with Projections to 1970 and 1975*, Research Report No. 5, Institute of International Agriculture, Michigan State University, East Lansing, 1968

US Department of Agriculture. *World Demand Prospects for Grain in 1980*, Foreign Agricultural Economic Report No. 75, Economic Research Service, Washington, DC, 1971

Grapefruit

Parker, Jr., A. F. 'An Econometric Analysis of the Florida Grapefruit Industry', PhD thesis, University of Florida, 1974

Hides

Cohen, K. *A Computer Model of the Shoe, Leather and Hide Sequence*, Englewood Cliffs: Prentice-Hall, 1960

Singh, B. 'An Econometric Study of Raw Materials in International Trade – A Case Study of Hides and Skins', PhD thesis, University of Pennsylvania, 1971

Hogs (Pork)

Bain, R. A. 'An Econometric Model of the Beef and Pork Sectors: Development and Application to Policy Analysis', PhD thesis, Cornell University, 1976

Chin, S. and Spearin, M. 'An Analysis of Quarterly Provincial and Regional Hog Supply Functions' in *Commodity Forecasting Models*, vol. 1, Agriculture Canada, Ottawa, 1978, pp. 5-13

Devisch, N. 'Application of the Systems Approach: An Information and Decision Model for the Hog Enterprise', PhD thesis, University of Missouri, 1976

Foote, R. J., Craven, A. and Williams, Jr. 'Pork Bellies: Quarterly 3-Equation Models Designed to Predict Cash Prices', Mimeograph, Texas Technical University, 1971

Harlow, A. A. *Factors Affecting the Price and Supply of Hogs*, Technical Bulletin No. 1068, Economic Research Service, US Department of Agriculture, Washington, DC, 1962

Hein, D. 'An Econometric Model of the US Pork Economy', *Review of Economics and Statistics*, 48 (1975): 370-375

Jaffrelot, J. J. 'A Model For Forecasting Provincial Hog Marketing' in *Commodity Forecasting Models for Canadian Agriculture*, vol I, Z. Hassan and H. B. Huff (eds.), No. 7812 Economics Branch, Agriculture Canada, 1978, pp. 61-77

Leuthold, R. M. 'An Analysis of Daily Fluctuations in the Hog Economy', *American Journal of Agricultural Economics*, 5 (November, 1969): 849-65

Martin, L. and Zwart, A. C. 'A Spatial and Temporal Model of the North American Pork Sector for the Evaluation of Policy Alternatives', *American Journal of Agricultural Economics*, 56 (1975): 55-66

Meadows, D. L. *Dynamics of Commodity Production Cycles*, Cambridge: Wright-Allen Press, 1970

Miller, S. E. 'Live Hog Futures Prices as Expected Prices in the Empirical Modeling of the Pork Sector', PhD thesis, Virginia Polytechnic Institute and State University, 1977

Naill, R. F. and Mass, D. 'Dynamic Modeling as a Tool for Managerial Planning: A Case Study of the US Hog Industry', Mimeograph, Thayer School of Engineering, Dartmouth College, Hanover, 1973

Ong, K. 'Quantitative Analysis of Applying Random Coefficient Regression Model to the Short Run Fluctuations for Hogs', PhD thesis, University of Illinois, 1973

Sadler, G. 'Short-Run Econometric Models for Live Hog Prices', PhD thesis, Texas Technical University, 1975

Viaene, J. 'An Econometric Model of the Market for Pigs in Belgium', Mimeograph, Fakulteit van de Landbouw Etenschappen, Rijksuniversiteit, Ghent, Belgium, 1974

Zellner, Jr., R. E. 'A Simultaneous Equation Analysis of Selected Terminal Hog
Markets', PhD thesis, University of Mississippi, 1971

Iron Ore

Elliott, John F. and Clark, Joel P. 'Mathematical Modeling of Raw Materials and
Energy Needs of the Iron and Steel Industry in the USA', Bureau of Mines
Open File Report 32-78, Washington, DC, 1977
Margueron, C. 'A Quantitative Analysis of the Supply-Demand Patterns in Iron
Ore: The Future Possibilities of Brazil', PhD thesis, Columbia University,
1972
Santos, A. 'International Trade in Iron Ore: An Econometric Analysis of the
Determinants of Trade Patterns', PhD thesis, Pennsylvania State University,
1976

Jute

Division of Agricultural Economics and Iowa State University Team. 'Kenaf
Demand in Thailand', Ministry of Agriculture and Cooperatives, Bangkok,
1975
Khan, A. S. 'An Economic Analysis of 1980 International Trade in Jute with
Special Reference to Pakistan', PhD thesis, University of Wisconsin, 1972
Labys, W. C. 'Simulation Analysis of an International Buffer Stock for Jute',
Journal of Development Studies, (1979)
Mujeri, M. K. 'The World Market for Jute: An Econometric Analysis', PhD
thesis, McMaster University, 1978

Lead

Charles River Associates, Inc. 'Economic Analysis of the Lead and Zinc Indus-
try', Prepared for Property Management and Disposal Service. Washington:
General Services Administration, 1970
Wharton Econometric Forecasting Associates. Existing In-House Model, Wharton
School of Finance and Commerce, 1975
Wise, K. T. 'The Effects of OSHA Regulations on the US Lead Industry: An
Economic Impact and Economic Modeling Analysis', PhD thesis, Massachusetts
Institute of Technology, 1979

Livestock

Arzac, E. R. and Wilkinson, M. 'Stabilization Policies for US Feed Grain and Livestock Markets', *Journal of Economic Dynamics and Control*, 1 (1979): 39-58
—— and Wilkinson, M. 'A Quarterly Econometric Model of US Livestock and Feed-
grain Markets and Some Policy Implications, *American Journal of Agricultural
Economics*, 61 (1979): 297-308

Crom, R. J. and Maki, W. R. 'A Dynamic Model of a Simulated Livestock-Meat Economy', *Agricultural Economic Research*, 17 (1965). Also see R. J. Crom, 'Development of a Systems Approach for Livestock Research in ERS', *American Journal of Agricultural Economics*, 57 (1975): 509–12

Egbert, A. C. and Reutlinger, S. 'A Dynamic Model of the Livestock-Feed Sector', *Journal of Farm Economics*, 47 (1965): 1288–305

Ferris, J. 'Linear Programming Analysis of the Feed Grain Livestock Economy of Great Britain in 1968, 1973, and 1977', Research Report No. 11, Institute of International Agriculture, Michigan State University, 1971

Filippello, N. A. 'A Dynamic Econometric Investigation of the Japanese Livestock Economy', PhD thesis, University of Missouri, Colombia, 1967

Foote, R. J. 'A Four-Equation Model of the Feed Livestock Economy and Its Endogenous Mechanism', *Journal of Farm Economics*, 35 (1953): 44–61

Fox, K. A. 'A Spatial Equilibrium Model of the Livestock-Feed Economy in the United States', *Econometrica*, 21 (1953): 547–66

Hildreth, C. and Jarrett, F. J. *A Statistical Study of Livestock Production and Marketing*, New York: John Wiley and Sons, 1955

Jolly, R. W. 'An Econometric Analysis of the Grain Livestock Economy in Canada With Special Emphasis on Commercial Agricultural Policy', PhD thesis, University of Minnesota, 1976

Judge, G. C., Havlicek, J. and Rizek, R. L. 'A Spatial Analysis of the US Livestock Economy' in G. Judge and T. Takayama (eds.), *Studies in Economic Planning Over Time and Space*, Amsterdam: North Holland Publishing Co, 1973

Len'kov, I. I. 'Optimization Model of Development Planning for Livestock Breeding', *Ekonomika i Matematicheski Metody*, 15 (1979): 92–101

Kost, W. E. 'Trade Flows in the Grain-Livestock Economy of the European Economic Community' in W. C. Labys (ed.), *Quantitative Models of Commodity Markets*, Cambridge: Ballinger Publishing Co, 1975

Maki, W. R. 'Forecasting Livestock Prices and Supply with an Econometric Model', *Journal of Farm Economics*, 45 (1963): 1670–4

Meadows, D. L. *Dynamics of Commodity Production Cycles*, Cambridge: Wright Allen Press, 1970

Propoi, A. 'Dynamic Linear Programming Models for Livestock Farms', *Behavioral Science*, 24 (1979)

Rahn, A. P. 'A Quarterly Simulation Model of the Livestock and Poultry Subsectors of Use in Outlook and Price Analysis', PhD thesis, Iowa State University, 1973

Sasaki, K. 'Spatial Equilibrium Analysis of Livestock Producers in Eastern Japan in G. Judge and T. Takayama (eds.), *Studies in Economic Planning Over Time and Space*, Amsterdam: North Holland Publishing Co, 1973

See also Beef, Cattle, Feedgrains, Hogs, Meat

Lumber

Adams, F. G. and Blackwell, J. 'An Econometric Model of the US Forest Products Industry', Discussion Paper No. 206, Department of Economics, University of Pennsylvania, Philadelphia, 1971

Chen, Hsi-Huang. 'A Dynamic Analysis of Supply and Demand for Lumber in the

United States, 1950-1972 and Projections to 1985', PhD thesis, University of Georgia, 1974

Field, D. B. 'Sortim: A Model for the Simulation of Regional Timber Markets', PhD thesis, Purdue University, 1974

McKillop, W. L. M. 'Supply and Demand for Forest Products – An Econometric Study', *Hilgardia*, 38 (March, 1967): 1-132

Robinson, V. L. 'An Econometric Analysis of the Softwood Lumber Market, 1947-67', PhD thesis, University of Georgia, 1972

Shim, Jae Kang. 'Spatial Equilibrium Analysis of the US Lumber Market: An Application of Quadratic Programming', PhD thesis, University of California at Berkeley, 1973

Manganese

Charles River Associates, Inc. 'Economic Analysis of the Manganese Industry', Prepared for Property Management and Disposal Service, Washington: General Services Administration, 1967

King, T. B. and Reddy, B. J. 'Analysis on the Effect of Price Increase on the Demand for Manganese', Paper presented at the National Academy of Sciences Workshops on Non-Fuel Mineral Demand Modeling, Airlie House, Warrenton, Virginia, June 1-2, 1981

Shaw, J. 'Manganese Model, Parts I and II', Miscellaneous Paper, Commodities Division, UN Conference on Trade and Development, Geneva, 1973

Meat

Bain, R. A. 'An Econometric Model of the Beef and Pork Sectors: Development and Application to Policy Analysis', PhD thesis, Cornell University, 1976

Bergstrom, A. R. 'An Econometric Study of Supply and Demand for New Zealand Exports', *Econometrica*, 23 (1955): 258-76

Chetwin, J. 'A Model of the United Kingdom Wholesale Meat Market', Mimeographed, Lincoln College, New Zealand, 1965

Crom, R. *A Dynamic Price-Output Model of the Beef and Pork Sectors*, Technical Bulletin No. 1426, Economic Research Service, US Department of Agriculture, Washington, DC, 1970

Duewar, L. A. and Maki, W. R. 'A Study of the Meat Products Industry Through Systems Analysis and Simulation of Decision Units', *Agricultural Economics Research*, 18 (1966): 79-83

Elam, T. E. 'A Model of the Monthly Structure of the US Beef-Pork Economy', PhD thesis, University of Tennessee, 1973

Fuller, W. A. and Ladd, G. W. 'A Dynamic Quarterly Model of the Beef and Pork Economy', *Journal of Farm Economics*, 43 (1961): 797-812

Haimerl, J. *A Blockrecursive Structural Model of the Cattle, Beef and Veal Market in West Germany*, Sonderhelt 41, Agrawirtschaft, A. S. Verlag, Hannover, 1970

Kettunen, L. 'Demand and Supply of Pork and Beef in Finland', Publication No. 11, Agricultural Economics Research Institute, Helsinki, 1968

Mahe, R. A. 'Modeling the French Beef and Pork Markets', Working Paper, INRA, Paris, 1979

Marian, B. W. and Walker, F. E. 'Short-Run Predictive Models for Retail Meat Sales', *American Journal of Agricultural Economics*, 60 (1978): 341–91

Myers, L. H. and Havlicek, Jr., Jr. 'Monthly Price Structure of the US Beef, Pork and Broiler Markets' in W. C. Labys (ed.), *Quantitative Models of Commodity Markets*, Cambridge: Ballinger Publishing Co, 1975

Shmueli, A. and Tapiero, C. S. 'The Israeli Meat Sector: An Econometric Model', Discussion Paper No. 777, Maurice Falk Institute, Jerusalem, 1977

Trierweiler, J. E. and Hassler, J. B. *Orderly Production and Marketing in the Beef-Pork Sector*, Research Bulletin 240, University of Nebraska Agricultural Experiment Station, Lincoln, 1970

Tryfos, P. *An Economic Model of the Canadian Red Meat System for Policy Analysis*, Ottawa: Agricultural Economics Research Council of Canada, 1974

Wallace, T. D. and Judge, G. G. *Econometric Analysis of the Beef and Pork Sectors of the Economy*, Oklahoma State University Technical Bulletin No. 75, Stillwater, 1959

Yandle, G. 'A Model of the New Zealand Domestic Market for Meat', Technical Paper No. 7, Agricultural Economics Research Unit, Lincoln College, Canterbury, New Zealand, 1969

See also Beef, Cattle, Hogs, Livestock

Mercury

Burrows, J. 'Analysis and Model Simulations of the Non-Ferrous Metal Markets: Mercury', Special Report, Cambridge: Charles River Associates, 1974

Wharton Econometric Forecasting Associates. Existing In-House Model, Wharton School of Finance and Commerce, 1975

Metal Scrap

Clark, J. P., Tribendis, J. and Elliott, J. 'An Analysis of the Effects of Technology, Policy, and Economic Variables on the Ferrous Scrap Market in the United States', Working Paper, Department of Material Science and Engineering, Massachusetts Institute of Technology, 1981

Molybdenum

Burrows, J. 'Analysis and Model Simulations of the Non-Ferrous Metal Markets: Molybdenum', Special Report, Cambridge: Charles River Associates, 1974

Slade, M. E. 'Dominant-Firm Pricing and Byproduct Supply: The Structure of the US Molybdenum Industry', PNRE Working Paper No. 73, Department of Economics, University of British Columbia, July 1981

Wharton Econometric Forecasting Associates. Existing In-House Model, Wharton School of Finance and Commerce, 1975

Multicommodity

Adams, F. G. 'Commodity Prices in the LINK System: An Empirical Appraisal of Commodity Price Impacts', Conference on Stabilizing World Commodity Markets: Analysis Practice and Policy, Airlie, VA, 1977

Alm, H., Duloy, F. and Gulbrandsen, O. 'Agricultural Prices and the World Food Economy', Institute for Economics and Statistics, University of Uppsala, March, 1969

Azis, A., Janakiraman, F., and Wener, A. B. 'A Computer Simulation Model for Assessment of Mineral Resources', *The XIV Symposium of the Council for the Applications of Computers and Mathematics in the Minerals Industry*, University Park, PA, 1976

Billerot, B. 'A Global Model of the Minerals Market', Working Paper, CEPRI – University of Paris at Dauphine, Paris, 1979

Blakeslee, L. L., Heady, E. O. and Framingham, C. F. *World Food Production, Demand, and Trade*, Ames: Iowa State University Press, 1973

Chen, Carl Chi-Jian. 'Quadratic Programming Models of United States Agriculture in 1980 with Alternative Levels of Grain Exports', PhD thesis, Iowa State University, 1975

Cromarty, A. 'An Econometric Model for United States Agriculture', *Journal of the American Statistical Association*, 54 (1959): 556–74

Deare, S. M. 'Spatial Agricultural Economy: A Theoretical Study with Special Reference to Brazil', PhD thesis, Yale University, 1973

Egbert, E. 'An Aggregate Model of Agriculture, Empirical Estimates and Some Policy Implications', *American Journal of Agricultural Economics*, 51 (February, 1969): 71–86

Evans, M. D. 'An Agricultural Submodel for the US Economy' in *Essays in Industrial Economics* – vol. II, L. R. Klein (ed.), Philadelphia: Wharton School of Finance and Commerce, 1969

Goreaux, L. and Manne, A. (eds.) *Multilevel Planning: Case Studies in Mexico*, Amsterdam: North-Holland Publishing Co., 1973

Guedry, L. J. 'An Application of a Multi-Commodity Transportation Model to the US Food Grain Economy' in G. Judge and T. Takayama (eds.), *Studies in Economic Planning Over Time and Space*, Amsterdam: North-Holland Publishing Co, 1973

Haidacher, R. C., Kite, R. C. and Matthews, J. L. 'Application of a Planning-Decision Model for Surplus Commodity Removal Programs' in W. C. Labys (ed.), *Quantitative Models of Commodity Markets*, Cambridge: Ballinger Publishing Co, 1975

Heady, E. O., Reynolds, T. M. and Mitchell, D. O. 'An Econometric Model of the US Farm Sector and Its Food Export Policies', Applied Statistics and Econometric Series No. 7, Gottingen (FRG): Vandenhoeck & Ruprecht, 1978

Heien, D. 'Price Determination Processes for Agricultural Sector Models', Presented at the Annual Meetings of the American Economic Association, Atlantic City, 1976

Hicks, N. L. 'The SIMLINK Model of Trade and Growth for the Developing World', Bank Staff Working Paper No. 220, World Bank, Washington, DC, 1975

Japan, Ministry of Agriculture and Forestry. *Sekai Shoduryo Jukyu Moderu ni*

Yoru Jukyu Tembo, 1980-nen, 1985-nen no Yosoku, (The World Food Models and the Projections of Agricultural Products for 1980, 1985), Nohron Tokei Kyokai, Tokyo, 1974

Krueger, P. K. 'Modeling Future Requirements for Metals and Minerals', *The XIV Symposium of the Council for the Application of Computers and Mathematics in the Mineral Industries*, University Park, 1976

Kunkel, David E., Gonzales, Leonardo A. and Hiwatig, Mario H. 'Application of Mathematical Programming Models Simulating Competitive Market Equilibrium for Agricultural Policy and Planning Analysis'

Levis, Alexander H. and Ducot, Elizabeth R. 'AGRIMOD: A Simulation Model for the Analysis of US Food Policies'. David J. Eaton and W. Scott Steele, *Analysis of Grain Reserves, A Proceedings*, Economic Research Service Report No. 634, US Department of Agriculture, Washington, DC, 1977

McFarquhar, A. M., Mitter, S. and Evans, G. 'A Computable Model for Projecting UK Food and Agriculture' in A. M. McFarquhar *Europe's Food and Agriculture*, A Comparison of Models for Projecting Food Consumption and Agricultural Production in Western European Countries to 1972 and 1974, Amsterdam: North-Holland Publishing Company, 1971

Norton, R. D. and Bassoco, L. 'A Quantitative Agricultural Planning Methodology', Bank Staff Working Paper No. 180, World Bank, Washington, DC, 1974

Rojko, A. S., Urban, F. S. and Naive, J. J. *World Demand Prospects for Grain in 1980 with Emphasis on Trade by the Less Developed Countries*, Foreign Agricultural Economic Report 75, US Department of Agriculture, ERS, 1971

Roy, D. E. 'An Econometric Simulation Model of US Agriculture Including Commodity Submodels', PhD thesis, Iowa State University, 1974

Scherr, B. A. 'The DRI Agricultural Model: A Summary', Working Paper No. 1, Data Resources, Inc., Lexington, MA, 1976

Simpson, J. R. and Adams, J. W. 'Disaggregation of Input-Output Models into Product Lines as an Economic Development Policy Tool', *American Journal of Agricultural Economics*, (1975): 584–90

Singh, I. J. 'A Dynamic Multicommodity Model of the Agricultural Sector: A Regional Application in Brazil', Conference on Commodity Markets, Models and Policies in Latin America, Lima, 1978

Stoecker, A. L. 'A Quadratic Programming Model of US Agriculture in 1980', PhD thesis, Iowa State University, 1974

Takayama, T. 'World Food and Energy Modeling: A Market Oriented Approach', Mimeographed, Department of Economics, University of Illinois, Urbana-Champaign, 1975

— and Hashimoto, H. 'World Food Projection Models: 1973-1974', *Illinois Agricultural Economics*, (1976): 1–8

Throsby, C. D. and Rutledge, D. J. 'A Quarterly Model of the Australian Agricultural Sector', *Australian Journal of Agricultural Economics*, 21 (1977): 157–68

Timms, W. 'International Linkage System of Food and Agriculture', Working Paper, University of Amsterdam, Amsterdam, 1979

US Bureau of Mines. 'Joint Aluminum/Copper Forecasting and Simulation Model', Final Report and Appendices A and B, Open File Report No. 114 (2)-1977, Prepared by Synergy, Inc. for US Department of the Interior, Washington, DC 1977

Wang, Kung Lee and Kokat, R. G. *An Inter-Industry Structure of the US Mining Industries*, IC 8338, United States Bureau of Mines, Washington, DC, 1967
Whitacre, R. C. 'An Evaluation of Japanese Agricultural Trade Policies with a Multi-Region-Multicommodity Model', PhD thesis, University of Illinois, 1979

Nickel

Adams, F. G. 'The Impact of Nickel Production from the Ocean Floor: An Econometric Appraisal', Prepared by the Economics Research Unit, University of Pennsylvania for the United Nations Conference on Trade and Development, Geneva, March, 1974
Charles River Associates, Inc. 'Economic Analysis of the Nickel Industry', Prepared for Property Management and Disposal Service, Washington, DC: General Services Administration, 1968
Copithorne, L. W. and Bagnell, R. 'An Economic Analysis of the Nickel Industry (An Application of Linear Programming)', *Proceedings of the Economic Council*, AIME, February 1973
Smithson, C. W., Anders, G., Gramm, W. P. and Maurice, S. C. 'Nickel Model' in C. W. Smithson *et al.*, *World Mineral Markets: An Econometric and Simulation Analysis*, Ontario: Canadian Ministry of Natural Resources, 1979

Nuts

Bushnell, P. G. 'Dynamic Analysis of the World Almond Market and the United States Almond Marketing Order', PhD thesis, University of California at Davis, 1979
Jellema, B. M. 'Analysis of the World Market for Groundnuts and Groundnut Products', PhD thesis, North Carolina State University, Raleigh, 1972
Mehta, V. 'India's Position in the World Peanut and Peanut Oil Markets', PhD thesis, North Carolina State University, Raleigh, 1972

Onions

Jesse, E. V. *Structure of the Intraseasonal Pricing Mechanism for Late Summer Onions, 1930-68*, Marketing Research Report No. 1004, Economic Research Service, US Department of Agriculture, Washington, DC, 1973
Suits, D. B. and Koizuni, S. 'The Dynamics of the Onion Market', *Journal of Farm Economics*, 38 (1956): 475-84

Oranges (Frozen Concentrated Orange Juice)

Dean, G. W. and Collins, N. R. 'World Trade in Fresh Oranges: An Analysis of the Effect of EEC Tariff Policies', Giannini Foundation Monograph No. 18, California Agricultural Experiment Station, Berkeley, 1967
Matthews, J. L., Womack, A. W. and Huang, N. W. 'The US Orange Economy:

Demand and Supply Prospects 1973/4 to 1984/5', *Fruit Situation*, 190 (February, 1974): 39-52

Powe, E. E. 'A Model for Evaluating Alternative Policy Decisions for the Florida Orange Subsector of the Food Industry', *American Economist*, 16 (Fall, 1973)

Raulerson, R. C. and Langham, M. R. 'Evaluating Supply Control Policies for Frozen Concentrated Orange Juice with an Industrial Dynamics Model', *American Journal of Agricultural Economics*, 52 (Fall, 1973)

Rausser, G. C. 'A Dynamic Model of the California-Arizona Orange Industry', PhD thesis, University of California, Davis, 1971

Zusman, P., Melamed, A. and Katzir, M. 'A Spatial Analysis of the EEC Trade Policies in the Market for Winter Oranges' in G. Judge and T. Takayama (eds.), *Studies in Economic Planning Over Time and Space*, Amsterdam: North-Holland Publishing Co, 1973

Palladium

Wharton Econometric Forecasting Associates. Existing In-House Model, Wharton School of Finance and Commerce, 1975

Peppers

Castro, R. J. 'Effects of Tariffs on Prices, Production, and Trade on Winter Green Peppers', PhD thesis, North Carolina State University, Raleigh, 1973

Petroleum

Adams, F. G. and Griffin, J. M. 'An Econometric-Linear Programming Model of the US Petroleum Industry', *Journal of American Statistical Association*, 67 (1972): 542-51

Hughes, B., Mesarovic, M. and Pestel, E. 'World Oil: Model Description and Scenario Assessment', Multilevel Regionalized World Modeling Project, Case Western Reserve University, Cleveland, 1974

Kennedy, M. 'An Economic Model of the World Oil Market', *Bell Journal of Economics and Management Science*, 5 (1974): 540-77

Lindsay, M. A. 'A Recursive Programming Model of the Development of US Petroleum Refining Capacity: 1955-73', PhD thesis, University of Wisconsin, 1974

Moore, C. L. and Zoltners, A. A. 'A Linear Programming Model for Determining an Optimal Regional Distribution of Petroleum Products', Mimeographed, University of Massachusetts, Amherst, 1975

Palma-Carillo, P. A. 'A Macroeconometric Model of Venezuela with Oil Price Impact Applications', PhD thesis, University of Pennsylvania, 1976

Pindyck, R. 'Gains to Producers from the Cartelization of Exhaustible Resources', MITEL76-012WP, Massachusetts Institute of Technology, 1976

Rice, P. and Smith, V. K. 'An Econometric Model of the Petroleum Industry', *Journal of Econometrics*, 6 (1977)

Wilkinson, J. W. 'An Econometric Study of the US Petroleum Industry', PhD Thesis, Temple University, 1974

Pharmaceuticals

Tsurimi, H. and Tsurimi, Y. 'An Oligopolistic Model of a Japanese Pharmeutical Company', Discussion Paper No. 22, Institute for Economic Research, Queens University, Kingston, Ontario, 1970

Phosphate

Hee, O. *A Statistical Analysis of the US Demand for Phosphate Rock, Potash, and Nitrogen*, IC 8418, United States Bureau of Mines, Washington, DC, 1967

Platinum

Charles River Associates, Inc. 'Economic Analysis of the Platinum Group Metals', Prepared for Property Management and Disposal Service, Washington: General Services Administration, 1967
Wharton Econometric Forecasting Associates. Existing In-House Model, Wharton School of Finance and Commerce, 1975

Pork (see Hogs)

Potatoes

Armbruster, W. V., Garoian, J. L. and Yonde, J. G. *Simulation of Farm Bargaining Policies in the Western Late Potato System*, Oregon State Agricultural Experiment Station, Technical Bulletin No. 119, Corvallis, 1972
Estes, E. A. 'Supply Response and Simulation of Supply and Demand for the US Potato Industry', PhD thesis, Washington State, 1979
Hee, O. *Demand and Price Analysis for Potatoes*, Technical Bulletin No. 1380, Economic Research Service, US Department of Agriculture, Washington, DC, 1967
Kristianslund, I. 'Analysis of Intraseasonal Potato Price Movements', PhD thesis, Michigan State University, 1972
Shane, R. C. 'An Interregional Analysis of the Effects of Increased Potato Production, Processing and Transportation Factor-Input Costs on the US Potato Industry', PhD thesis, Washington State, 1979
Zusman, P. 'Econometric Analysis of the Market for California Early Potatoes', *Hilgardia*, 33 (1962): 539-668

Refuse and Wastes

Randers, J. and Meadows, D. 'The Dynamics of Solid Waste Generation' in *Toward Global Equilibrium: Collection of Papers*, Dennis and Donella Meadows (eds.), 1975

Rice

Adams, F. G. and Behrman, J. R. *Econometric Models of World Agricultural Commodity Markets*, (One of eight models) Cambridge: Ballinger Publishing Co, 1976

Boonma, C. 'Modeling Rice and Corn Markets in Thailand', PhD thesis, University of Illinois at Urbana-Champaign, 1972

Chaipravat, Olarn. 'International Rice Buffer Stock Operations, A Simulation Study', Conference on Stabilizing World Commodity Markets: Analysis, Practice and Policy, Airlie, VA, March, 1977

— and Pariwat, Sayan. 'An Econometric Model of World Rice Markets', Discussion Paper DP/76/14, Department of Economic Research, Bank of Thailand, Bangkok, 1976

David, Christina Crisostomo. 'A Model of Fertilizer Demand in the Asian Rice Economy: A Micro-Macro Analysis', PhD thesis, Stanford University, 1976

Grant, W. R., Mullins, T. and Morrison, W. R. *World Rice Study: Disappearance, Production, and Price Relationships Used to Develop the Model*, Economic Research Service Report No. 608, US Department of Agriculture, ERS, 1975

Holder, Jr., Shaw, D. L. and Snyder, J. C. *A Systems Model of the US Rice Industry*, Technical Bulletin No. 1453, Economic Research Service, US Department of Agriculture, Washington, DC, 1970

Nasol, R. L. 'Demand Analysis for Rice in the Philippines', *Journal of Agricultural Economics and Development*, 2 (1971): 1-13

Ohga, Kegi. 'The FAO World Rice Model', Working Paper, FAO, Rome, 1979

Pandey, V. K. and Takayama, T. 'Temporal Equilibrium of Rice and Wheat in India' in G. Judge and T. Takayama (eds.), *Studies in Economic Planning Over Time and Space*, Amsterdam: North-Holland Publishing Co, 1973

Tsuji, H. 'An Econometric Analysis of the Effects of Technological Improvements in Rice Production on Rice Trade Among Thailand, Indonesia and the World', vol. 2, *Proceedings of the Conference on Agriculture and Economic Development*, Tokyo: Japan Economic Research Center, 1972

— 'An Econometric Study of the Effects of National Rice Policies', PhD thesis, University of Illinois, 1973

Vilas, Andres Troncoso. 'A Spatial Equilibrium Analysis of the Rice Economy in Brazil', PhD thesis, Purdue University, 1975

Rubber

Behrman, J. R. 'Econometric Model Simulations of the World Rubber Market' in *Essays in Industrial Economics* – vol. III, L. R. Klein (ed.), Philadelphia: Wharton School of Finance and Commerce, 1971

Cheong, T. 'An Econometric Model of the Malayan Rubber Industry', PhD thesis, London School of Economics and Political Science, 1972

Grilli, E., Helterline, R. and Pollak, P. 'An Econometric Model of the World Natural Rubber Economy', *Metroeconomica*, 31 (1978)

— Helterline, R. and Pollak, P. 'An Econometric Model of the World Rubber Economy', World Bank Staff Commodity Paper No. 3, January, 1979

Kolbe, H. and Timm, H. *Die Bestimmungsfaktoren der Preisentwicklung auf dem Weltmarkt fur Naturkautschuk: Eine Okonometrische Modellanalyse*, NR 10, HWWA-Institut fur Wirtschaftsforschung, Hamburg, June, 1972

Reutens, A. 'An Econometric Analysis of the International Rubber Economy', PhD thesis, University of Illinois at Urbana-Champaign, 1974

Tan, C. S. 'World Rubber Market Structure and Stabilization: An Econometric Study', PhD dissertation, Australian National University, 1982

Teken, I. B. 'Supply and Demand for Indonesian Rubber', PhD thesis, Purdue University, 1971

Shrimp

Doll, J. P. 'An Econometric Analysis of Shrimp Ex-Vessel Prices, 1950-1968', *American Journal of Agricultural Economics*, 54 (1972): 431-40

Gillespie, E. C., Hite, J. S. and Lytle, J. S. *An Econometric Analysis of the US Shrimp Industry*, South Carolina Agriculture Experiment Station Bulletin No. 2, Clemson, 1969

Timmer, C. P. 'A Projection Model of the US Shrimp Market', *Food Research Institute Studies*, 8 (1968): 243-56

Silver

Burrows, J., Hughes, W. and Vallette, L. 'An Econometric Analysis of the Silver Industry', Charles River Associates, Cambridge, MA, 1972

Charles River Associates, Inc. 'Economic Analysis of the Silver Industry', Prepared for Property Management and Disposal Service, Washington: General Services Administration, 1969

Soybeans (Oil, Meal)

Evans, R. S., Jr. 'Soybean Acreage Response: An Analysis of Price and Policy Impacts', PhD thesis, Virginia Polytechnic Institute and State University, 1975

Free, J. W. *The Future of the South in the Soybean Processing Industry, 1970-1975*, Bulletin No. 168, Southern Cooperative Series, Tennessee Valley Authority, November, 1971

Houck, J. P. and Mann, J. S. *An Analysis of Domestic and Foreign Demand for US Soybean and Soybean Products*, Technical Bulletin No. 265, University of Minnesota Agricultural Experiment Station, 1968

— Ryan, M. E. and Subotnik, A. *Soybeans and Their Products: Markets, Models and Policy*, Minneapolis: University of Minnesota Press, 1972

Leunis, J. V. and Vanderborre, R. 'An Interregional Analysis of the US Soybean Industry' in G. Judge and T. Takayama (eds.), *Studies in Economic Planning Over Time and Space*, Amsterdam: North-Holland Publishing Co, 1973

Matthews, J. L., Womack, A. W. and Hoffman, R. G. 'Formulation of Market Forecasts for the US Soybean Economy with an Econometric Model', *Fats and Oils Situation*, 260 (November, 1971): 26–31

Meilke, K. D. and Young, L. 'A Quarterly North American Soybean Forecasting Model', Working Paper No. 4, Policy Planning and Economic Brands, Agriculture Canada, 1980

— and Griffith, G. R. 'Incorporating Policy Variables in an Econometric Model of the World Soybean/Rapeseed and Products Markets', School of Agriculture Economics and Extension Education, University of Guelph, 1981

Meyers, W. H. 'Summary of Soybean Model', Unpublished paper, Economics, Statistics and Cooperations Service, US Department of Agriculture, Washington, DC, 1978

Vandenborre, R. J. *Economic Analysis of Relationships in the International Vegetable Oil and Meal Sector*, Agricultural Economics Experiment Station Bulletin No. 106, University of Illinois, Urbana-Champaign, 1970

Wahi, P. L. 'An Econometric Analysis and Temporal Price Equilibrium of US Soybean Oil', PhD thesis, University of Illinois, 1972

Williams, G. W. 'Economic Structure of the Brazilian Soybean Industry: A Prototype Model', MS thesis, Purdue University, December, 1977

Steel

Abe, M. A. 'Dynamic Microeconomic Models of Production, Investment and Technological Change of the US and Japanese Iron and Steel Industries' in G. Judge and T. Takayama (eds.), *Studies in Economic Planning Over Space and Time*, Amsterdam: North Holland, 1973

Beeck, J. C. 'An Econometric Model of Steel Prices in the EEC', Mimeographed, Central Planning Bureau, The Hague, 1972

Clark, J. and Church, A. 'Process Analysis Modeling of the Stainless Steel Industry', Paper presented at the National Academy of Sciences Workshops on Non-Fuel Mineral-Demand Modeling, Airlie House, Warrenton, VA, 1981

Clavio, F. 'Un Modele de la Siderugid Belgo-luxenbourgeoise Simulations et Previsions', *Recherches Economique de Louvain*, 39 (1973): 459–84

Elliott, J. F. *Mathematical Modeling of Raw Materials and Energy Needs of The Iron and Steel Industry in the US*, Phase I-A Model of the Raw Materials Requirements of the US Steel Industry, and Phase II-Metallic Supply for Steelmaking: A Dynamic System, Reports OFR6(1)-76 and OFR6(2)-76, US Bureau of Mines, Washington, DC, 1973 and 1975

Fabian, T. 'Process Analysis of the US Iron and Steel Industry' in A. S. Manne and H. M. Markowitz (eds.), *Studies in Process Analysis: Economy-Wide Production Capabilities*, Cowles Foundation for Research in Economics Monograph No. 18, John Wiley & Sons, New York, 1963

Higgins, C. I. 'An Econometric Description of the US Steel Industry' in *Essays in Industrial Economics* – vol. II, L. R. Klein (ed.), Philadelphia: Wharton School of Finance and Commerce, 1969

Katrack, F. E. 'Analysis of the Supply of and Demand for Steel in the United States', PhD dissertation, Massachusetts Institute of Technology, 1978

Kendrick, D. *Programming Investment in the Process Industries* (A Model of the Brazilian Steel Industry), Cambridge: The MIT Press, 1967

Kinoshita, K. 'An Econometric Analysis of the Steel Industry of the United States, 1950-1970', Paper presented at the Third World Congress of the Econometric Society, Toronto, Canada, August 22-26, 1975

Labys, W. C. 'Simulation of a Basing Point System', MBA thesis, Graduate School of Business, Duquesne University, 1962

Mo, W. Y. and Wang, K. L. *A Quantitative Economic Analysis and Long-Run Projections of the Demand for Steel Mill Products*, US Bureau of Mines, IC 8451, Washington, DC, 1970

Nelson, J. P. 'An Interregional Recursive Programming Model of the US Iron and Steel Industry: 1947-67', PhD thesis, University of Wisconsin, 1970

Russell, C. S. and Vaugh, W. J. *Steel Production: Processes, Products, and Residuals*, Johns Hopkins Press, Baltimore, MD, 1976

Shriner, R. D. 'An Econometric Analysis of the Demand and Supply for Scrap Iron and Steel', PhD thesis, Indiana University, 1974

Tsao, C. S. and Day, R. H. 'A Process Analysis Model of the US Steel Industry', *Management Science*, 17 (1971): 588-608

Vaughn, W. J. 'A Residuals' Management Model of the Iron and Steel Industry: A Linear Programming Approach (Parts 1 and 2)', PhD thesis, Georgetown University, 1975

Watanabe, T. and Kinoshita, S. 'An Econometric Study of the Japanese Steel Industry' in L. Klein (ed.), *Essays in Industrial Econometrics*, vol. III, Philadelphia, PA: Economics Research Unit, University of Pennsylvania, 1969, pp. 99-162

Sugar

Abou-Bakr, A. 'The US Sugar Position in the World Sugar Economy', PhD thesis, Washington State, 1976

Adams, F. G. and Behrman, J. R. *Econometric Models of World Agriculture Commodity Markets*, (One of eight models) Cambridge: Ballinger Publishing Co, 1976

Bateman, M. 'Analyzing and Forecasting World Sugar Prices', Conference on Commodity Markets, Models and Policies in Latin America, Lima, 1978

Bates, H. and Schmitz, A. *A Special Equilibrium Analysis of the World Sugar Economy*, Giannini Foundation Monograph, Berkeley, May, 1969

Flores, A. S. 'Spatial Equilibrium Analysis of the US Sugar Industry Under Alternative Policy Measures', PhD thesis, University of Hawaii, 1972

Gemmill, G. 'The World Sugar Economy: An Econometric Analysis of Production and Policies' in W. C. Labys, M. I. Nadiri and J. Nunez del Arco (eds.), *Commodity Markets and Latin American Development: A Modeling Approach*, New York: National Bureau of Economic Research, 1980

Niles, J. N. and French, B. C. 'A Simulation Model of Grower-Processor Coordination in the Beet Sugar Industry', Giannini Foundation Research Report No. 321, University of California at Berkeley, 1974

Pringle, G. E. 'A Temporal Spatial Analysis of Sugar Production and Marketing in Puerto Rico', PhD thesis, University of Wisconsin, 1969

Ryland, G. J. and Guise, J. W. B. 'A Spatio-Temporal Quality Competition Model of the Australian Sugarcane Processing Industry', *American Journal of Agricultural Economics*, 57 (1975): 431–8

Sugai, Yoshimiko. 'A Quota System Policy and Its Impact on the Labor Market in the Sugarcane Industry: Analysis Through a Dynamic Linear Programming Procedure, San Paulo, Brazil', PhD thesis, Iowa State University, 1974

Tewes, T. 'Sugar: A Short-Term Forecasting Model of the World Market, With A Forecast of the World Market Price for Sugar in 1972–1973', *The Business Economist*, 4 (Summer, 1972): 89–97

Wymer, C. R. 'Estimation of Continuous Time Models with an Application to the World Sugar Market' in W. C. Labys (ed.), *Quantitative Models of Commodity Markets*, Cambridge: Ballinger Publishing Co, 1975

Sulphur

Hee, O. 'Industrial Demand for Sulphur and Alternative Inputs', Mimeographed, US Bureau of Mines, Washington, DC, February, 1972

Laulajainen, R. 'The US Frasch Industry, 1955–1975: A Study in System Dynamics', The British Sulphur Corporation Ltd, *Sulphur*, 129 (March – April, 1977): 33–9

Tantalum

Charles River Associates, Inc. 'Economic Analysis of the Tantalum Industry', Prepared for Property Management and Disposal Service, Washington: General Services Administration, 1967

Tea

Adams, F. G. and Behrman, J. R. *Econometric Models of World Agricultural Commodity Markets*, (One of eight models) Cambridge: Ballinger Publishing Co, 1976

Murti, V. N. 'An Econometric Study of the World Tea Economy 1948–1961', PhD thesis, University of Pennsylvania, 1961

UN Conference on Trade and Development. 'The Effect of Supply Change on Short-Term Movements of Tea Prices', UNCTAD/CD/Misc. 47, Geneva, 1972

Textiles

den Hartog, H. and Frankel, M. 'An Econometric Model of the Textile and Clothing Industries in the Netherlands', Mimeographed, Central Planning Bureau, The Hague, 1972

Jones, M. and Clavijo. 'Un Modele de L'industrie du Textile Belge', *Recherches Economiques de Louvain*, 39 (1973): 485–502

Miller, R. L. *A Short-Term Econometric Model of Textile Industries*, Discussion Paper No. 188, Institute for Economic Research, University of Washington, Seattle, 1971

Moreno-Calvo, H. 'Econometric Study of Demand and Supply Determinants in the US Carpeting Industry', PhD thesis, Clemson University, 1973

Naylor, T. H., Wallace, W. H. and Sasser, W. E. 'A Computer Simulation Model of the Textile Industry', *Journal of the American Statistical Association*, 62 (1967): 1338-64

Tin

Chabra, J., Grilli, E. and Pollak, P. 'The World Tin Economy: An Econometric Analysis', IBRD Staff Working Paper, World Bank, 1978

Desai, M. 'An Econometric Model of the World Tin Economy, 1948-1961', *Econometrica*, 34 (1966): 105-34

Grilli, E. 'A Revised Tin Model', *A System of Linked Models for Commodity Market Analysis*, IBRD Report, World Bank, Washington, DC, 1976

Mariano, R. S. 'Forecasts and Analysis of the Tin Market', Prepared for Wharton Econometric Forecasting Associates, Inc, Philadelphia, September, 1974

Pinto, F. 'Tin Model', *The Simlink Model of Trade and Growth for the Developing World*, IBRD Staff Working Paper No. 220, World Bank, October, 1975

Smith, G. W. and Schink, G. R. 'The International Tin Agreement: A Reassessment', *Economic Journal*, (1976)

Tobacco

Mann, J. S. 'A Dynamic Model of the US Tobacco Economy', *Agricultural Economics Research*, 25 (1973): 81-92

Sutton, R. W. 'An Econometric Analysis of the Structure of the US Tobacco Industry', PhD thesis, University of Kentucky, 1974

Vernon, J., Rives, N. and Naylor, T. H. 'An Econometric Model of the Tobacco Industry', *Review of Economics and Statistics*, 51 (1969): 149-57

Tomatoes

Brandt, J. A. 'An Econometric Analysis of the Processing Tomato Industry', PhD thesis, University of California, Davis, 1977

Brooker, J. R. 'Systems Analysis of the US Winter Fresh Tomato Industry', PhD thesis, University of Florida, 1973

Chern, Wen Shyong. 'Supply Response and Price-Demand Relationships for California Processing Tomatoes', PhD thesis, University of California at Berkeley, 1975

Lee, W. B. 'The Competitive Nonlinear Spatial Equilibrium Analysis: An Empirical Study of the US Tomato Industry', Mimeographed, Bloomsburg State College, Bloomsburg, PA, 1973

Richardson, P. W. 'A Short-Run Econometric Analysis of the Demand and Import

Supply of a Horticultural Good: Tomatoes', *Applied Economics*, 6 (1974): 157–69

Tungsten

Burrows, J. C. *Tungsten: An Industry Analysis*, Lexington: D. C. Heath and Co, 1971
— 'Analysis and Model Simulations of the Non-Ferrous Metal Markets: Tungsten', Special Report, Cambridge: Charles River Associates, 1974
Tan, C. Suan. 'The World Tungsten Economy, An Econometric Model', *Resources Policy*, (December, 1977): 281–91
Wharton Econometric Forecasting Associates. Existing In-House Model, Wharton School of Finance and Commerce, 1975

Turkeys

Bawden, D., Carter, H. O. and Dean, G. W. 'Interregional Competition in the United States Turkey Industry', *Hilgardia*, 37 (1966): 1–95
Blomo, V. J. and Farris, D. E. *Seasonal Demand and Supply for Turkeys*, Departmental Information Report No. 72–10, Texas Agricultural Experiment Station, College Station, 1972

Vanadium

Charles River Associates, Inc. 'Economic Analysis of the Vanadium Industry', Prepared for Property Management and Disposal Service, Washington, DC: General Services Administration, 1967

Vegetables

Adams, R. M. 'A Quadratic Programming Approach to the Production of California Field and Vegetable Crops Emphasizing Land, Water, and Energy Use', PhD thesis, University of California at Davis, 1975
Hammig, M. D. 'Supply Response and Simulation of Supply and Demand for the US Fresh Vegetable Industry', PhD thesis, Washington State, 1978
Matetic, J. R. 'An Economic Anlaysis of the Chilean Fresh Fruit and Vegetable Export Sector', PhD thesis, University of Minnesota, 1971
Shuffett, M. D. *The Demand and Price Structure for Selected Vegetables*, Technical Bulletin No. 1105, United States Department of Agriculture, Washington, DC, 1954
Simmons, R. L. and Pomareda, C. 'Equilibrium Quantity and Timing of Mexican Vegetable Exports', *American Journal of Agricultural Economics*, 57 (1975): 472–9
Tramel, T. and Seale, A. D., Jr. 'Reactive Programming of Supply and Demand

Relations – Application to Fresh Vegetables', *Journal of Farm Economics*, 41 (1959): 1012-22

Water

Gouensky, I. V. 'Dynamic Linear Programming Model for Deriving Agricultural Water Demands' in C. C. Sasky and A. Propoi (eds.), *Dynamic Linear Models for the Study of Agriculture Systems*, 1982

Heady, E. O. and Madsen, H. C. 'National and Interregional Models of Water Demand for Land Use and Agricultural Policies' in G. Judge and T. Takayama (eds.), *Studies in Economic Planning Over Space and Time*, Amsterdam: North-Holland Publishing Co, 1973

Horowitz, Uri. 'A Dynamic Model Integrating Demand and Supply Relationships for Agricultural Water, Applied to Determining Optimal Intertemporal Allocation of Water in a Regional Water Project', PhD thesis, Iowa State, 1974

Parks, L. 'Estimation of Water Production Functions and Farm Demand for Irrigation Water, with Analysis of Alternatives for Increasing the Economic Returns of Water on Chilean Farms', PhD thesis, University of California at Davis, 1976

Watermelon

Suits, D. 'An Econometric Analysis of the Watermelon Market', *Journal of Farm Economics*, 37 (1955): 237-51

Wheat

Adams, F. G. and Behrman, J. R. *Econometric Models of World Agricultural Commodity Markets*, (One of eight models) Cambridge: Ballinger Publishing Co, 1976

Ahn, C. Y. and Singh, I. J. 'The Future of Agriculture in South Brazil: Some Policy Projections with a Dynamic Model of the Wheat Region, Rio Grande Do Sol (1978-85)', Mimeographed, Department of Agricultural Economics and Rural Sociology, Ohio State University, Columbus, 1973

Barr, T. N. 'Demand and Price Relationships for the US Wheat Economy', *Wheat Situation*, 226 (1973): 15-25

Blonde, D. 'An Econometric Model of the World Wheat Market', Working Paper, UNCTAD, Geneva, 1978

Chai, J. C. 'An Econometric Analysis of the Demand and Price Structure of Wheat For Food by Classes in the US', PhD thesis, University of Minnesota, 1967

Doyle, J. 'World Wheat Economy: Development of Dynamic Analysis of an Imperfect Market', PhD thesis, Kansas State University, 1976

Hoyt, R. C. 'A Dynamic Econometric Model of the Milling and Baking Industries', PhD thesis, University of Minnesota, 1972

Hutchison, J. E., Naive, J. J. and Tsu, S. K. *World Demand Prospects for Wheat in 1980 with Emphasis on Trade by Less Developed Countries*, Foreign Agricultural Economic Report No. 62, US Department of Agriculture, ERS, 1970

Labys, W. C. and Halliday, R. 'Model of Disequilibrium Adjustments Between the Wheat Spot and Futures Markets', Working Paper, West Virginia University, 1980

Lattimore, R. and Zwart, A. C. 'Medium Term World Wheat Forecasting Model', *Commodity Forecasting Models for Canadian Agriculture*, vol. II, Agriculture Canada, Ottawa, 1978, pp. 87–120

Lee, P. S. T. 'An Econometric Analysis of Wheat Markets of Taiwan and Japan', PhD thesis, Washington State University, Pullman, 1973

Liu, Chun-lan Lee. 'Optimal Temporal and Spatial Pricing and Allocation of Wheat in the International Market', PhD thesis, University of Illinois at Urbana-Champaign, 1975

Meinken, R. W. *The Demand and Price Structure for Wheat*, Technical Bulletin No. 1136, United States Department of Agriculture, Washington, DC, 1968

Mo, Y. *An Econometric Analysis of the Dynamics of the United States Wheat Sector*, Technical Bulletin No. 1395, United States Department of Agriculture, Washington, DC, 1968

Reutlinger, S. 'A Simulation Model for Evaluation Worldwide Buffer Stocks for Wheat', *American Journal of Agricultural Economics*, 58 (1976): 1–12

Schmitz, A. and Bawden, D. *World Wheat Economy: An Empirical Analysis*, Giannini Foundation Monograph No. 32, University of California at Berkeley, 1973

Shei, S. J. and Thompson, R. L. 'The Impact of Trade Restrictions on Price Stability in the World Wheat Market', *American Journal of Agricultural Economics*, 59 (1977): 628–38

Toyoda, Yhoshihira. 'A Spatial Equilibrium Model of World Wheat Trade with Market Constraints', Working Paper, University of North Carolina at Raleigh, 1974

Vannerson, F. L. 'An Econometric Analysis of the Postwar US Wheat Market', PhD thesis, University of Wisconsin, 1968

Warner, D. L. 'An Econometric Model of the World Wheat Economy', PhD thesis, Princeton University, 1979

Wine

Biondolillo, A. L. 'Social Cost of Production Instability in the Grape Wine Industry: Argentina', PhD thesis, University of Minnesota, 1972

Labys, W. C. 'Preliminary Results of an Econometric Model of the International Wine Market', Mimeograph, Graduate Institute of International Studies, Geneva, 1973

Wohlgenant, M. K. 'An Economic Analysis of the Dynamics of Price Determination: A Study of the California Grape-Wine Industry', PhD thesis, University of California at Davis, 1979

Wool

Adams, F. G. and Behrman, J. R. *Econometric Models of World Agricultural Commodity Markets*, (One of eight models) Cambridge: Ballinger Publishing Co, 1976

Duane, P. *Analysis of Wool Price Fluctuations: An Economic Analysis of Price Formation in a Raw Materials Market*, Wool Economic Research Report No. 25, Australian Government Publishing Service, Canberra, Australia, 1967

Durbin, S. I. 'A Sample Wool Marketing Simulation Model', MSc thesis, Massey University, New Zealand, 1969

McKenzie, C. J. 'Quarterly Models of Price Formation in the Raw Wool Market', MSc thesis, Lincoln College, Canterbury, New Zealand, 1966

Witherell, W. H. *Dynamics of the International Wool Market: An Econometric Analysis*, Research Memorandum No. 91, Econometric Research Program, Princeton University, 1967

Zinc

Adams, R. G. 'The Chase Econometric Zinc Forecasting Model: A Pragmatic Approach', Paper presented at the National Academy of Sciences Workshops on Non-Fuel Mineral-Demand Modeling, Airlie House, Warrenton, VA, June 1–2, 1982

Bush, William R. 'Econometric Forecasting of the World Zinc Industry', Society of Mining Engineers of AIME, Preprint #79–35, 1979

Cavander, D. C. 'The US Zinc Industry: An Econometric Study', PhD thesis, Iowa University, 1976

Kovisars, L. 'World Production, Consumption and Trade in Zinc – An LP-Model', US Bureau of Mines Contract J-0166003, Stanford Research Institute, 1976

Smithson, C. W. *et al.* 'Zinc Model' in C. W. Smithson *et al.*, *World Mineral Markets: An Econometric and Simulation Analysis*, Ontario: Canadian Ministry of Natural Resources, 1979

Wharton Econometric Forecasting Associates. Existing In-House Model, Wharton School of Finance and Commerce, 1975

Note

1. Because of the large number of energy models and energy modeling studies, it has not been possible to provide a comprehensive listing. Rather, we have cited those studies which to our knowledge contribute to a survey of the range of energy models.

INDEX

Printed in the United States
by Baker & Taylor Publisher Services